# ALIVE IN CHRIST

GRADE 8

**The Church**

aliveinchrist.osv.com

**Our Sunday Visitor**

The Subcommittee on the Catechism, United States Conference of Catholic Bishops, has found this catechetical series, copyright 2014, to be in conformity with the *Catechism of the Catholic Church*.

**Nihil Obstat**
Rev. Fr. Jeremiah L. Payne, S.Th.L.
Censor Librorum, Diocese of Orlando

**Imprimatur**
✠ Most Rev. John Noonan
Bishop of Orlando
January 20, 2014

For permission to reprint copyrighted materials, grateful acknowledgment is made to the following sources:

Excerpts from the English translation of *Rite of Penance* © 1974, International Commission on English in the Liturgy Corporation (ICEL); excerpts from the English translation of *A Book of Prayers* © 1982, ICEL; excerpts from the English translation of *Book of Blessings* © 1988, ICEL; excerpts from the English translation of *The Roman Missal* © 2010, ICEL. All rights reserved.

Scripture selections taken from the *New American Bible, revised edition* © 2010, 1991, 1986, 1970 by the Confraternity of Christian Doctrine, Washington, D.C., and are used by license of the copyright owner. All rights reserved. No part of the *New American Bible* may be reproduced in any form without permission in writing from the copyright owner.

English translation of the *Catechism of the Catholic Church for the United States of America* copyright © 1994, United States Catholic Conference, Inc.—Libreria Editrice Vaticana. English translation of the *Catechism of the Catholic Church: Modifications from the Editio Typica* copyright © 1997, United States Catholic Conference, Inc.—Libreria Editrice Vaticana. Used by permission. All rights reserved.

Excerpts from the English translation of the *Compendium of the Catechism of the Catholic Church* copyright © 2006 Libreria Editrice Vaticana. All rights reserved. The exclusive licensee in the United States is the United States Conference of Catholic Bishops, Washington, D.C. and all requests for United States uses of the *Compendium of the Catechism of the Catholic Church* should be directed to the United States Conference of Catholic Bishops.

Quotations from papal and other Vatican documents are copyright © Libreria Editrice Vaticana.

Alive in Christ Grade 8 Student Book
ISBN: 978-1-61278-019-1
Item Number: CU5109

1 2 3 4 5 6 7 8  015016  18 17 16 15 14
Webcrafters, Inc., Madison, WI, USA; June 2014; Job# 113687

© Our Sunday Visitor

## UNIT 4   The Church

# A New Year

## ♡ Let Us Pray

**Leader:** O, Lord, let us be your witnesses and show the world how you are alive in us and we are alive in you.

"May God be gracious to us and bless us;
    may his face shine upon us.
So shall your way be known upon the earth,
    Your victory among all the nations.
May the peoples praise you, God;
    May all the people praise you!" **Psalm 67:2–4**

**All:** Help us show the world that we are alive in you, Lord.

## ✝ Scripture

So then you are no longer strangers and sojourners, but you are fellow citizens with the holy ones and members of the household of God, built upon the foundation of the apostles and prophets, with Christ Jesus himself as the capstone. Through him the whole structure is held together and grows into a temple sacred in the Lord; in him you also are being built together into a dwelling place of God in the Spirit.

**Ephesians 2:19–22**

### Have you ever thought...

- What does being Catholic mean to you?
- How does the Church keep you connected to Jesus Christ?

# Getting Started

Every chapter in your book begins with a Getting Started section
that introduces you to the topics that will be covered in the chapter.
You'll discover important points about Jesus, Sacred Scripture,
Sacred Tradition, and Church history. In this section you will
also complete charts, webs, tables, and other graphic organizers
with information you have already learned about chapter topics.
Sometimes you will return to these pages to complete the charts
as you work through the chapters.

In this box you will find directions for
completing the graphic organizers and charts.

Fill in the chart with some things you already
know about the Catholic Church.

| The Catholic Church | |
| --- | --- |
| **Our Mission** | The Church's mission is to spread the Good News of God's Kingdom. |
| **Our Members** | |
| **Our Leadership** | |
| **Our Prayer and Worship** | |

**The Church and My Life Today**  As a member of the Catholic Church, your relationship with Jesus and the Church is a part of your life every day. Our faith is connected to who we are and therefore everything we do. Place a check mark next to the statements that most apply to you. Draw a star next to things you have questions about.

○ I take time to pray every day.

○ I read the Bible at least once a week.

○ I think about the teachings of Jesus and the Church when I'm making decisions.

○ My relationship with Jesus influences my life.

○ I participate in Mass every week.

○ I've told someone outside of my Church about my faith.

○ I trust that God has a plan for my life.

○ I think it's important to serve others.

**What is one thing from the list above that you want to work on this year?**

_____

_____

_____

_____

_____

_____

_____

_____

**Who or what do you think will help you do this?**

_____

_____

_____

_____

_____

_____

_____

# Eighth Grade

**Where will this year take you?**

A new year is ahead of you. Your book will guide you on your journey in life and faith this year as you discover more about your relationship with Jesus Christ and the Catholic Church, and learn how to make it stronger.

This symbol lets you know that the reading that follows is from Sacred Scripture. In every chapter you will spend time with God's Word, meeting Jesus and learning about your faith in a different and exciting way. You'll get to know the Church better through understanding her history and **Sacred Tradition**, and how people and events have changed, while the Word of God has remained the same. You'll find out what was important to early Christian followers and why those things are still important to Catholics today. You'll ask questions about topics that matter to you, and discover what Jesus and the Church have to say about them. You'll also have opportunities to Go to the Source—to read more about certain passages of Scripture and their background and apply it to what you have learned, and to your life today.

## Scripture

He put all things beneath his feet and gave him as head over all things to the church, which is his body, the fullness of the one who fills all things in every way.
**Ephesians 1:22–23**

### Go to the Source
Read *Ephesians 1:15–23* to see what else Saint Paul has to say about the Church as Christ's body. What does Saint Paul hope for his fellow believers? How does that message apply to the Church today?

Each chapter in your book begins and ends with prayer. Every time you start class, you will have the chance to thank God, ask for his help, pray for others, and praise God just for being who he is. You'll learn about different prayer forms—prayers of praise and adoration, blessing, intercession, petition, and thanksgiving—and how to practice these forms in personal prayer and devotional practices.

Every chapter also includes tools to help you interact with chapter content and better understand what you're learning. You may be underlining, highlighting, completing thoughts, or more.

**Sacred Tradition** God's Word to the Church, safeguarded by the Apostles and their successors, the bishops, and handed down verbally—in her Creeds, Sacraments, and other teachings—to future generations

Each chapter also contains Catholic Faith Words, important vocabulary terms that help you better understand core Catholic teachings—the "what" and "why" of your faith. These terms are highlighted and defined throughout your book.

Your book also contains features such as Where It Happened, which explains the location and context of events in biblical or Church history. You'll see photographs from historical sites as they appear today, often as special places of pilgrimage for people of all Christian communities.

The Catholics Today feature connects you to Church history and how your faith is still in action right now. You'll learn about how Catholics all over the world live their faith by the ways we pray, the stands we take, and the choices we make.

At the end of each chapter you will find a Catholics Believe section, which summarizes what you have learned about Church teachings, and how Catholics put the core doctrines of our faith into practice.

In the back of your book you will also find the Catholic Social Teaching: Live Your Faith section. The principles of Catholic Social Teaching help build a just society and show how to live lives of holiness. You'll learn about how the Catholic Church and her members respond to the physical and spiritual needs of people, especially through the Corporal and Spiritual Works of Mercy, and the issues facing everyone around the world today.

The Our Catholic Tradition section in the back of your book provides valuable information on Sacred Scripture, Sacred Tradition, prayer, devotions, and other reference material. There is also a Church History timeline to help you visualize the growth of the Catholic Church from her very beginning.

## LIST AND DISCUSS

List three things you want to find out about what the Catholic Church does and what it means to be a part of the Catholic Church community.

1. _____
2. _____
3. _____

Discuss your thoughts with a classmate you don't know well. Share your questions with each other and then find out what others in your class are wondering about.

# The Church in Sacred Scripture

You have already learned that the Bible is made up of two parts: the Old Testament and the New Testament. Together, they make up what we call Sacred Scripture, or the inspired Word of God written by humans, and their unity comes from the unity of God's plan of salvation for all people. That plan and God's truth are recorded in both Testaments as our **salvation** history, part of the history of the Church herself.

The Catholic canon of Scripture, or authorized version of the Bible, contains seventy-three books. Forty-six books make up the Old Testament, and twenty-seven books can be found in the New Testament. We cannot read and understand the New Testament without the background of the Old Testament, or the other way around!

Catholic Faith Words

**salvation** the loving action of God's forgiveness of sins and the restoration of friendship with the Father brought by Jesus Christ

The Old Testament tells about God the Father's relationship with the Hebrew people before the birth of Jesus, his presence in their lives, and the covenant, or sacred agreement, he made with them. The Old Testament includes the laws, history, and stories of God's Chosen People.

The New Testament tells about the birth, life, ministry, teachings, suffering, Death, and Resurrection of Jesus Christ, and also tells the story of the early Church and how it spread. Jesus was a Jew who preached about the Kingdom of God to his fellow Jews at the time. Jesus fulfilled the promise of the

*Christ among the Doctors in the Temple,* **Paolo Veronese**

📖 Go to the Source
Read *Isaiah 7:14; 9:5–6* to discover the prophetic promise Isaiah made of Jesus as Messiah.

Old Testament prophets of a Messiah. He also fulfilled the Law of Moses as explained in the Old Testament, by giving the people a new law of love. He taught that God's covenant of love is for everyone, not just the Chosen People.

In the New Testament we discover accounts, stories, and parables that tell of God's love through Jesus and the Holy Spirit. The Gospels according to Matthew, Mark, Luke, and John proclaim the Good News of Jesus today, just as they did to the early followers of Christ.

The Gospels were formed in three stages; first, in the life and teaching of Jesus, then through the early Christians' oral tradition of storytelling and preaching. Finally, the stories, teachings, and sayings of Jesus were collected in the written Gospels themselves.

When we study the Scriptures—in the Old Testament and the New Testament—we learn not only about God's past saving actions, but also about how he is still saving us today, leading and guiding the Church. Jesus in present in the Seven Sacraments and in the Church's liturgy and worship.

As you come to know Jesus and the Church better through studying the New Testament

and seeing how he accomplished so much during his time on Earth, you will come to realize in a deeper way how Christ's actions and the Word of God in Scripture and Tradition continue to guide and strengthen Catholics in the present time. You are connected with the early Christian followers, and God is calling you to be part of your parish and school community and part of the greater Catholic community.

## DESCRIBE

Describe one thing you already know about the history of the Catholic Church.

_____

_____

_____

What is one thing you would like to know about how the early Church grew?

_____

_____

_____

## Jesus Christ, the Catholic Church, and You

You might have thought you'd never get to eighth grade. Many things in your life are changing: at home, with your friends, and inside of you. You might surprise yourself, and others, with some of the things you feel, do, and say.

Sometimes you might feel like you are stuck between two worlds, with high school right around the corner. The good news is that this year can help get you ready for the responsibilities and exciting new times you'll have. But it's just as important to focus on the here and now. This year, you will get to know yourself better, and begin to understand what choices you want to make and why. You'll have fun with friends and family, and push yourself in ways you might not have imagined. Think of eighth grade as the start of a great adventure.

Even while so much in your life is changing, there is one thing you can count on to remain the same: the love of God, who never changes. His wisdom, his Church, and his love will always be there for you. Your family and school and parish are also there to help you as you continue your faith journey.

We live in a world where everything changes all the time, and not always for the better. There are few things we can depend on to help us no matter what. That's why our Catholic faith is so important. Things are different, and better, when you let the **Holy Trinity**—God the Father, his Son, Jesus, and the Holy Spirit—into your life. Learning about the Holy Trinity will help you through the ups and downs in your life, and give you the strength to become who God wants you to be: someone who is Alive in Christ.

### Catholic Faith Words

**Holy Trinity** the mystery of one God in three Divine Persons: Father, Son, and Holy Spirit

## Get Ready

Jesus loves for who you are right now. He calls you to begin this next part of your life with hope, trusting in the Father's plan for you. As you move through this book, you will learn about what it means to be part of the Catholic Church, and discover how the Church continues Jesus' work in the world. You'll look at the things happening in your life through the eyes of Christ, and you'll discover that your faith community can help you make good choices and show everyone you meet that you are a disciple of Christ.

Fill in the chart with your thoughts about the next year. Over the next few months, update your chart with your progress or how your thoughts have changed.

| The Next Year | |
|---|---|
| What I know about Jesus: | _____ |
| What I know about the Bible: | _____ |
| My goals for the coming year: | _____ |
| My faith helps my goals by: | _____ |
| How is Christ alive in me now? | _____ |
| How can I be alive in Christ? | _____ |

## Our Catholic Life

Each chapter in your book has an Our Catholic Life section. It builds on what you have read in the chapter and focuses in a special way on **what it means to be Catholic**. Text, images, and an activity will help you better understand how to grow closer to Jesus and the Church. Topics covered will include learning more about the Catholic faith, background on the meaning and celebration of the Seven Sacraments, discovering how to live as Christ calls us to, understanding different forms of prayer, advice on how to be an active member of your Church, and ways to help others come to know Jesus Christ through our own words and actions.

> What are you looking forward to learning most this year?

## People of Faith

### Holy Men and Women

You will also be introduced to People of Faith, men and women from all periods of Church history who loved God and did his work to help build the Kingdom on Earth. Some were figures such as Apostles, some were priests, monks, or religious sisters, and some served as part of the laity, without taking vows or being ordained. Some were young people who realized their call early, and some made commitments to the Church at a later age. They are officially recognized by the Catholic Church as Venerables, Blesseds, and Saints. You will learn about their lives and the people they met, influenced, or were influenced by, and discover how their lives changed as they accepted God's grace and made a commitment to live a Christian life.

For more, go to **aliveinchrist.osv.com**

## REFLECT

Think of some of the roles in the Catholic Church that you already know about, such as priests or deacons or altar servers. What impact do these people make in your parish or community?

_____

_____

_____

What questions do you have about the Church and your part in it?

_____

_____

_____

_____

_____

## ♥ Celebration of the Word

**Leader:** Let us take time, here and now, to gather for prayer, in the name of the One who calls us to follow his call.

Jesus call us together and form us as your Body, moving and acting in the world today.

"Keep watch over yourselves and all the flock of which the Holy Spirit has made you overseers. Be shepherds of the church of God, which he bought with his own blood."
**Acts 20:28**

**Reader 1:** Where there is inequity, where people don't have the things they need,
Where children go hungry and people are hurting,
Let us be your witnesses, Lord.

**All:** We are called to act with justice.

**Reader 2:** Where there is hatred, where accusations fly,
Where eyes are lowered, fingers pointed, and tempers rise,
Let us be your love, Lord.

**All:** We are called to love tenderly.

**Reader 3:** Where there is a job to be done, where others can benefit from our gifts and abilities,
Where people long to have hope, and to hear the Good News,
Let us be your servants, Lord.

**All:** We are called to serve one another.

**Leader:** We are your Body, your hands and heart and voice in the world.
You call us to act with love and justice, to serve you in those around us.
Give us the guidance and strength to follow your call and to be alive in you.
We ask this in your name.

**All:** Amen.

## About the Pre-Test

As you begin the year, you may be asked to complete the Pre-Test that starts on the next page. The Pre-Test corresponds with major concepts you will learn this year, and your teacher will use the results to determine individual and class knowledge related to the topics. This Pre-Test and the Post-Test at the end of the year will help your teacher assess your knowledge and understanding of Catholic teachings, beliefs, and practices.

**Circle the letter of the response that correctly answers the question or completes the statement.**

1. God made a ____, or a sacred promise or agreement, with the Hebrew people, involving mutual commitments.
   a. covenant
   b. vow
   c. conversion
   d. tradition

2. Which of the following together are the sources of God's Divine Revelation to us?
   a. Conversion and Confession
   b. Salvation and Grace
   c. Sacred Scripture and Sacred Tradition
   d. Apostles and the Church

3. Which devotion honors Jesus' Real Presence in the Eucharist?
   a. the Liturgy of the Hours
   b. the Stations of the Cross
   c. Adoration of the Blessed Sacrament
   d. the Litany of the Blessed Virgin Mary

4. The Transfiguration is when Jesus ____.
   a. instituted a sacramental remembrance of himself
   b. showed his parents that he would teach others about God
   c. revealed his Divine glory to his disciples on a mountaintop
   d. taught the Beatitudes, which give us a blueprint for living

5. The three offices of Christ are Priest, Prophet, and ____.
   a. Savior
   b. Shepherd
   c. King
   d. Pastor

6. Saint Paul said that our bodies are temples of ____.
   a. the Church
   b. the Holy Spirit
   c. the Seven Sacraments
   d. sacred meaning

7. Who was the first martyr to be killed for professing belief in Jesus?
   a. Paul
   b. Peter
   c. Stephen
   d. Lazarus

8. By virtue of our ____, we are called to take part in the mission of the Church.
   a. Confirmation
   b. confession
   c. salvation
   d. Baptism

9. The ____ refers to the pilgrim Church on Earth, those being purified in Purgatory, and the blessed already in Heaven.
   a. Holy Communion
   b. Mystical Body of Christ
   c. Communion of Saints
   d. hierarchy

**10.** When a Church teaching is \_\_\_, it is free from error.

   **a.** sacramental

   **b.** traditional

   **c.** infallible

   **d.** apostolic

**11.** The Church is \_\_\_, or catholic, because of her mission to share the Gospel with the world.

   **a.** sacramental

   **b.** universal

   **c.** liturgical

   **d.** righteous

**12.** What is the name for the practice of making other people or things more important to us than God is?

   **a.** superstition

   **b.** blasphemy

   **c.** idolatry

   **d.** perjury

**13.** The most important function of a family is to \_\_\_.

   **a.** serve as an economic unit

   **b.** foster the social life of the parents

   **c.** cultivate the faith life of its members

   **d.** stimulate intellectual growth of the children

**14.** Over time, personal sin can become so ingrained into a group of people that it becomes \_\_\_.

   **a.** social sin

   **b.** Original Sin

   **c.** mortal sin

   **d.** venial sin

**15.** The \_\_\_ name some of the minimum requirements given by Church leaders for deepening our relationship with God and the Church.

   **a.** Ten Commandments

   **b.** Precepts of the Church

   **c.** offices of Christ

   **d.** Theological Virtues

**16.** Catholic marriage is a permanent \_\_\_ between a baptized man and woman.

   **a.** conversion

   **b.** character

   **c.** charism

   **d.** covenant

**17.** The \_\_\_ is the public prayer that the Church uses to mark each day as holy.

   **a.** Eucharist

   **b.** Rosary

   **c.** Lord's Prayer

   **d.** Liturgy of the Hours

**18.** When holy water is used in blessings or in a ritual, it is meant to recall \_\_\_.

   **a.** the Eucharist

   **b.** our Baptism

   **c.** the Annunciation

   **d.** the Stations of the Cross

**19.** Which is a feast honoring Mary that is also a Holy Day of Obligation?

   **a.** feast of the Annunciation

   **b.** feast of the Assumption

   **c.** feast of the Visitation

   **d.** feast of Our Lady of Lourdes

20. Who issued the Edict of Milan in A.D. 313 to give Romans freedom of worship?
    a. Saint Benedict
    b. Martin Luther
    c. the Council of Trent
    d. the Emperor Constantine

21. This God-given gift allows us to judge whether actions are right or wrong.
    a. free will
    b. conscience
    c. doctrine
    d. Tradition

22. What do we call showing contempt or lack of reverence for God's name?
    a. blasphemy
    b. idolatry
    c. heresy
    d. piety

23. This Sacrament is founded on the commissioning of the Apostles by Jesus to share in his ministry and work.
    a. Baptism
    b. Confirmation
    c. Holy Orders
    d. Matrimony

24. This group of people serve(s) through their Baptism and Confirmation in personal life, family life, social life, and parish life.
    a. laity
    b. priests
    c. monks
    d. clergy

25. These are strong habits of doing good that help you make moral decisions.
    a. doctrine
    b. virtues
    c. Creeds
    d. psalms

26. A ___ is a formal statement of what is believed about the Holy Trinity and the Church.
    a. Gospel
    b. creed
    c. prayer
    d. Sacrament

27. Pentecost occurred ___ days after Easter.
    a. twenty-five
    b. forty
    c. seven
    d. fifty

28. Who was Lazarus' sister and Jesus' friend?
    a. Maria
    b. Ruth
    c. Esther
    d. Martha

29. Ecumenism is a movement working toward unity and ___ among all Christians.
    a. Church
    b. community
    c. prayer
    d. Sacraments

30. The Magisterium is the ___ office of the Church.
    a. counseling
    b. sacramental
    c. teaching
    d. liturgical

Name the three Divine Persons of the Holy Trinity.

**31.** _____

**32.** _____

**33.** _____

Name the Marks of the Church.

**34.** _____

**35.** _____

**36.** _____

**37.** _____

Think about the following images of Jesus. Describe what each means in terms of Jesus' relationship with God.

**38.** Light of the World

_____

_____

**39.** Bread of Life

_____

_____

**40.** Vine

_____

_____

**41.** How can the Catholic Church be "one" as Jesus prayed for?

_____

_____

**42.** What is more important to your faith: the fact that the Church is one, or the fact that she is diverse?

_____

_____

**43.** What is the Paschal Mystery?

_____

_____

**44.** What do you think friendship with Jesus means?

_____

_____

**45.** What is the mission of the Catholic Church?

_____

_____

**46.** What is the difference between the Old and New Testament books of the Bible?

_____

_____

_____

**47.** Which four books of the Bible do we call the Gospels?

_____

_____

**48.** Name two parables Jesus told in the Gospels.

_____

_____

**49.** Why could we call Mary the most important woman in history?

_____

_____

_____

**50.** Describe how the Church is a community to you.

_____

_____

# All Souls Day

 **Let Us Pray**

**Leader:** Father, we give you thanks for your great love, a love that is stronger than death. Help us to trust in the promise of your Son, Jesus, that those who believe will have life eternal.

"For he stands at the right hand of the poor,
   to save him from those who pass judgment on him."
   **Psalm 109:31**

**All:** Father God, help us to trust in the promise of your Son.

## Scripture

"For if we have grown into union with him through a death like his, we shall also be united with him in the resurrection. We know that our old self was crucified with him, so that our sinful body might be done away with, that we might no longer be in slavery to sin. For a dead person has been absolved from sin. If, then, we have died with Christ, we believe that we shall also live with him. We know that Christ, raised from the dead, dies no more; death no longer has power over him." **Romans 6:5–9**

### Have you ever thought...

- How are we related to other Christians who have died?

- What happens when we die if we are not ready for Heaven?

## United in Christ

All Souls Day is celebrated on November 2, the day after All Saints Day. On All Souls Day, Catholics remember deceased family members and friends and pray that their souls will be with God in Heaven. All Souls Day is part of Ordinary Time, the season in which the Church celebrates the life and ministry of Jesus. During Ordinary Time, the priest most often wears green vestments, and the Church also remembers Mary and the Saints as part of her sanctoral cycle.

God's promise and gift of life in union with him forever requires an acceptance on the part of every person. We accept God's gift of Heaven by offering a heart that is free of sin and completely open to his grace. When our earthly life is over, God allows us to continue to grow in holiness—to be purified. The Church gives the name *Purgatory* to this final purification.

Those who have died depend on us to continue to love them through our prayer and sacrifices. We ask God to help them to come to the fullness of life with him waiting for them in Heaven. While we can and should do this all year, the Church remembers the dead in a special way on All Souls Day.

Ever since the beginning of the Church, Catholics have prayed for the dead. The idea of a specific day to remember the poor souls began in Benedictine monasteries in the sixth century. In the eleventh century, Saint Odilo established November 2 as the date that his monastery would offer special prayers for the dead. Other monasteries followed, and the entire Church eventually adopted the feast.

Today, the feast is marked with solemn remembrances and up to three Masses. In some places, the priests bless graves and recite the Rosary at the cemetery. These things are all done to show that we remember the faithful departed and stand in solidarity with them.

> How does All Souls Day give us hope?

> Why is it important to set aside a day to remember the Souls in Purgatory?

# Faithfulness in Action

When we stand in solidarity with the souls in Purgatory, we are being faithful to them. A person who is faithful is loyal. A loyal friend sticks with you through good times and bad. When you think you cannot run any further, a teammate will inspire you to the finish line. If you have trouble studying, a dependable classmate will tutor you. In turn, you owe these people loyalty when things are not going their way. It's just what a faithful person does.

## Fruits of the Holy Spirit

The twelve **Fruits of the Holy Spirit** are qualities that can be seen in us when we let the Holy Spirit work in our hearts. This season we are focusing on **faithfulness**.

**Faithfulness** is fidelity. It helps a person keep to his or her promises and follow through on commitments to God and others. You can depend on and trust a faithful person. To cultivate faithfulness, you must recognize your obligations to God, to the Church, and to others. Then, you must follow through on them as best you can.

It is comforting to know that faithfulness extends beyond this life. We must continue to be faithful to those who have died as we pray for them and others and do good works in their name. Our loving actions will help them on their journey to eternal happiness—the fullness of God's love. We trust that they will do the same for us when our life in this world ends.

## CONSIDER

When we offer our sympathy to people who have lost someone, there are often holy cards available with the deceased person's name and sometimes their dates of birth and death, followed by Scripture or a prayer. On the lines below, write a Bible passage for a card for someone you love, and explain your choice.

_____

_____

_____

_____

_____

_____

## ♥ Prayer for All Souls Day

*Pray the Sign of the Cross together.*

**Leader:** Today we remember the souls of all who have died.

**All:** May they rest in peace. Amen.

**Leader:** "The souls of the righteous are in the hand of God,
> and no torment shall touch them.

**Group 1:** They seemed, in the view of the foolish, to be dead;
> and their passing away was thought an affliction
> and their going forth from us, utter destruction.

But they are in peace.

**Group 2:** For if to others, indeed, they be punished,
> yet is their hope full of immortality;

Chastised a little, they shall be greatly blessed,
> because God tried them
> and found them worthy of himself.

**Group 1:** As gold in the furnace, he proved them,
> and as sacrificial offerings he took them to himself.

In the time of their visitation they shall shine,
> and dart about as sparks through stubble;

They shall judge nations and rule over peoples,
> and the LORD shall be their King forever.

**Group 2:** Those who trust in him shall understand truth,
> and the faithful shall abide with him in love:

Because grace and mercy are with his holy ones,

and his care is with the elect." **Wisdom 3:1–9**

**Leader:** We go forth with God's grace and mercy.

**All:** We go forth to faithfully serve the Lord. Amen.

▶ *Sing or play "On Eagle's Wings"*

# A Time for Preparation

## ♡ Let Us Pray

**Leader:** Let us praise the Lord God,

" . . . surely he will speak of peace . . .
Near indeed is his salvation for those who fear him;
        glory will dwell in our land."  **Psalm 85:9–10**

**All:**  Near indeed is his salvation. Amen.

### 📖 Scripture

"Behold, I am sending my messenger ahead of you;
    he will prepare your way.
A voice of one crying out in the desert:
    'Prepare the way of the Lord,
    make straight his paths.'
John the Baptist appeared in the desert proclaiming
a baptism of repentance for the forgiveness of sins."
**Mark 1:2–4**

### Have you ever thought...

• Who is a prophet that helps you
  to be aware of God in your life?

• How are we like the people who
  listened to John speak?

© Our Sunday Visitor

## Living as Prophets

John the Baptist is sometimes called the "last of the prophets of Israel," but that is not completely accurate. In a certain way, we are called to be prophets, too.

Through Baptism, we are commissioned to share in the three-fold ministry of Jesus—Priest, Prophet, and King. We are priests because we serve God's people. We are kings because, as adopted sons and daughters of God, we share in the royalty of Christ. We are prophets because we proclaim God's Word. During Advent, the words that we proclaim are those of waiting and watchfulness.

The Gospel according to Mark begins with Baptism, as did our own faith journey. In the opening lines of the Gospel, John the Baptist brings the faith of the Old Testament into the New Testament by revealing to the Judean people that another person, God's Son, will arrive soon. John says that Jesus will baptize with the Holy Spirit.

We have been baptized with the Holy Spirit. In Advent, the first season of the Church year, we are called to renew our baptismal commitment, to be prophets of the Second Coming.

During Advent, the Church is decorated in purple, and the priest wears purple vestments. In this season we prepare our hearts, our homes, and our world for Jesus' Second Coming, we look happily forward to the upcoming Christmas feast, and we pray for a change of heart and for God's forgiveness, and for those in need.

> How are you a prophet?
> In what ways can you prepare for both Christmas and the Second Coming of Christ?

## Preparing through Patience

Looking toward the future, to a feast several weeks away, requires patience. Looking even further into the future, to the end of the world, requires even more patience. Advent helps us to develop one of the Fruits of the Holy Spirit—patience.

**Patience** is steadfastness in the face of adversity or provocation because we trust God is with us and will somehow make things good and right. During Advent we have so many things to do, and we make timetables for accomplishing them. When we are delayed, we become impatient.

What may help us grow in patience is to look at the source of the delays. Perhaps you find it difficult to get to school on time. Consider what will solve the problem, perhaps including getting your clothes and homework ready the night before.

In other situations, we might not have control. Perhaps you need to do extra chores to help get ready for the holidays, or feel like you have no free time to be with friends. Use those moments to pray for patience. Advent is a good time to recognize that we are not always in charge, and that God is willing to help us learn to grow in holiness in any situation.

### Fruits of the Holy Spirit

The twelve **Fruits of the Holy Spirit** are qualities that can be seen in us when we let the Holy Spirit work in our hearts. This season we are focusing on **patience**.

### WRITE

On the lines below, write about some situations that make you impatient.
Briefly write about how you can use the situations to acquire patience.

| Situations | My Plan for Patience |
| --- | --- |
| | |
| | |
| | |
| | |
| | |

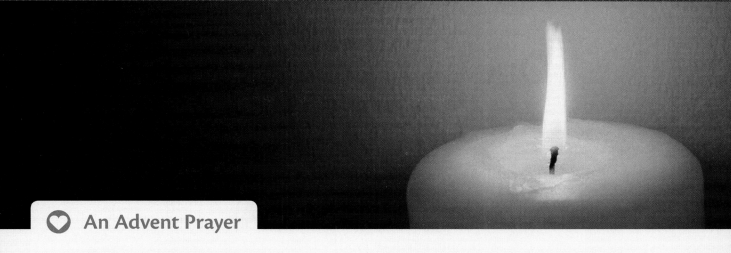

## ♥ An Advent Prayer

*Pray the Sign of the Cross together.*

**Leader:** "But do not ignore this one fact, beloved, that with the Lord one day is like a thousand years and a thousand years like one day."

**All:** Lord, help us to see that our minds are too limited to understand how limitless you are.

**Reader 1:** "The Lord does not delay his promise, as some regard 'delay,' but he is patient with you, not wishing that any should perish but that all should come to repentance."

**All:** Thank you for your patience with me, oh Lord. I am slow to change.

**Reader 2:** "But the day of the Lord will come like a thief, and then the heavens will pass away with a mighty roar and the elements will be dissolved by fire, and the earth and everything done on it will be found out."

**All:** Lord, help us trust that you will come in love and judge us all with justice.
2 Peter 3:8–10

**Leader:** Now go forth to live in holiness, devotion, and patience, as we wait in joyful hope for the Lord's coming again.

**All:** We shall live according to his promise. Amen.

▶ *Sing or play "Ready the Way"*

# Our Lady of Guadalupe

## ♥ Let Us Pray

**Leader:** Dear God, you sent Mary to be our mother, and to be a model of goodness for us.

"[Her] deed of hope will never be forgotten by those who recall the might of God." **Judith 13:19**

**All:** Amen.

## ✝ Scripture

"Mary set out and traveled to the hill country in haste to a town of Judah, where she entered the house of Zechariah and greeted Elizabeth. When Elizabeth heard Mary's greeting, the infant leaped in her womb, and Elizabeth, filled with the Holy Spirit, cried out in a loud voice and said, 'Most blessed are you among women, and blessed is the fruit of your womb. And how does this happen to me, that the mother of my Lord should come to me? For at the moment the sound of your greeting reached my ears, the infant in my womb leaped for joy. Blessed are you who believed that what was spoken to you by the Lord would be fulfilled.'" **Luke 1:39-45**

© Our Sunday Visitor

### Have you ever thought...

- Was Mary's goodness visible when she was a child?
- Why does Mary appear to people after she was assumed into Heaven?

# Mary, Our Help

The story of the feast of Our Lady of Guadalupe begins in 1531 in Mexico City. While on his way to Mass one day, Juan Diego, an Aztec farm worker, mat maker, and one of the first Catholics in Mexico, met a beautiful woman who said she was the Blessed Mother.

Mary asked that a house be built for her where she could share Jesus with her visitors. She wanted people to share their troubles with her, and she said that she would "curb all their different pains, their miseries and sorrows." Mary asked Juan Diego to tell the bishop about her visit.

The bishop asked Juan Diego for a sign that the woman was the Blessed Mother. When Juan Diego relayed the request, Mary told him to return to their meeting place the next morning, December 12.

That morning, Juan Diego could not meet Mary because he was trying to help his dying uncle. Instead, Mary found him. She said, "Do not fear any illness or vexation, anxiety or pain. Am I not here who am your mother? Are you not under my shadow and protection?" At that instant, Juan Diego's uncle recovered. Mary sent Juan Diego to a place where he would find roses blooming despite the frozen ground. The flowers were for the bishop. Juan placed them in his cloak.

When the peasant opened his cloak for the bishop, out fell the flowers. Even more surprisingly, Mary's image was imprinted on the cloak. This convinced the bishop that Juan Diego had met Mary.

Today, a large cathedral in Mexico City stands where Mary appeared. Juan Diego's cloak, with the image of Our Lady, is there, a reminder to Mary's visitors that they are under her protection.

The Church celebrates the feast of Our Lady of Guadalupe on December 12 because on that date Juan Diego gave the flowers to the bishop. The feast always falls in the season of Advent and reminds us that Mary our Mother will guide us when we need her help.

> How can Mary help us with our "miseries and sorrows"?

> Why do some people need proof that God works in their lives? What proof do we have of God working in our lives?

A chapel in the Basilica of Our Lady of Guadalupe, in Mexico City, the most visited shrine in the Americas.

# Mary's Goodness

Mary showed goodness in her actions on Earth. She went to visit her cousin Elizabeth when Elizabeth was pregnant. She asked Jesus to help when the wine ran out at the wedding at Cana. She asked her Son for healing for Juan Diego's uncle. She anticipated the needs of others and did what she could to meet those needs.

**Goodness** is one of the twelve Fruits of the Holy Spirit. Goodness is showing love and honor to God. It is desiring and doing what is best for another person. When people show goodness, they anticipate what others need, and they supply it without being asked.

## Fruits of the Holy Spirit

The twelve Fruits of the Holy Spirit are qualities that can be seen in us when we let the Holy Spirit work in our hearts. This season we are focusing on goodness.

Do you recognize the goodness around you? A volunteer coach's goodness supports the needs of children on teams and in the community. Neighbors who bring food to families in crisis demonstrate goodness. You can practice goodness when you perform acts of kindness for others. When you make choices to perform good, loving actions, God's goodness grows in you.

## IDENTIFY

Think of three situations where you could demonstrate goodness at home, at school, and with friends. How can you anticipate and fill the needs of others? Write about the situation and what you can do.

**At home:**

_____

_____

**At school:**

_____

_____

**With friends:**

_____

_____

## ♥ Prayer to Our Lady of Guadalupe

*Pray the Sign of the Cross together.*

**Leader:** Lord, open our hearts to understand your message through Mary.

**All:** Help us imitate her goodness.

**Leader:** Mary, you show us how to be kind and good.

**All:** Help us be like you.

**Leader:** Mary, you sought out people who needed help.

**All:** Help us be like you.

**Leader:** Our Lady of Guadalupe, we find you among the poor, the small, those the world counts for nothing.

You remind us of our priorities.

You remind us how precious each of us is to you and to your Son, our Lord, Jesus Christ.

You comfort us in our suffering. You challenge us to use our strengths. You call us to do whatever He tells us.

May we heed your message given to us at Tulpetlac: to acknowledge God's love, to protect the innocent, to replace our fear with trust, to keep our priorities in order. We ask this through the mercy and grace of Our Lord, Jesus Christ.

**All:** Help us serve others for your sake.

**Leader:** Let us quietly reflect on Mary's example of goodness. Then let us go forth to imitate Mary by showing God's love through our goodness.

We ask this through Christ our Lord.

**All:** Amen.

▶ *Sing or play "Hail Mary, Gentle Woman"*

# The Word Made Flesh

## ♥ Let Us Pray

**Leader:** Lord God, the coming of Jesus, your Son, brings you great glory.

"Sing to the LORD a new song;
    sing to the LORD, all the earth.
Sing to the LORD; bless his name." **Psalm 96:1–2**

**All:** Bless the name of the Lord. Amen.

## 📖 Scripture

"In the beginning was the Word,
    and the Word was with God,
    and the Word was God.
He was in the beginning with God.
    All things came to be through him,
    and without him nothing came to be.
    What came to be
    through him was life,
    and this life was the light of the human race;
    the light shines in the darkness,
    and the darkness has not overcome it. ...
And the Word became flesh
    and made his dwelling among us,
    and we saw his glory,
    the glory as of the Father's only Son,
    full of grace and truth." **John 1:1–5, 14**

### Have you ever thought...

- How do you know when you are truly loved?
- What does Jesus' birth tell us about God's love?

© Our Sunday Visitor

## God's Word Among Us

At a given point in history, the Second Divine Person of the Trinity, Jesus Christ, enters the world and is born into our human nature. The Church gives us the entire Christmas season, which begins with the Christmas Eve Vigil on December 24 and ends with the Baptism of the Lord, after Epiphany, to contemplate this mystery of the Incarnation. The mystery of God taking on human flesh is so wondrous that we celebrate it for the entire Christmas season. During this season, the priest wears white or gold vestments, and the Church is decorated in those colors as well.

The feast of Christmas celebrates that Jesus is both human and Divine—fully God and fully man. We reaffirm this every time we recite the Nicene Creed. The readings for the Mass during the day on Christmas help us understand the Incarnation as an expression of God's Word, or promise, to us.

The feasts of the season help us contemplate the Incarnation and how it applies to us. In the week between Christmas and New Year's, we honor early martyrs, including Saint Stephen and the Holy Innocents. These feasts remind us that the gift of faith can lead to great earthly trials as well as great glory. Epiphany, the original feast of Christ's birth, celebrates the coming of the Magi, the travelers from the East. The Gospel according to Matthew tells us their story to help us to understand that Jesus came for all people, not just for the Chosen People, the Jews. Jesus is the manifestation of God's overwhelming generosity, the sacrifice of his Son that we might be saved.

> John tells us that "God so loved the world that he gave his only Son." Do you think it is possible to understand a love that deep?

> What do you think it would take for people to focus on this meaning of Christmas instead of all the other things that get in the way?

# Happily Receiving and Giving

Christmas is all about being generous. We think about God's generosity in sharing Jesus with the world. We think about Jesus' generosity in coming to live with us on Earth. We think about Mary's generosity in sharing her newborn Son with many visitors and in the Temple.

**Generosity** is the Fruit of the Holy Spirit that helps us give or serve out of gratitude to God. The season shows how much we have to be grateful for. We make connections with family and friends at social events. We enjoy songs and celebrations that come from

## Fruits of the Holy Spirit

The twelve **Fruits of the Holy Spirit** are qualities that can be seen in us when we let the Holy Spirit work in our hearts. This season we are focusing on **generosity**.

our cultural roots. We seek and find the light that illuminates our souls.

So with gratitude inspired by the generosity of others, we are moved to be generous ourselves. In the Christmas season's spirit of giving, we gladly share significant parts of ourselves, to mirror the great gifts we have received.

© Our Sunday Visitor

## SUMMARIZE

Here are two Bible citations for passages about giving and generosity. Read the passages. Then on the lines below each citation, summarize what the passage means to you.

Mark 12:41–44

1 John 3:17–18

_____ _____

_____ _____

_____ _____

## ♥ Prayer for the Christmas Season

*As you begin the prayer, gather around the Nativity scene. Pray the Sign of the Cross together.*

**Leader:** Glory to God in the highest, and on earth peace to people of good will.

**All:** We praise you,
we bless you,
we adore you,
we glorify you,
we give you thanks for your great glory,
Lord God, heavenly King,
O God, almighty Father.

Lord Jesus Christ, Only Begotten Son,
Lord God, Lamb of God, Son of the Father,
you take away the sins of the world,
   have mercy on us;
you take away the sins of the world,
   receive our prayer;
you are seated at the right hand of the Father,
   have mercy on us.

For you alone are the Holy One,
you alone are the Lord,
you alone are the Most High,
Jesus Christ,
with the Holy Spirit,
in the glory of God the Father.

**All:** Amen.

**Leader:** Let us pray a prayer of blessing.

**All:** God of every nation and people,
from the very beginning of creation
you have made manifest your love:
when our need for a Savior was great
you sent your Son to be born of the
   Virgin Mary.
To our lives he brings joy and peace,
justice, mercy, and love.

**Leader:** Lord,
bless all who look upon this manger;
may it remind us of the humble birth
   of Jesus,
and raise our thoughts to him,
who is God-with-us and Savior of all,
and who lives and reigns forever and ever.
Book of Blessings

**All:** Amen.

▶ *Sing or play "Joy to the World"*

# Go Toward the Light

## ♥ Let Us Pray

**Leader:**  Lord God,

"Let the words of my mouth be acceptable,
   the thoughts of my heart before you,
LORD, my rock and my redeemer."  **Psalm 19:15**

**All:**  We ask this through Christ, our Lord. Amen.

### 📖 Scripture

"You were once darkness, but now you are light in the Lord. Live as children of light, for light produces every kind of goodness and righteousness and truth. Try to learn what is pleasing to the Lord. Take no part in the fruitless works of darkness; rather expose them, for it is shameful even to mention the things done by them in secret; but everything expose by the light becomes visible, for everything that becomes visible is light."  **Ephesians 5:8–14a**

### Have you ever thought...

• How does someone become more accomplished at something?

• How do we get the strength to be disciples of Jesus?

## Preparation and Renewal

Lent is the season observed by the Church between Ash Wednesday and Holy Thursday. It is a time of new beginnings in the Church. Parishes prepare to welcome new members. Candidates complete their preparations to receive the Sacraments of Initiation at the Easter Vigil. Priests wear purple vestments as a sign that this season calls us to change and to do penance.

Lent provides us an opportunity to begin anew as well. In solidarity with the candidates for full initiation, we seek to grow in holiness, in right relationship with God and neighbor. We find ways to leave our sinful past and refocus our lives on what really matters: our relationship with God, and with others.

One of the most helpful means of achieving this is taking part in the Sacrament of Penance and Reconciliation. This Sacrament leads us to confront the darkness and sinfulness of our lives. We measure ourselves against the Commandments and the Precepts of the Church. Then we ask for forgiveness so that we might love God more deeply and our neighbor in his name. We move forward hopefully.

One of the traditional practices of Lent is fasting. Fasting is regulating the amount of food a person eats. Catholics are required to fast when they reach 18 years of age. Many young people give up sweets or other favorite foods as a form of self-discipline. Other young people use Lent as an opportunity to acquire good habits. Building up self-control in this manner can have benefits that stretch far beyond the Easter season.

> Why is renewal important for the Church? For individuals?

> What Lent traditions do you practice?

# A Means to an End

Lent is a good time to build **self-control.** Self-control is about striving to overcome temptation and do God's will. When we use self-control, we restrain our natural impulses and try to master our personal desires and passions. We can develop self-control by denying ourselves pleasures, such as favorite foods or television shows. With God's help, we can develop self-control by building up good habits, including being on time, considering the feelings of others, and obeying those in authority over us.

Jesus is our model of self-discipline. Luke 4:1–13 tells how Jesus fasted in the desert for forty days before he was tempted by the

devil. To overcome Satan's temptation, Jesus focused on what he knew to be true. Jesus did not allow Satan to undermine his knowledge of himself, his place in the world, and his relationship with the Father.

We can be like Jesus and master temptation by focusing on what is important to a life of discipleship and becoming the people God wants us to be. Lent gives us a framework that will help us do that.

## Fruits of the Holy Spirit

The twelve Fruits of the Holy Spirit are qualities that can be seen in us when we let the Holy Spirit work in our hearts. This season we are focusing on self-control.

## IDENTIFY

Think of the self-control and discipline an Olympic athlete has to have. Consider how he or she has to practice self-control in order to achieve the gold (for instance, not eating anything they want). Then answer these questions.

What are three ways you practice self-control in order to achieve a goal?

1. _____
2. _____
3. _____

What acts of self-control help you receive the fullness of life God has in store for you?

_____

_____

_____

## ♥ The Confiteor

*Pray the Sign of the Cross together.*

**Leader:** Let us take a moment to reflect on our sins and ask God for his mercy and forgiveness.

A reading from the Acts of the Apostles.

"Repent, therefore, and be converted, that your sins may be wiped away, and that the Lord may grant you times of refreshment and send you the Messiah already appointed for you, Jesus, whom heaven must receive until the times of universal restoration of which God spoke through the mouths of his holy prophets from old." **Acts 4:18–21**

The word of the Lord.

**All:** Thanks be to God.

**Leader:** Let us now ask God's forgiveness.

**All:** I confess to almighty God
and to you, my brothers and sisters,
that I have greatly sinned
in my thoughts and in my words,
in what I have done
and in what I have failed to do,
through my fault, through my fault,
through my most grievous fault;
therefore I ask blessed Mary ever-Virgin,
all the Angels and Saints,
and you, my brothers and sisters,
to pray for me to the Lord our God.

**Leader:** Let us offer each other the Sign of Peace.

 *Sing or play "Be Merciful, O Lord"*

# Triduum

## ♥ Let Us Pray

**Leader:**   Lord Jesus, we are not worthy of your sacrifice.

"Let your face shine on your servant;
save me in your mercy."   **Psalm 31:17**

**All:**   We thank you for your kindness, Lord. Amen.

### 📖 Scripture

"Before the feast of Passover, Jesus knew that his hour had come to pass from this world to the Father. He loved his own in the world and he loved them to the end. ... So when he had washed their feet and put his garments back on and reclined at table again, he said to them, 'Do you realize what I have done for you? You call me "teacher" and "master," and rightly so, for indeed I am. If I, therefore, the master and teacher, have washed your feet, you ought to wash one another's feet. I have given you a model to follow, so that as I have done for you, you should also do.'"   **John 13:1; 12–15**

**Have you ever thought...**

• Why did Jesus want his Apostles to understand that, if they love him, they must serve each other?

• Why does it seem that some people are more loving than others?

# Our Days of Remembrance

The Triduum, the solemn time from Holy Thursday through Easter Sunday evening, links us with Jesus' Jewish heritage and his sacrifice for our salvation. When we participate in the liturgy during the Triduum, we celebrate the whole of salvation history.

On Holy Thursday, we gather for the Evening Mass of the Lord's Supper at the same time of day that Jesus and his followers gathered. They were celebrating the Jewish remembrance of Passover, when God led the Israelites out of slavery in Egypt. The readings of the day from the Lectionary for Mass begin with the story of the Passover Meal, and then recount the celebration of the Passover Meal by Jesus and his Apostles. You will remember that during that Last Supper, Jesus blesses, breaks, and shares the bread that becomes his very Body and the cup of wine that becomes his Blood.

The next day, Good Friday, we enter a church that is undecorated. Mass is not celebrated that day. We are there to watch and wait. We honor the Cross that was the instrument of our salvation. We hear the Passion again, walking with Jesus through his betrayal, scourging, and journey to Calvary. We are with the women and John as they see Jesus suffer and die on the Cross. We feel the finality of the rock being rolled across the tomb's opening. What saves us from desolation is knowing the rest of the story, which we will celebrate during the Easter Vigil Liturgy.

The Easter Vigil is the high point of the Church's liturgical year. It is our

Palestinian Christians carry a large wooden cross on Good Friday along the Via Dolorosa, the route tradition says Jesus took to his Crucifixion.

confirmation that Jesus Christ has conquered sin and death and brought us the hope of eternal life, and our confirmation of Christ as the Son of God.

We begin in silence and darkness, listening again to the story of our salvation in Old Testament readings. The Gospel reading is short, but powerful. With the women at the tomb, we learn that Jesus has risen to new life and is with us again. The cantor sings the Exsultet, celebrating this event. As the evening unfolds, we welcome new members into the Church and renew our own commitment by repeating our Baptismal vows. We recognize the great love that Jesus has for us, and we want to return it.

> Why is the celebration of the Death and Resurrection of Jesus so central to the life of all Catholics?

> What part of the Triduum do you most identify with? And why?

## Moved to Charity

Jesus has shown his love for us through his Passion, Death, and Resurrection. Nothing that anyone can do will ever exceed his gift to us. We want to reciprocate, but what could we possibly do that would even begin to repay him?

Jesus knows that we are unable to equal his gift to us. God wants us to accept his gift of love and love him in return. By doing that, we share his love with the world. We can do that by acting with charity. **Charity** is another name for love. It directs people to love God above everything else and to love our neighbors as we love ourselves. In loving, we forget our own needs and desires. We want to see that others are taken care of before we are. True charity focuses on meeting the needs of others.

Jesus taught us about love and charity. He asked us to follow the New Commandment and provided a model for our actions, from honoring the sweetness of children to washing the dusty feet of his Apostles. We, too, can perform acts of charity.

### Fruits of the Holy Spirit

The twelve **Fruits of the Holy Spirit** are qualities that can be seen in us when we let the Holy Spirit work in our hearts. This season we are focusing on **charity**.

### DESCRIBE

Read 1 Corinthians 13:1–7. In each column, write a word that describes what love is and what love is not. Use what your own experience has taught you about love. For instance, you may know that love is loyal because your friend has stuck by you through some hard times.

| What Love Is | What Love Is Not |
|---|---|
| _____ | _____ |
| _____ | _____ |
| _____ | _____ |
| _____ | _____ |

## ♥ Prayer for Holy Week

*Pray the Sign of the Cross together.*

**All:** Our blessing-cup is a Communion with the Blood of Christ.

**Leader:** "How can I repay the Lord
for all the great good done for me?
I will raise the cup of salvation,
and call on the name of the Lord."

**All:** Our blessing-cup is a Communion with the Blood of Christ.

**Reader 1:** "Dear in the eyes of the Lord
is the death of his devoted.
Lord, I am your servant, your servant,
the child of your maidservant,
you have loosed my bonds."

**All:** Our blessing-cup is a Communion with the Blood of Christ.

**Reader 3:** "I will offer a sacrifice of praise,
and call on the name of the Lord.
I will pay my vows to the Lord
in the presence of all his people."

**All:** Our blessing-cup is a Communion with the Blood of Christ.   Psalm 116:12-13, 15-16bc, 17-18; Response cf. 1 Corinthians 10:16

**Leader:** Let us go forth to act with charity toward all people.

**All:** Let us act with charity. Amen.

▶ *Sing or play "Bread for the World"*

# New Freedom

## ♥ Let Us Pray

**Leader:** Lord God, we speak out with a voice of joy.

"Let it be heard to the ends of the earth:
The Lord has set his people free."  Based on Isaiah 48:20

**All:** We are set free. Alleluia! Amen.

## 📖 Scripture

Then the two recounted what had taken place on the way, and how he was known to them in the breaking of bread.

While they were still speaking about this, he stood in their midst and said to them, "Peace be with you." But they were startled and terrified and thought that they were seeing a ghost. Then he said to them, "Why are you troubled? And why do questions arise in your hearts? Look at my hands and my feet, that it is I myself. Touch me and see, because a ghost does not have flesh and bones as you can see I have." And as he said this, he showed them his hands and his feet. While they were still incredulous for joy and were amazed, he asked them, "Have you anything here to eat?" They gave him a piece of baked fish; he took it and ate it in front of them.  Luke 24:35–43

© Our Sunday Visitor

### Have you ever thought...

- How does Jesus' Resurrection change all of human history?
- How does knowing that God loves you with a love beyond imagining make a difference today?

## An Extended Celebration

The fifty days from Easter Sunday to Pentecost are one continuous celebration. The seven Sundays within this time combine to reveal the Easter mystery to us. The Sundays are called the "Sundays of Easter," not the "Sundays after Easter," to indicate that they are part of an uninterrupted remembrance.

The Sunday Scriptures for the season tell us much about the Risen Lord and how we will cope when he returns to his Father.

We hear the stories of his appearances to the Apostles, of how Thomas doubted, of his walk along the road to Emmaus. We hear Jesus tell Peter to feed his lambs and sheep. We learn again about the Good Shepherd, and we are alerted to watch for the Holy Spirit.

These Gospels are shared in a special way with the new members of the Church. They have studied for many months and spent Lent in intensive preparation for the Easter Vigil, when they were welcomed into the Church and received the Sacraments of Initiation.

During Easter season the first reading at Mass, which is normally from the Old Testament, gives way to readings from the Acts of the Apostles. We hear the stories of the faith and courage of those first believers. In doing so, our own faith is strengthened and we receive the Eucharist with a deeper understanding and appreciation of Christ's Real Presence. This celebration of new life in the Church continues through the Feast of the Ascension, which occurs forty days after Easter, and to Pentecost, when we celebrate the coming of the Holy Spirit. These are fifty days of joy.

> Why does the Easter celebration continue for so long?

> How do new members enrich our life in the Church?

# Finding Joy

The new members of the Church reflect the joy we feel in the happy news of Jesus' Resurrection. This is not mere happiness, the feeling we get when we play with a puppy or laugh at a joke. This is **joy**, a Fruit of the Holy Spirit that comes from the growing awareness that God and his love are with us no matter our personal circumstances or achievements. And this joy is sustained over

> ### Fruits of the Holy Spirit
>
> The twelve **Fruits of the Holy Spirit** are qualities that can be seen in us when we let the Holy Spirit work in our hearts. This season we are focusing on **joy**.

the season. It won't leave us as long as we maintain our focus on Jesus' Resurrection.

But keeping that focus can be difficult. As we move through the Easter season, sometimes its message can become less real to us. The somber moods of Holy Week give way to glorious Easter celebrations and then fade. We call each Sunday Mass "a little Easter" for a great reason. At every Mass we are present once again at the Death and Resurrection of Jesus. He offers himself as a sacrifice for us in his Body and Blood. Death has no power over us. We can share in divine life. For that reason we are an Easter People: a people who live with the joy and thanksgiving for the gift of Christ's love.

## DESCRIBE

Imagine you are one of the people listed below on Easter morning. Send a text message from that person describing what you are seeing and/or feeling. Read the Resurrection stories in the Bible and recall how each of these people came to learn that Jesus was alive.

| Mary Magdalene | Peter | Disciples on the Road to Emmaus |
|---|---|---|
| _____ | _____ | _____ |
| _____ | _____ | _____ |
| _____ | _____ | _____ |
| _____ | _____ | _____ |
| _____ | _____ | _____ |
| _____ | _____ | _____ |

## ♥ Prayer for the Easter Season

*Pray the Sign of the Cross together.*

**Reader 1:** "Answer me when I call, my saving God.

When troubles hem me in, set me free; take pity on me, hear my prayer."

**All:** "LORD, show us the light of your face!"

**Reader 2:** "Know that the LORD works wonders for his faithful one; the LORD hears when I call out to him."

**All:** "LORD, show us the light of your face!"

**Reader 3:** "But you have given my heart more joy."

**All:** "LORD, show us the light of your face!"

**Reader 4:** In peace I will lie down and fall asleep,

for you alone, LORD, make me secure."

**All:** "LORD, show us the light of your face!" **Psalm 4:2, 4, 7-8, 9**

**Leader:** Let us pray the prayer that Jesus taught us.

**All:** Our Father, who art in heaven, hallowed by thy name; thy kingdom come, thy will be done on earth as it is in heaven.

Give us this day our daily bread, and forgive us our trespasses, as we forgive those who trespass against us; and lead us not into temptation, but deliver us from evil. Amen.

**Leader:** We go forth, ready to sustain our Easter joy.

**All:** We do this through Jesus, your Son. Amen.

▶ *Sing or play "Yours Today"*

# Pentecost

## ♥ Let Us Pray

**Leader:** Let us always remember that

"The love of God has been poured into our hearts through the holy Spirit that has been given to us." Romans 5:5

**All:** His Spirit lives in us. Alleluia! Amen.

## 📖 Scripture

When the time for Pentecost was fulfilled, they were all in one place together. And suddenly there came from the sky a noise like a strong driving wind, and it filled the entire house in which they were. Then there appeared to them tongues as of fire, which parted and came to rest on each one of them. And they were all filled with the holy Spirit and began to speak in different tongues, as the Spirit enabled them to proclaim. **Acts 2:1–4**

### Have you ever thought...

- Is the Holy Spirit as present today as he was on that first Pentecost?

- How does being open to the Spirit's presence make a difference in people's lives?

## The Coming of the Spirit

Just as Holy Thursday has its roots in the Jewish Passover, Pentecost is linked to a Jewish harvest feast, Shavuot. This is the celebration of the spring growing season's end, a time to be happy with the new wheat that the land had provided. Shavuot falls fifty days after Passover. The Jews were assembling in Jerusalem to celebrate Shavuot when the Holy Spirit descended upon Jesus' followers.

Saint Paul refers to Shavuot in 1 Corinthians 15:20–24. He links the feast to Jesus' ministry. Jesus is like the "first fruits," the part of the harvest that was offered to God. Just as grain rises from dead ground, Jesus rose from his grave to new, eternal life.

We are part of the harvest, too, as we will be gathered and given to God at the Last Judgment. We, too, will share in eternal life. However, before we are gathered into the Kingdom, we have work to do here on Earth. The Holy Spirit guides us in that mission.

Pentecost is celebrated fifty days after Easter, when the Church celebrates the day the Holy Spirit descended on the Apostles and Mary. During Pentecost, the priest wears red vestments, and members of the Church are reminded that like the Apostles and Mary, we, too, have received the Gifts of the Holy Spirit through the Sacraments of Baptism and Confirmation.

The Feast of Pentecost commemorates the last action of the Paschal Mystery that we have been celebrating since Holy Week: Jesus' sending the Holy Spirit to guide us. At Pentecost, we were formed into the Body of Christ. We became the Church in a new covenant with Christ.

> What mission will the Holy Spirit guide us to do?

> How are we part of God's harvest?

# Peace from Confusion

The story of Pentecost is full of action: wind, flames, crowds, preaching, and astonishment. From the disorder and confusion emerged order, and a group of frightened individuals became a community of believers. The gift of the Holy Spirit's presence makes us the Church. The disorder caused by the Original Sin of our first parents has been righted by the sacrifice of Jesus and the coming of the Holy Spirit. Great calm, or peace, came through the Spirit's actions.

As a Fruit of the Holy Spirit, **peace** is a state in which we experience freedom from worry as God's love fills our hearts. We know that the world cannot be always organized. But we can work to establish harmony, to give the world a glimpse of the calm that will prevail when Jesus comes again. In the Beatitudes, Jesus, our Prince of Peace, says, "Blessed are the peacemakers" (Matthew 5:9). In bringing his peace to the world we bless it with God's order, where each person is treated with dignity and respect and has what they need to live.

### Fruits of the Holy Spirit

The twelve Fruits of the Holy Spirit are qualities that can be seen in us when we let the Holy Spirit work in our hearts. This season we are focusing on peace.

© Our Sunday Visitor

## WRITE

Write one way each situation listed below could be resolved peacefully.

A country goes to war because they want to take over the land that produces good crops.

_____

People want to blame someone for neighborhood problems.

_____

Siblings are always complaining to their parents about who gets more.

_____

## ♥ Prayer for Pentecost

*Pray the Sign of the Cross together.*

**Leader:** "Bless the LORD, my soul!
LORD, my God, you are great indeed!

You are clothed with majesty and splendor,
robed in light as with a cloak."

**All:** Send forth your Spirit, they are created
and you renew the face of the earth.

**Leader:** "How varied are your works, LORD!
In wisdom you have made them all
the earth is full of your creatures;
...Bless the LORD, my soul! Halleluia!"

**All:** Send forth your Spirit, they are created
and you renew the face of the earth.

**Leader:** "All of these look to you
to give them food in due time.

When you give it to them, they gather;
when you open your hand, they are well
filled."

**All:** Send forth your Spirit, they are created
and you renew the face of the earth.

**Leader:** "You take away their breath, they
perish
and return to their dust.

Send forth your spirit, they are created,
and you renew the face of the earth."

**All:** Send forth your Spirit, they are created
and you renew the face of the earth.
Psalm 104:1-2, 24, 30, 35, 27-28, 29-30

**Leader:** Go in peace.

**All:** Thanks be to God.

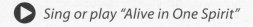 *Sing or play "Alive in One Spirit"*

# REVELATION

*How do we learn to be holy through the example of God, Jesus, and the Church?*

## CHURCH HISTORY TIMELINE

**326**   The first Basilica of Saint Peter is consecrated

**756**   Birth of the Papal States

**1506**   Construction begins on New Basilica of Saint Peter

**1929**   Lateran treaty establishes Vatican City

Go to page 348 for more

## Our Catholic Tradition

- God made humans in his image and likeness so we could be in relationship with him. God calls each of us to be in relationship with him and to honor the covenant and live by natural and revealed law. (CCC, 45, 54)

- God reveals himself to us in Sacred Scripture and Sacred Tradition, and we are called to respond in love by what we say and do. Faith is both a gift from God and a free, human choice. (CCC, 80, 176, 177)

- The Church is a sign of the holiness of God. Being holy is one of the Marks of the Church, and she helps us grow in holiness, especially through prayer and worship. (CCC, 867)

## Our Catholic Life

- With a soul, reason, and free will, humans can set their priority and direction in life toward friendship with God. Jesus is the model for living out this relationship. (CCC, 356, 357)

- God's Revelation is contained in his written Word of Sacred Scripture and Sacred Tradition entrusted to the Apostles and safeguarded by them and their successors, the bishops, and handed down verbally to future generations. (CCC, 84)

- Each of us is called to be holy in the ordinary circumstances of our lives. God created humans to share in his glory, to be holy, and to be joined fully with him. (CCC 319, 2013, 2014)

# In God's Image

## ♥ Let Us Pray

**Leader:** Holy God, we praise and bless you for your presence with us. Thank you for helping us to remember that we are holy and chosen.

"I praise you, because I am wonderfully made;
wonderful are your works!"  **Psalm 139:14**

**All:** God, help me to see clearly what matters in my life.

### 📖 Scripture

"God created mankind in his image;
    in the image of God he created them;
    male and female he created them.

God blessed them and God said to them: Be fertile and multiply; fill the earth and subdue it. Have dominion over the fish of the sea, the birds of the air, and all the living things that crawl on the earth. …God looked at everything he had made, and found it very good."  **Genesis 1:27–28, 31**

### Have you ever thought...

- What does it mean to be created in God's image?

- How can we know the right way to live?

# Getting Started

In this chapter, you will learn about God's desire for people to live in his image and to be in relationship with him. He wants to have a personal relationship with each of us, and his law helps us live in his love and his image.

## Catholic Faith Words

- soul
- free will
- covenant
- Ten Commandments
- Decalogue

 Answer the questions below to tell what you already know about the uniqueness of humans and their special role in God's creation.

## Living in His Image

| | |
|---|---|
| **What makes humans different from the rest of creation?** | _____<br>_____<br>_____<br>_____ |
| **How do these things relate to being made in God's image?** | _____<br>_____<br>_____<br>_____ |
| **What are some ways God helps us to live as he intends?** | _____<br>_____<br>_____<br>_____ |

**Commitments**  On the lines below, write about commitments you have made to different people and things. Which commitments are most important to you? Why?

**Friends**

_____

_____

**Family**

_____

_____

**God**

_____

_____

**Myself**

_____

_____

**Clubs or Sports**

_____

_____

**Church**

_____

_____

_____

_____

**School**

_____

_____

_____

_____

# Joined with God

## Why did God create us?

We all have expectations put on us and our time. Our family and friends need us, and schoolwork takes time. With all of these demands, you might wonder what's really important. The challenge is to find out what really matters, and to build your life around that.

## Our Purpose

As humans, we all share the same purpose. By our very nature, we are made to have a relationship with God: to be his friend, to know and love him, and to help others do the same. This is our purpose in life. How we respond to the expectations placed on us, and create expectations for ourselves, should be based on which ones lead us toward friendship with God.

Because God wanted to have a relationship with humans, he made us different from the rest of his creation. You were made in God's image and likeness, with a body and a **soul**—the spiritual principle, or part, of a human person that is individual, created by God, and will exist forever.

With only a body, human beings would be like all the other animals. Because God has breathed his own Divine Spirit into every human person, you are both a physical and spiritual being. You have an intellect that makes it possible for you to think, reason, and judge, and a **free will**—the God-given ability to choose between good and evil.

God created us with free will so we can have the freedom to choose good, to choose to love him above all things, and to love our neighbors as we love ourselves. This unique combination makes you an image of God.

You are related to God. The journey of life involves the ways that you live out that relationship with God.

> **How would you describe your journey of faith so far?**

## Jesus' Example

Jesus showed us that our happiness comes from trusting in God the Father and being one with him. This is what God created us for, and when our lives are lived with this purpose, everything else leans toward it.

Jesus taught us what friendship with God is all about. The choices he made, the ways he prayed, and the priorities he had in life showed us how to love God and others. He recognized the dignity of all people, even when society did not. He welcomed people others ignored, forgave people who were truly sorry, and cared for people in need. He showed compassion. He was also responsible to Mary and Joseph, and he followed the rituals and feasts of his Jewish faith.

Having a relationship with God the Father was not something separate from the rest of Jesus' life. It was part of who he was when with his family, friends, and followers. It was part of the choices he made and the things he did, whether eating a meal with his disciples or performing a miracle to feed 5,000 people.

### Catholic Faith Words

**soul** the spiritual principle of a human person that is individual, created by God, and will exist forever

**free will** the God-given freedom and ability to make choices. God created us with free will so we can have the freedom to choose good.

© Our Sunday Visitor

Jesus once told his disciples not to worry about what they were going to wear or eat.

## Scripture

"Look at the birds in the sky; they do not sow or reap, they gather nothing into barns, yet your heavenly Father feeds them. Are not you more important than they?"
**Matthew 6:26**

He was not telling them that material concerns were not important, but he didn't want them to be constantly worried about them. He wanted them to depend upon God and to be focused first on God's Kingdom.

> **What is really important to you? What is really worth worrying about?**

> **How would things change for you if you followed Jesus' advice about worrying?**

Jesus was able to model a complete relationship with God because he is fully human and fully Divine. As Saint Paul said, Jesus was the "image of the invisible God" (**Colossians 1:15**). Through Baptism, we are as brothers and sisters of Christ. We are in some ways an image of the invisible God. Though not perfect like Christ, each of us shares in the image of Christ.

## NAME

Because you have been united with Christ in Baptism, you have put on Christ to become more like him. Name some things that you recognize in yourself that are "like" Christ.

_____

_____

_____

_____

Name some ways you recognize that you need to grow more "like" him.

_____

_____

_____

_____

# Called to Covenant

**What is a covenant with God?**

Even though we are free to make choices, we do not always choose what is right. Sometimes we show God's goodness, and at other times we fail. Whether people are good or bad, God never stops offering his love. But people might still wonder, "If God is so good and loving, why is there sin and evil in the world?"

God created our first parents, Adam and Eve, in his image and likeness. They shared fully in his holiness and goodness. They also shared in God's gift of freedom but chose to disobey him. Because of their choices and actions, they lost the holiness and goodness first received from God.

Yet, God remained perfect in his love for Adam and Eve. Instead of abandoning them, he promised that all humans would once again share fully in his life.

He made a **covenant** with them and their descendants, first Noah, then Abraham. A covenant is like a contract between two persons, but it is more serious and heartfelt than a legal contract. It is a sacred promise or agreement between God and humans

involving mutual commitments. In the Old Testament accounts, God showed over and over again that he would remain faithful to the covenant he made to be their God and for them to be his People.

> **What covenant or sacred promise do you share with God?**

## Called by Name

God seemed to surprise people in the Old Testament with the way he called them to serve him.

- Abraham was called to journey to the land of Canaan, where God would make of his descendants a great nation. (See Genesis 12.)

- Jacob was chosen to be given the family birthright even though his brother Esau was older. (See Genesis 27.)

- God called Samuel to be a prophet, even though he was only a servant to the prophet Eli. (See 1 Samuel 3.)

© Our Sunday Visitor

**Go to the Source**
Read *Genesis 12:1–9* and think about how you would respond if God called you like he did Abraham.

God calls all people to live in covenant friendship with him. It is always possible to say "yes" to God, because God provides help in showing how to live in this relationship. Many figures in the Old Testament provided examples of what it means to live in a covenant relationship with God. They reacted to God's call in different ways, but each is an example of trusting in him and his will.

| Living Out the Covenant | |
|---|---|
| Noah | In the section of the Book of Genesis that we call pre-history, we hear the story of Noah. With his family, he trusted that God would keep them safe through the flood. God made a covenant with Noah never to wash away all living creatures on Earth again. |
| The Chosen People | They were the descendants of Abraham and Sarah, and God promised to make of them a great nation. Even when they turned from God, they were forgiven and called back to the covenant. |
| Moses | God saved Moses from his abandonment as an infant and raised him to lead the people of Israel in rebellion against their Egyptian captors. Moses then led the people out of Egypt and through the Red Sea when God parted the water. God gave Moses the Ten Commandments as a sign of his covenant love. |
| Ruth | Ruth was a Moabite who became part of the Chosen People through marriage. She became an example of self-sacrifice and good moral character through her gift of faith in God. |
| Solomon | As King of Israel, Solomon was noted for a wisdom that reflected God's care for his People. |
| Susanna | She trusted that God's wisdom in the prophet Daniel would prove that the accusations against her were false. She became a model of truthfulness for her family and all of God's People. |
| Jeremiah | Though at first he did not believe he was capable or worthy of being a prophet, he finally put his trust in God and answered the call. He constantly reminded the people that God would remove their hardened hearts and replace them with new hearts. |

## LIST

List three responsibilities you have as part of your personal relationship with God.

**My personal relationship with God calls me to:**

1. _____

2. _____

3. _____

**Moses carries the tablets of the Decalogue in the film *The Ten Commandments***

# Guided by the Law

**How does the law help us live in God's image?**

The law serves as God's way of helping us live out the covenant and grow closer to him because it helps us recognize evil.

The law is first of all based on nature, because it is through human nature that people participate and share in God's goodness. Natural moral law refers to the precepts about goodness that are written by God in our hearts and accessible through our God-given reason. This natural moral law shows that each person created in God's image has a fundamental human dignity. Natural moral law, or simply natural law, is the foundation for the rights and responsibilities all humans share.

## Laws of Love

The revealed laws of God, like the **Ten Commandments**, guide us in making choices. Revealed law:

- shows us how to live in relationship with God and others
- sets before us the virtues (like faith, hope, and charity) that help us live as God's children in his image
- helps us to recognize what is evil and what creates separation or division from God and others, and
- gives us insight about how to make God's love a real part of our lives

If human nature had remained perfect, humans would not have needed the laws of the Ten Commandments because these rules would have come from the heart and spirit of each person. The Ten Commandments, also called the **Decalogue**, from a Greek phrase that means "ten words," are based on natural moral law, but have also been revealed by God as a way of instructing us in how to live the life God intends for us.

God gave Moses the Ten Commandments on Mount Sinai so that the people would have a guide for learning how to live in God's image and follow the covenant— through their love for God (Commandments 1–3) and their love for each other (Commandments 4–10).

The Ten Commandments are found in the Old Testament, but the two versions given have some variations. (See Exodus 20:2–17 and Deuteronomy 5:6–21.) Saint Augustine used the Ten Commandments to teach baptismal candidates and Church members.

Natural law:

- helps humans distinguish between good and evil,
- shows the way to put that which is good into practice,
- is universal because it applies to every human being,
- varies in the way it is applied because humans are asked to use the gift of reason to make choices,
- is unchangeable and permanent throughout all of history, and
- provides the basis for all other moral laws and rules.

The Ten Commandments apply to all human beings in matters that are serious and also in ways that are less serious but important. For example, everyone knows that killing is a most serious sin (going against the Fifth Commandment). But the Commandment also applies to hurting someone with abusive language.

## Catholic Faith Words

**Ten Commandments** the ten fundamental moral laws given by God to Moses, and recorded in the Old Testament, to help his People live by the covenant

**Decalogue** another name for the Ten Commandments; from the Greek phrase meaning "ten words"

## IDENTIFY

**The Commandments** Write the correct number of the Commandment next to its text. Then draw a star next to a Commandment you will work on following this week.

_____ You shall not steal.

_____ You shall not covet your neighbor's goods.

_____ I am the Lord your God: you shall not have strange gods before me.

_____ You shall not bear false witness against your neighbor.

_____ You shall not take the name of the Lord your God in vain.

_____ You shall not covet your neighbor's wife.

_____ Remember to keep holy the Lord's Day.

_____ You shall not commit adultery.

_____ Honor your father and your mother.

_____ You shall not kill.

# IN SUMMARY    Catholics Believe

God made humans in his image and likeness so we could be in relationship with him.

- With a soul, reason, and free will, humans can set their priority and direction in life toward friendship with God. Jesus is the model for living out this relationship.
- God established a covenant with his People, promising to be faithful to them and to be their God. God calls each of us to be in relationship with him and to honor the covenant.
- The natural moral law and revealed law—especially the Ten Commandments—guide people in what is good and evil, what is faithful living, and what it means to truly be an image of God.

## Our Catholic Life

Rules are in place and enforced in every part of our lives, from rules about classroom behavior to traffic signs. Some are easy to follow, but others are more difficult or require explanation. Some are common sense, but others have been made in response to events or problems in society. The **Ten Commandments** go beyond everyday "rules." You have probably heard them since you were a young child, and over time you've understood them better. They are God's laws for living in relationship with him and with each other, and they are at the heart of God's covenant. God gave the Ten Commandments to the Israelites, but they apply to our lives even now, at every age.

> **Which Commandments are easiest for you to follow? Which are most difficult?**

## People of Faith

### Saint Marcella, 325–410

Marcella married young, but she was widowed within her first year of marriage. Afterward, she invited a group of noble ladies to meet at her home, where they lived a life of self-discipline and self-denial to grow more deeply in their relationship with God through Christ. Because of the way she lived in faith and sacrifice, Saint Jerome called Marcella "the glory of the ladies of Rome." Marcella's relationship with God pointed her toward a life rich in the Spirit of God. The Church celebrates her feast day on **January 31**.

 For more, go to
**aliveinchrist.osv.com**

## IDENTIFY

Imagine your life with no expectations or demands from others. You have to set all the expectations for yourself regarding your home life, school, friendships, and relationship with God. What expectations would you give yourself that would help you be an image of God to others?

_____

_____

_____

_____

_____

_____

_____

_____

_____

## ♥ Prayer of Petition

**Leader:** God, as we hear in the book of Genesis, on that sixth day, you made all of the living creatures of our planet. Last of all, you created man, male and female. From the first man and woman, we have been gloriously made in your own image.

**Reader 1:** A reading from Genesis 1:24–25. "Then God said: Let the earth bring forth every kind of living creature: tame animals, crawling things, and every kind of wild animal. And so it happened … God saw that it was good."

**Leader:** Let's pray for the Earth's animals.

**Reader 2:** A reading from Genesis 1:26: "Then God said: Let us make human beings in our image, after our likeness. Let them have dominion over … all the creatures that crawl on the earth."

**Leader:** Let's ask God to guide the way we treat animals and the environment.

**Reader 3:** A reading from Genesis 1:27–28.

"God created mankind in his image;
in the image of God he created them;
male and female he created them.

God blessed them and God said to them: Be fertile and multiply; fill the earth and subdue it."

**Leader:** Let's ask God to help us respect the gift of sexuality and all people because they are made in his image.

**Reader 4:** A reading from Genesis 1:29–31: "God also said: See, I give you every seed–bearing plant on all the earth … to be your food; and to all the wild animals, all the birds of the air, and all the living creatures that crawl on the earth, I give all the green plants for food. And so it happened. God looked at everything he had made, and found it very good."

**Leader:** Let's thank God for the variety of plants, bushes, and trees that grow all over the Earth; they feed us.

**All:** God, your plan of Creation was a perfect plan. We often fail to take good care of this Earth. We don't protect the dignity and life of other human beings. Help us remember to do so. Amen.

▶ *Sing or play "Almighty Creator"*

Go to **aliveinchrist.osv.com** for an interactive review.

**A** **Work with Words**  Circle the letter of the choice that best completes the sentence.

1. The ___ is the spiritual principle that is created by God and will exist forever.
   a. intellect
   c. soul
   b. spirit
   d. body

2. ___ is the God-given freedom and ability to make choices without being forced to choose or act in a certain way.
   a. Intellect
   c. Free choice
   b. Free will
   d. Covenant

3. A ___ is a sacred promise or agreement between God and humans involving mutual commitments.
   a. covenant
   c. vow
   b. contract
   d. Commandment

4. Another name for the Ten Commandments is the ___.
   a. natural law
   c. Decalogue
   b. revealed law
   d. Decalaw

5. Your ___ makes it possible for you to think, reason, and judge.
   a. intellect
   c. heart
   b. conscience
   d. soul

**B** **Check Understanding**  Complete each sentence with the correct term from the Word Bank.

| | |
|---|---|
| Natural moral law | law |
| Jeremiah | Moses |
| Solomon | Revealed law |
| spirit | Decalogue |

6. God chose _____ to lead his People out of Egypt and gave him the Ten Commandments.

7. The _____ helps people recognize the evil that leads them away from God.

8. _____ is universal because it applies to every human being.

9. _____, like the Ten Commandments, guides us in making choices.

10. The prophet _____ constantly reminded the people that God would take away their hardened hearts and replace them with a new heart.

**C** **Make Connections**  Write a brief response about a relationship in which you have seen or experienced a human reflection of God's covenant love. How did the relationship illustrate that love? What effect did that love have on you or the others involved?

_____

_____

_____

_____

_____

# Revelation and Faith

## ♥ Let Us Pray

**Leader:** Holy Lord, you have made yourself known to us through words and actions. Increase our faith!

"You will show me the path to life,
   abounding joy in your presence,
   the delights at your right hand forever." **Psalm 16:11**

**All:** Help us be open to your ways, Lord. Make our faith stronger.

### 📖 Scripture

"What good is it, my brothers, if someone says he has faith but does not have works? Can that faith save him? If a brother or sister has nothing to wear and has no food for the day, and one of you says to them, 'Go in peace, keep warm, and eat well,' but you do not give them the necessities of the body, what good is it? So also faith of itself, if it does not have works, is dead."

**James 2:14–17**

**Have you ever thought...**

- What does it mean to truly live our faith?
- How does faith make a difference in our lives?

# Getting Started

In this chapter, you will learn more about God's Revelation and explore how we respond in faith to what God has made known to us. You will look at how faith affects the way we live.

Catholic Faith Words

- Sacred Tradition
- faith
- Church
- councils
- virtue
- Theological Virtues

In the chart below, write names of some people who showed great faith from the Old Testament and the New Testament. Then write how each person demonstrated his or her faith.

## Examples of Faith

### Old Testament

- _____
  _____
  _____
  _____
- _____
  _____
  _____
  _____

### New Testament

- _____
  _____
  _____
  _____
- _____
  _____
  _____
  _____

**The Practice of Faith**  Faith and works go hand-in-hand (see James 2:14–17). Maybe you've heard the expression, "practice what you preach." As Catholics, we practice what we believe. On the chart lines, list a Catholic belief in the left-hand column. Across from the belief, name one way that you practice that belief. In other words, how do you live what you believe?

| Catholics Believe | | Catholics Practice |
| --- | --- | --- |
| God created us in his image and likeness. | → | We treat each other with respect. |
| | → | |
| | → | |
| | → | |
| | → | |
| | → | |
| | → | |
| | → | |
| | → | |
| | → | |
| | → | |
| | → | |

# God Made Known

### Where do we find God's Revelation?

We all have doubts and uncertainties at times, even about God and his presence in the world. Sometimes it's hard to have faith, especially when things aren't going very well. You might even wonder what it means to have faith, to believe in God and all that he has made known to us. Faith is a gift that God gives to each of us. We each can accept this gift of faith, or reject it. By following up on the questions or doubts we have, we can get to the bottom of things. We can understand our faith better.

## Sacred Scripture and Sacred Tradition

In order that the people would continue to hear the Good News of God's love, Jesus asked his followers to tell others all about him. The Apostles did just that, and, inspired by the Holy Spirit, they passed on the Good News through their preaching, writing, and baptizing.

The newly baptized believers first relied on the accounts and teachings of the Apostles and others who had known Jesus. They later turned to the letters of Saint Paul and other disciples, then to the Gospels recorded by Matthew, Mark, Luke, and John.

As the Church grew, the Apostles' successors, the bishops, looked to Sacred Scripture, especially the Gospel accounts about Christ, and they handed on verbally God's Word entrusted to them. They helped Christians interpret God's Word contained in Sacred Scripture and Sacred Tradition. **Sacred Tradition** is God's Word to the Church, safeguarded by the Apostles and their successors, the bishops, and handed down verbally—in her Creeds, Sacraments, and other teachings—to future generations.

Sacred Scripture and Sacred Tradition together are the sources of God's Revelation to us. Scripture is the basis of the written Word of God, and Tradition is the Word of God handed down verbally since the time of the Apostles. Contained in them is the Deposit of Faith. We need both to help us understand who God is and our relationship with him.

© Our Sunday Visitor

## Scripture

"This is good and pleasing to God our savior, who wills everyone to be saved and to come to knowledge of the truth."
1 Timothy 2:3–4

**Statue of Saint Paul the Apostle in front of St. Peter's Basilica, the Vatican, Rome**

## Handing It On

The Church strives to spread the message of God's Revelation by finding just the right words and actions that will help people say "yes" to God. In this way, the Church's leaders continue to share and apply the Word of God to the circumstances of our time, helping us to more fully know Jesus and live out his message.

In doctrine, the Church sets down in writing the important beliefs that are central for living a life of faith. An important example of this is a creed, or brief summary or statement of beliefs. Both the Apostles' and Nicene Creed capture the Sacred Tradition handed down from the Apostles.

We proclaim the Nicene Creed at Mass. In worship, like the Mass and the Seven Sacraments, the Church comes together to give God thanks and praise. In the life of the members of the Church, we see the faith of Christians put into action, especially for those who are in need of God's help.

### Catholic Faith Words

**Sacred Tradition** is God's Word to the Church, safeguarded by the Apostles and their successors, the bishops, and handed down verbally—in her Creeds, Sacraments, and other teachings—to future generations

## THINK

What's one thing about your faith that you feel is certain?

_____

_____

_____

_____

What's one thing that you want more clarity about?

_____

_____

_____

_____

# We Respond in Faith

**What does it mean to have faith?**

Most of us enjoy receiving a gift and hope it will be something we like. If we get something useless, we may pretend we like it, but then put it aside. The gift of **faith** that God gives to us is similar because he freely gives it. We may either accept or reject it.

Faith is a gift from God, but it is also your response to God's invitation to share in his life. It is your acceptance of what God has made known through Sacred Scripture and Sacred Tradition, and by your willingness to let his love make a difference in your life. You show your faith through the things you think, the decisions you make, and your actions. Faith involves the whole of you: your heart, will, mind, and soul. Faith is a way of seeing life and the people around you as if through God's eyes.

Having faith in God influences our whole life. Because of faith, we come to an understanding of God's greatness and how unique we are. Faith leads us to be thankful to God for all he has given us and show our gratitude for others as well. Faith helps us to understand and respect the unity and dignity of people, and lets us put our trust in God, no matter what is happening in our lives.

Because people are imperfect, we need God's help to have faith. This is why Jesus poured out the Holy Spirit when he died. The Holy Spirit makes Christ present to us. With the Holy Spirit's help, it is possible for someone to have faith. But no one is ever forced to have faith. We are drawn toward faith by the work of the Holy Spirit in our hearts and lives. It is by God's grace—the free gift of his own life and help—that we are able to believe.

## Catholic Faith Words

**faith** the Theological Virtue that makes it possible for us to believe in God and all that he has revealed. Faith leads us to obey God. It is both a gift from God and a free, human choice.

**Church** the community of all baptized people who believe in the Holy Trinity and follow Jesus

**councils** gatherings of bishops during which they speak about the faith of the Church, her teachings, and important issues

Having faith and believing in God is always a free decision. And it takes work. We have to respond to the gift God has given us so that our faith can grow and mature. One way we can strengthen our faith is by reading Sacred Scripture. Another is by asking Jesus to help us believe and increase our faith as one father did in the Gospel according to Mark: "I do believe, help my unbelief!" (Mark 9:24). We rely on the Holy Spirit to do both.

> **When have you caught yourself believing in something that did not seem possible?**

## Belief: An Act of the Church

Not only is "believing," or having faith, a human act, but it is also an act of the community of people who believe in the Trinity. The community of baptized believers who believe in the Holy Trinity and follow Jesus is the **Church**. No one is alone when they have faith in God the Father, Son, and Holy Spirit. Our faith in God flows from the faith of the Church.

In turn, the faith of the Church offers us support and helps us to become stronger in faith throughout our lifetime. Everything that the Church does and teaches relates to God's Word revealed in Sacred Scripture and Sacred Tradition.

One of the ways that the Catholic Church interprets and explains Sacred Tradition is by gathering bishops in **councils** to speak about the faith of the Church, her teachings, and important issues.

The last council was the Second Vatican Council, or Vatican II, between 1962 and 1965. Vatican II took place in Vatican City, Rome, beginning in October 1962. The council of over 2,500 bishops met in Saint Peter's Basilica. This council produced teachings on the topics listed in the chart:

| Topics of Vatican II | |
|---|---|
| • Revelation | • What the Church Is |
| • Liturgy and Worship | • How the Church Lives in the Modern World |
| • Religious Freedom | • Communications |
| • Ecumenism | • Bishops, Priests, Laity, and Religious Life |
| • Missions | • Education |
| • Eastern Churches | • Non-Christians |

## IDENTIFY

Imagine that you are a parent and you want to help your child to grow in faith. Identify five important things that you would do to help your child grow in faith.

1. _____

2. _____

3. _____

4. _____

5. _____

*David Kills Goliath*, by Reni Guido, 17th Century.

## Strength through Faith

**How does faith affect the way I live?**

Faith is much more than belief in creeds and doctrines. If we look at some of the important people in Sacred Scripture, we see that faith made a difference in the way they lived their lives. We can see the Holy Spirit giving them the initial promptings to turn to God the Father. The Holy Spirit is in our hearts, too, guiding us to see and believe in what the Son has revealed.

We find accounts in all four of the Gospels that Jesus often healed or forgave someone because they had faith in him. He would tell them that their faith in him had saved them. Jesus' followers understood the importance of faith for life.

### Scripture

"The apostles said to the Lord, 'Increase our faith!'

The Lord replied, 'If you had faith the size of a mustard seed, you would say to [this] mulberry tree, "Be uprooted and planted in the sea," and it would obey you.'"

**Luke 17:5–6**

> **What do you think Jesus is telling his followers in this passage?**

### The Effects of Faith

- ○ Abraham and Sarah were able to take the risk of moving to a foreign land because they believed that God would keep his promise to make them the parents of a great nation.

- ○ David was willing to face the giant because he believed God would help him even though he was so much smaller than Goliath.

- ○ The Apostle Paul, after he converted to belief in Jesus, continued to preach the Gospel even when people tried to imprison and persecute him.

- ○ Mary, the Mother of Jesus, had such faith in God and trusted in him so much that she said "yes" to the angel at the Annunciation.

- ○ Peter was the first of all the Apostles to identify Jesus' divinity, saying, "You are the Messiah, the Son of the living God" (**Matthew 16:16**).

Place a check mark next to the person whose experience you most identify with.

## Catholic Faith Words

**virtue** a good spiritual habit that strengthens and enables you to do what is right and good. They develop over time with our practice and openness to God's grace.

**Theological Virtues** gifts from God that help us believe in him, trust in his plan for us, and love him as he loves us; they are faith, hope, and charity

With openness to God as a gift from God, faith is one of the Theological Virtues. A **virtue** is a good spiritual habit that enables you to do what is right and make good moral decisions. Virtues guide our conduct and our emotions. The word *theological* is a combination of the two Greek words for "God" and "word."

The three **Theological Virtues**, faith, hope, and charity (also called "love"), point us toward God. These gifts from God make it possible for Christians to live in relationship with God. They help us believe in him, trust in his plan for us, and love him as he loves us. They are the three virtues from which all other virtues flow. If a follower does not have them, it would be difficult to possess any other virtues. Saint Paul writes "So faith, hope, love remain, these three; but the greatest of these is love" (1 Corinthians 13:13).

- Faith helps us to see beyond what is purely human, to recognize the mystery of God in our hearts, in other people, and in all of creation.

- Hope sets our vision in the future, helping us realize that no matter what happens on Earth, God will keep his promise to bring us to everlasting life. It helps us put our trust in God and his plan for us.

- Charity, or love, makes faith and hope concrete—through love of God we join with the Church in working with God to spread his Kingdom and make his reign known.

> **Why do you think Saint Paul says that the greatest of the Theological Virtues is love?**

**Anchors are often shown as symbols of the Theological Virtue of hope.**

## IN SUMMARY  Catholics Believe

God reveals his love to us, and we are free to respond in love by what we say and do.

- God's Revelation is contained in his written Word of Sacred Scripture and his Word in Sacred Tradition safeguarded by the Apostles and their successors, the bishops, handed down from generation to generation.

- Faith is both a Theological Virtue (a gift from God) and a human choice and action. Faith is an individual act and act of the Church as a whole; the faith of the Church nourishes and strengthens the faith of each of us.

- Faith makes a difference in our lives; others can see by the way we live that we believe in God.

## Our Catholic Life

You may have heard this saying before: "Faith without works is dead." It is a summary of the passages in James 2:14–26, in which James explains the effect our faith should have on our lives even outside of our Church. The Catholic Church demonstrates the power of her faith by performing **good works** all over the world, whether in relief settings or in missionary work. Good works are performed locally, too, in parishes and our neighborhoods. Catholic Churches work with each other and those from other faith communities to improve the lives of people in schools, neighborhoods, towns, and cities. We do this to show our gratitude for everything God has given us, and to honor the human dignity of everyone, because we are all made in God's image.

> How are you involved in the good works performed in your school or parish?

## People of Faith

### Saint Thomas, d. 72

Saint Thomas is best known for his response to reports of Jesus' Resurrection. Because he didn't believe that Jesus had risen from the dead, he is called "Doubting Thomas." Sacred Tradition says that after Pentecost, Thomas preached in India. A large group there still call themselves "Christians of Saint Thomas." When Thomas came to the city of King Misdai, he converted the king's wife and son. For this, he was led out of the city to a hill, and pierced through with spears by four soldiers. The Church celebrates his feast day on **July 3**.

📶 For more, go to
**aliveinchrist.osv.com**

My Lord and My God

## INTERVIEW

Think of a Saint about whom you know. Imagine that you get an opportunity to spend time with him or her. What three questions you would like to ask about his or her relationship with God?

1. _____
   _____
   _____

2. _____
   _____
   _____

3. _____
   _____
   _____

## ❤ Celebration of the Word

**Leader:** Let us begin with the sign of our faith, the Sign of the Cross.

In today's reading, we hear the cry, "I do believe, help my unbelief!"

A reading from the holy Gospel according to Mark.

*Read Mark 9:14–29.*

The Gospel of the Lord.

**All:** Praise to you, Lord Jesus Christ.

**Leader:** Lord, you alone provide the grace to help us believe.

With all our heart, we pray to you:

**All:** Lord, I believe; help my unbelief.

**Leader:** When we are in doubt,
when we feel weak,

when we feel you have abandoned us,

**All:** Lord, I believe; help my unbelief.

**Leader:** When we want to make choices we know are wrong,

when we wonder whether or not
you are real,

when we lose all our hope,

**All:** Lord, I believe; help my unbelief.

**Leader:** When everything seems to be going right,

when we have more to be thankful for than to ask for,

when we need to remember that all our blessings come from you,

**All:** Lord, I believe; help my unbelief.

**Leader:** When we have lost our way,
when it seems like our prayers go unanswered,

when we doubt ourselves,

**All:** Lord, I believe; help my unbelief.

▶ *Sing or play "Open My Eyes"*

Go to **aliveinchrist.osv.com** for an interactive review.

**A** **Work with Words** Complete each sentence with the correct term from the Word Bank.

| | |
|---|---|
| Church | virtue |
| councils | the Gospel |
| Sacred Tradition | inspiration |
| canon | faith |

1. _____ is the Word of God safeguarded by the Apostles and their successors, the bishops, handed down verbally through the generations.

2. One of the ways that the Church interprets and applies Sacred Tradition is by gathering

 bishops in _____ to speak about the faith of the Church, her teachings, and important issues.

3. _____ is the Theological Virtue that makes it possible for us to believe in God and the things that he has revealed to us.

4. The _____ is the community of baptized believers who believe in the Holy Trinity and follow Jesus.

5. A good spiritual habit that strengthens and enables you to do what is right is known as a

 _____.

**B** **Check Understanding** Indicate whether the following statements are true or false. Then rewrite false statements to make them true.

6. Sacred Scripture and Sacred Tradition together are sources of God's Revelation to us. **True/False**

 _____

 _____

7. The Sacrament of Reconciliation is founded on the commissioning of the Apostles by Jesus to share in his ministry and work as Church leaders. **True/False**

 _____

 _____

8. Sacred Scripture is God's Word handed down verbally to the Church in her Creeds, Sacraments, and other teachings. **True/False**

 _____

 _____

9. The Theological Virtues—mercy, grace, and peace—are the three virtues from which all other virtues flow. **True/False**

 _____

 _____

10. Sacred Tradition and Sacred Scripture together ensure that what the Church writes and hands down through the generations comes from God. **True/False**

 _____

 _____

**C** **Make Connections** On a separate sheet of paper, write a one-paragraph response to the questions: Think of someone—described in the Bible or from your life—who has great faith. What role does faith play in that person's life? What have you learned from that person about your own faith?

# The Church Is Holy

## ❤ Let Us Pray

**Leader:** Father, most Holy One, give us the faith and the holiness
we need to follow your Son, Jesus, and to discover your
will for our lives.

"Know that the LORD is God,
   he made us, we belong to him …
His mercy endures forever,
   his faithfulness lasts through every generation."
**Psalm 100:3–5**

**All:** Holy God, you sent your Son Jesus to show us the way
to you. We bless and praise you!

## 📖 Scripture

"He said to [his] disciples, 'Therefore I tell you, do not worry about your life and what you will eat, or about your body and what you will wear. For life is more than food and the body more than clothing. Notice the ravens: they do not sow or reap; they have neither storehouse nor barn, yet God feeds them. How much more important are you than birds! … seek his kingdom, and these other things will be given you besides. Do not be afraid any longer, little flock, for your Father is pleased to give you the kingdom. Sell your belongings and give alms. Provide money bags for yourselves that do not wear out, an inexhaustible treasure in heaven that no thief can reach nor moth destroy. For where your treasure is, there also will your heart be.'"
**Luke 12:22–23, 31–34**

### Have you ever thought...

- How can anyone completely trust in God?
- What does it really mean to be holy?

# Getting Started

In this chapter, you will explore God's holiness and what it means to be holy in our everyday lives. God's holiness and the holiness of the Church help us grow in holiness.

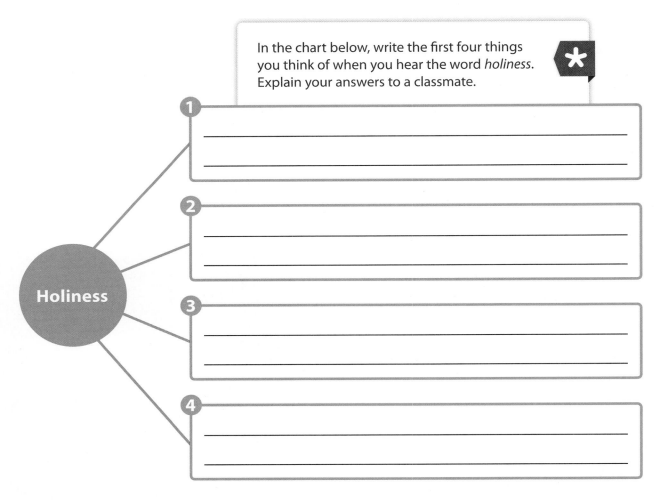

In the chart below, write the first four things you think of when you hear the word *holiness*. Explain your answers to a classmate.

**Holiness**

1. _____
   _____

2. _____
   _____

3. _____
   _____

4. _____
   _____

## Catholic Faith Words

- holiness
- angels
- holy
- Marks of the Church

## SOLVE

**To Be Holy** In the Gospel according to Luke, Jesus offers us insight into what it means to be holy. Solve the word search below to find some of the advice this Gospel gives.

| | | | | | | | |
|---|---|---|---|---|---|---|---|
| S | E | E | K | G | O | D | B |
| J | Z | N | Q | U | P | X | N |
| G | I | V | E | A | L | M | S |
| J | Z | N | Q | B | O | V | Y |
| W | R | A | M | D | V | R | A |
| D | O | N | T | F | E | A | R |
| B | L | G | N | R | X | L | P |
| P | R | E | P | A | R | E | T |

What is your definition for holiness?

_____

_____

_____

_____

_____

_____

_____

_____

Share with a classmate one way you have witnessed or experienced holiness.

© Our Sunday Visitor

Visitors explore space travel history at a planetarium in Poland.

# The Holiness of God

**How can we really be holy?**

Sometimes people think that holiness is about living in a monastery or spending the whole day in prayer. Some people are called to do that. But **holiness** is also about the ordinary events of life. Holiness is becoming more God-like, living in his presence and with his love no matter where you are. Holiness involves opening your heart to God's presence and growing deeper into relationship with God every day. God calls every person to be holy in some unique way.

## Sharing God's Glory

On each of the six days of creation, God looked upon what he had made and said that it was "good." Everything reflected his own goodness and holiness. So all of creation is related because everything was created by God and shows his goodness.

God created the variety of creatures each with a different purpose and order. He made them to be interdependent. But God made human beings special. He created us in his image, with an intellect and free will, and he set us over all creation to care for it. God wanted people to live in ways that would reflect his own goodness and holiness.

## Scripture

"When I see your heavens, the work of
  your fingers,
  the moon and stars that you set in place—
What is man that you are mindful of him,
  and a son of man that you care for him?
Yet you have made him little less than a god,
  crowned him with glory and honor.
You have given him rule over the works
  of your hands,
  put all things at his feet."  **Psalm 8:4–7**

When the holiness of God is seen and communicated in creation and in humans, this is the glory of God. We have many chances to share in God's glory so that the whole human race will come to realize this gift of sharing in God's own holiness. When we live for the good of others, we show God's glory. And God promises that the fullness of glory will be ours when we finally arrive in his heavenly Kingdom.

> **How have you experienced God's friendship in a way that surprised you?**

## Messengers

From time to time God has sent messengers to make known and help people understand his plan for all of creation. These messengers are **angels**, spiritual beings that praise God and serve him. They can think and choose like humans, but they do not have bodies. The word *angel* comes from Greek and Hebrew words that mean "messenger from God." Although there are many angels in the stories of Sacred Scripture, three of them are named:

### Gabriel ("the strength of God")

- helps the prophet Daniel understand the mysteries and prophecies God wants him to communicate (see Daniel 7 and 10)
- announces to Zechariah that he will have a son named John, who becomes John the Baptist and the cousin of Jesus
- announces the birth of Jesus to Mary at the Annunciation

### Raphael ("the healing of God")

- appears by name only in the Book of Tobit (12) to heal Tobit of blindness and to help his wife struggle against evil

### Michael ("who is like God")

- also appears with the prophet Daniel as the one who will help God's followers in their struggles, especially at the end of time (see Daniel 10 and 12)

- is mentioned in the Letter to Jude as one who fights with the devil
- leads the battle in Heaven recorded in the Book of Revelation (see Revelation 12)

*Tobias and the Archangel Raphael* attributed to Vecellio Tiziano

## Catholic Faith Words

**holiness** a state of becoming more God-like, living in his presence and with his love

**angels** spiritual beings that praise God and serve him as messengers to help people understand God's plan or to keep them safe from harm

### WRITE

List some things you do as a part of your routine every day. Then write what the difference might be to this event if you saw that moment as an opportunity to grow in holiness. For example, choosing what to eat for breakfast can remind you of God's command to care for our bodies.

_____

_____

_____

_____

_____

_____

# The Holiness of the Church

**Who will help you grow in holiness?**

Our world is covered with lakes and streams that are filled with life because water flows into one area and flows out somewhere else. Sometimes we find a stagnant body of water. Because there is no movement or outlet for the water, living organisms cannot survive.

It is much the same with the holiness of God that is given to every person and to the Church. If we try to keep God's holiness for ourselves, we become lifeless. But when we share the goodness of God with others, we grow more and more in God's life. We are each called to holiness because the Church is called to be **holy**, as Christ himself is holy.

## Catholic Faith Words

**holy** a mark of the Church. The Church is holy because she is set apart for God and his purposes and God is holy. Christ gave himself up to make the Church holy and gave the Church the gift of the Holy Spirit to give her life.

**Marks of the Church** the essential characteristics that distinguish Christ's Church and her mission: one, holy, catholic, and apostolic

## The Holiness of Jesus

As the perfect and complete Revelation of God, Jesus shows God's holiness

- by taking on our burdens
- by being the way to the Father
- by speaking with the voice of God
- by the way he lived the Beatitudes
- by reaching out to the lost, the needy, and sinners
- by being the perfect model of love

Being holy is one of the **Marks of the Church**—the four essential characteristics that distinguish Christ's Church: one, holy, catholic, and apostolic. The Church can be identified by these characteristics.

Because the Church is the Body of Christ, the holiness of the Church comes from

*Jesus Rescues the Sinful Woman* by Hendrick Krock

Christ. The Church is holy because the Holy Spirit gives us life and lives within us, guiding us as individuals and a community.

The Church helps each of us to follow Jesus' example and to become holy, sometimes in small ways, sometimes in great ways.

## Prayer and Worship

In the prayer and worship of the Church, Catholics meet God in a personal way and are strengthened to grow in holiness. This is why the Church invites us to pray at all times and in all places.

### Prayer and Worship

- ○ **Sacraments of Healing (Penance and Reconciliation and the Anointing of the Sick)** strengthen us in body and spirit when we have failed or when we are weakened by sickness.

- ○ **Special devotions, like the Stations of the Cross,** help us recall the presence of God in our lives and the help God offers at all times.

- ○ **Adoration of the Blessed Sacrament** helps us remember and honor in a special way Jesus' unique presence in the Eucharist.

- ○ **Sacraments at the Service of Communion (Matrimony and Holy Orders)** mark our commitment to follow God's call.

- ○ **The Liturgy of the Hours (prayed by ordained men, consecrated religious, and many laypeople)** marks every part of the day as holy.

- ○ **Feasts of the liturgical year** remind us of events and people that are important models for holiness.

- ○ **Personal prayer** gives us an opportunity to speak with God in a way that relates to the circumstances of our own life.

- ○ **Eucharist, or the Mass,** is the central act of worship because we hear God's Word, remember the Death and Resurrection of Christ, and are intimately joined to Christ in Holy Communion.

**✱**

1. Highlight the type of prayer or worship you most often take part in.

2. Draw a star next to a type that interests you or that you have questions about.

## IDENTIFY

In Colossians 3:12, Saint Paul asks us to clothe ourselves in Christ. Read that passage from Scripture. Think of a concrete example of how Jesus lived as Paul suggests. Compare your answers with a classmate.

# Holiness in Action

**What does it mean to be holy?**

Saint Paul tells us that a person without love is like a noisy gong or a clanging cymbal. A person may do nice things and speak very persuasively, but if words and actions do not flow from love, that person is nothing. (See 1 Corinthians 13:1–2.) Being holy means being in love with God and expressing that love of God through love for all creation and all people.

Prayer is an important part of being holy, but it is not the only part. Holiness that comes from love shows in your actions. Saint John taught this when he said that the way we can tell someone is in union with Christ is by the way that person lives like Christ. (See 1 John 2:5–6.)

 **Go to the Source**

Read *1 John 4:16–21*. How would you describe the relationship between love of God and love of our brothers and sisters?

## We Grow in Holiness

When people are baptized, they receive the light of Christ, and the Church prays that the light of faith will always be bright. They also receive a baptismal garment, and the Church prays that the dignity of the baptized person will always be strong.

The prayers of Baptism recognize that the gift of holiness develops and grows through a person's lifetime. Those prayers also recognize that sometimes people will face difficulties or evil as they learn how to grow in holiness and love.

- The members of the Church help each other grow in holiness.
- They support and encourage each other.
- They pray together and learn together.
- They listen to the Word of God and reflect on how to put God's Word into practice.
- They remember God's mercy when they fail and find God's grace to help them become more holy.

## CREATE

Use the letters in the acrostic to make a list of some of the ways the Church helps and supports you and some ways you help and support other members of the Church.

_____

_____

_____

_____

_____

_____

_____

_____

## IN SUMMARY  Catholics Believe

The Church is a sign of the holiness of God.

- Each of us is called to be holy in the ordinary circumstances of our lives. God created humans to share in his glory, to be holy, and to be joined fully with him.

- The Church is holy because Christ is holy and because the Holy Spirit lives within her. The Church helps us grow in holiness, especially through prayer and worship.

- A life of holiness is built on love; the love that God first gives us and his love that we share with our brothers and sisters.

## Our Catholic Life

Just as God blesses us, we are a blessing to God and others. As Catholics, our lives, our actions, our thoughts, and our words give praise to God because we show God's goodness wherever we are. We bless God in prayer. Because God blesses us, we can return that blessing. When we pray a **prayer a of blessing**, we are really asking God, who is the source of all blessings, to bless. We can bless people, places, and things. Parents bless their children, teachers bless their students, priests and deacons bless parishioners, and we bless ourselves with the Sign of the Cross. You can read more about prayers of blessing on page 380 of the Our Catholic Tradition section of your book.

> When have you felt God's blessing on you? When have you asked for it for someone else?

## People of Faith

### Blessed Miguel Pro, 1891–1927

Miguel Agustin Pro Juarez become a Jesuit at the age of 20. During a time of anti-Catholicism in his native Mexico, Miguel spent his life in a secret ministry, living like a daring spy. He was falsely accused of trying to assassinate a former Mexican president and sentenced to death without a trial. At his execution, Father Pro refused a blindfold. As he died, he bravely said, "Viva Cristo Rey," which means "Long live Christ the King!" Pope Saint John Paul II beatified Father Pro in 1988. The Church celebrates his feast day on **November 23**.

For more, go to **aliveinchrist.osv.com**

## IDENTIFY

Name some people who you think model holiness. Describe someone younger than you, someone your age, and someone older than you.

**Younger:**

_____

**Your age:**

_____

**Older:**

_____

What do these people have in common? What can you do to be more like them?

_____

_____

## ❤ Prayer of Service

**All:** In the name of Father, the Son, and the Holy Spirit, Amen.

**Leader:** Heavenly Father, over the centuries, women and men of faith have served you in many ways.

We pray for guidance and assure you of our longing to serve you in our day and in our time.

Let us pray.

**Side 1:** We know and believe that Jesus, your Son,
followed your plan and trusted in your will for his life.

We are here—we come to do your will.

**All:** We come to do your will.

**Side 2:** We know and believe that we are your children,
and that you want us to be happy
and to trust in your plan for us all.

We are here—we come to do your will.

**All:** We come to do your will.

**Side 1:** We know and believe that our world is hurting,
is wounded and in need of servants
who follow and respond to your voice;
servants willing to help and to heal
a weary and broken world.

We are here—we come to do your will.

**All:** We come to do your will.

**Side 2:** Heavenly Father,
send us your Spirit.
Give us the faith and the holiness needed
to be your people, your servants,
committed to you and to your will.

**All:** We ask this through Christ, our Lord. Amen.

▶ *Sing or play "Psalm 40: Here I Am, Lord"*

Go to **aliveinchrist.osv.com** for an interactive review.

**A**   Work with Words   **Circle the letter of the choice that best completes the sentence.**

1. ____ is becoming more God-like, living in his presence and with his love
   a. Beatification
   c. Holiness
   b. Justification
   d. Glorification

2. Human beings are created by God to be unique because we are made in his image with a(n) ____, and he set us over all creation to care for it.
   a. intellect
   c. challenge
   b. free will
   d. both a and b

3. The word ____ comes from Greek and Hebrew words that mean "messenger from God."
   a. Messiah
   c. savior
   b. angel
   d. Christ

4. Being holy is one of the ____ of the Church (the four essential or distinguishing characteristics of the Church).
   a. Doctrines
   c. Traditions
   b. Marks
   d. Characters

**B**   Check Understanding   **Indicate whether the following statements are true or false. Then rewrite false statements to make them true.**

5. All of creation is related because everything, including human beings, has been created by God. **True/False**

_____

_____

6. The Angel Gabriel leads the battle in Heaven that is recorded in the Book of Revelation. **True/False**

_____

_____

7. The four essential or distinguishing characteristics of the Church are one, holy, catholic, and sacramental. **True/False**

_____

_____

8. The Liturgy of the Hours gives special honor to Jesus' presence in the Eucharist. **True/False**

_____

_____

9. Holiness that comes from love is seen primarily in prayer and actions. **True/False**

_____

_____

10. Members of the Church grow in holiness as they listen to the Word of God and reflect on how to put God's Word into practice. **True/False**

_____

_____

**C**   Make Connections   **On a separate sheet of paper, respond to the questions. Which type of prayer or worship is most meaningful to you? How do you encounter God through this experience?**

**A** Work with Words  **Match the words on the left with the correct definitions or descriptions on the right.**

____ **1.** soul

____ **2.** free will

____ **3.** covenant

____ **4.** Decalogue

____ **5.** Sacred Tradition

____ **6.** virtue

____ **7.** angel

____ **8.** Marks of the Church

____ **9.** natural moral law

____ **10.** revealed law

____ **11.** Liturgy of the Hours

____ **12.** councils

**a.** a sacred promise between God and humans involving mutual commitments

**b.** the four essential characteristics that distinguish Christ's Church and her mission

**c.** another name for the Ten Commandments

**d.** a good spiritual habit that strengthens and enables you to do what is right and good

**e.** spiritual principle of a human person that is individual, created by God, and will exist forever

**f.** from Greek and Hebrew words that mean "messenger from God"

**g.** is God's Word to the Church, safeguarded by the Apostles and their successors, the bishops, and handed down verbally to future generations

**h.** the God-given freedom and ability to make choices. God created us with this so we can have the freedom to choose good.

**i.** this is universal because it applies to every human being

**j.** rules for living that guide us in making choices

**k.** a practice of prayer that marks every part of the day as holy

**l.** gatherings of bishops during which they speak about the faith of the Church, her teachings, and important issues

**B** Check Understanding  **Complete each sentence with the correct term from the Word Bank. Not all terms will be used.**

13. _____ and Sacred Tradition are the source of God's Revelation to us.

14. _____ is God's Word to the Church, safeguarded by the Apostles and their successors, the bishops, and handed down verbally—in her Creeds, Sacraments, and other teachings—to future generations.

15. The Sacrament of _____ is founded on the commissioning of the Apostles by Jesus to share in his ministry and work in a special way as Church leaders.

16. The _____ faith, hope, and charity, are the three virtues from which all other virtues flow.

17. Human beings are created uniquely by God, the only creatures made in his image with a(n) _____.

18. The four essential characteristics that distinguish Christ's Church are one, catholic, apostolic, and _____.

19. _____ gives special honor to Jesus' unique presence in the Eucharist.

20. Members of the Church grow in _____ as they listen to the Word of God and reflect on how to put God's Word into practice.

21. _____ is the Theological Virtue that makes it possible for us to believe in God and all that he has revealed.

| Word Bank |
| --- |
| Adoration of the Blessed Sacrament |
| free will |
| holy |
| Theological Virtues |
| Faith |
| Holy Orders |
| Sacred Scripture |
| holiness |
| Reconciliation |
| Sacred Tradition |

**C** Make Connections **Write a short answer to the following questions or prompts.**

**22.** God has a purpose for our lives: to know him, to love him, and to serve him. What does this purpose mean for your life?

_____

_____

_____

_____

_____

**23.** Write a purpose statement for your life that reflects your goals and desires as they are shaped by your relationship with God.

_____

_____

_____

_____

_____

**24.** Jesus Christ was the fulfillment of God's own Revelation. What aspects of God's nature become more clear to you through the life of Jesus? Provide specific examples from Jesus' life to support your answer.

_____

_____

_____

_____

_____

**25.** How do the virtues help you to respond to challenges in your life?

_____

_____

_____

_____

_____

# TRINITY

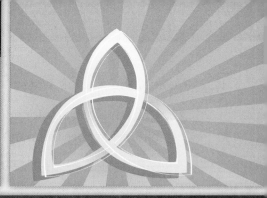

*How is Jesus the perfect sign of the Father made visible in the world through the work of the Holy Spirit?*

## CHURCH HISTORY TIMELINE

**313** Edict of Milan establishes religious freedom for Christians

**325** The First Council of Nicaea

**1274** Saint Thomas Aquinas finishes the *Summa Theologiae*

**1978** Pope Saint John Paul II is elected Pope

Go to page 348 for more

## Our Catholic Tradition

- We relate to the three Divine Persons of the Trinity in different ways. We are children of God the Father, brothers and sisters of Christ, and Temples of the Holy Spirit. The Holy Spirit furthers God's work on Earth. (CCC, 257)

- We belong to the People of God through Baptism and belief in Christ. The Church is part of God's plan for all people to come to know him and love him, and all her members have a role in spreading his message. (CCC, 778)

- The Church is both a visible, structured organization and the Mystical Body of Christ, in which the Holy Spirit lives uniting the Church, guiding her, and giving the community and each of us life. (CCC, 771, 809)

## Our Catholic Life

- Jesus' Transfiguration revealed his Divine glory as the Son of God, and shows us God the Father, Son, and Holy Spirit. (CCC 554–556)

- Through Baptism, each of us shares in Christ's mission as Priest, Prophet, and King. We offer our lives and prayer to God, and we show others the Good News through our words and actions, and through how we serve and lead others. (CCC 1546–1547)

- The Gifts of the Holy Spirit help us to give witness to Christ and live faithful lives, and the Fruits of the Holy Spirit are the results of those gifts working in our lives. (CCC 1831–1832)

# The Trinity Made Known

## 💙 Let Us Pray

**Leader:** Loving God, all praise and glory and honor are yours forever! We praise you Father, Son, and Holy Spirit.

"Great is the LORD and worthy of much praise,
whose grandeur is beyond understanding." **Psalm 145:3**

**All:** Holy Spirit, give us knowledge and understanding of who God is. Please guide us.

### 📖 Scripture

"At that very moment he rejoiced [in] the holy Spirit and said, 'I give you praise, Father, Lord of heaven and earth, for although you have hidden these things from the wise and the learned you have revealed them to the childlike. Yes, Father, such has been your gracious will. All things have been handed over to me by my Father. No one knows who the Son is except the Father, and who the Father is except the Son and anyone to whom the Son wishes to reveal him.'"
Luke 10:21–22

### Have you ever thought...

• How does Jesus reveal God the Father to us?

• What does God's being the Holy Trinity teach us about him?

# Getting Started

In this chapter, you will learn about Jesus' Transfiguration and what it revealed about the Trinity. You will discover how the Holy Spirit furthers God's work on Earth and shows us his power through the Church.

In the chart below, record what you know about ways that we encounter Jesus and explain what each one means on the lines next to it. This first one is begun for you.

## Encountering Jesus

1. _During the Mass_ : _____

_____

_____

_____

_____

_____

2. _____ : _____

_____

_____

_____

_____

_____

3. _____ : _____

_____

_____

_____

_____

_____

## DESCRIBE

**Relationships**  To be in relationship with someone is to know that person. It can mean you are related, but it always means that you have an association or connection with someone. Our relationships typically fall into categories such as primary, secondary, and acquaintances. In the first three boxes below, write a phrase or sentence to describe the nature of the relationships in each category and list some people you would consider to be in each. In the fourth box, describe how someone could move from being your acquaintance to a secondary or primary relationship.

**Primary:**
_____
_____
_____
_____
_____
_____
_____

**Secondary:**
_____
_____
_____
_____
_____
_____
_____

**Relationships**

**Acquaintances:**
_____
_____
_____
_____
_____
_____

**Moving from Acquaintance to Primary:**
_____
_____
_____
_____
_____
_____
_____

© Our Sunday Visitor

# A Glimpse into God

**What did the Transfiguration reveal about Jesus?**

Sometimes we think we have someone figured out. Then that person does something that surprises us, showing us a whole different side of his or her personality.

As Jesus' disciples grew in relationship with him, they began to see Jesus in different ways. His followers had seen him preaching and healing. They knew he was special, but they had to grow in their understanding of who he really was.

## Right Before Their Eyes

We read in the Gospel according to Luke that one day, Jesus took Peter, James, and John up a mountain to pray. His Apostles didn't expect anything out of the ordinary. However, they found out that Jesus was much more than their teacher and friend. As Jesus prayed, an incredible thing happened. Suddenly, his face changed and his clothes glowed whiter than anything imaginable. Then two men, also in shining clothing like an angel's, appeared out of nowhere and began talking with Jesus.

The Apostles realized that the two men with Jesus were historic leaders of the Jewish people: Moses, the Lawgiver, and Elijah, the prophet, were standing before them, talking with their friend! The disciples had never seen this glorious side of Jesus before. They had walked many dusty miles with him and stayed in places that were far from heavenly. The experience was almost too much for Jesus' friends. Then it became even more amazing when a cloud came and darkened the mountaintop, and they heard a voice from the cloud proclaim, "This is my chosen Son; listen to him" (Luke 9:35).

As the voice finished speaking, the Apostles looked around. The cloud was gone. Moses and Elijah were gone. Jesus alone stood before them. (See Luke 9:34–36.)

### Catholic Faith Words

**Transfiguration**  the revelation of Jesus' Divine glory to the Apostles Peter, James, and John

Jesus spans the distance between God and humanity. He provides the bridge between Heaven and Earth. His mission in the Trinity is to bring humanity back to God the Father.

> **What separates us from God? How does Jesus act as a bridge?**

## On the Mountaintop

Throughout Scripture, we find examples of God choosing to reveal important messages on mountaintops. In this particular mountaintop episode, the disciples witnessed the **Transfiguration** of the Lord, the event in which the revelation of Jesus' Divine glory was shown to them.

© Our Sunday Visitor

**📖 Go to the Source**
Read *Luke 9:28–36* to find out what Elijah, Moses, and Jesus were discussing. What parallel can be made between what the Old Testament figures said to Jesus and what they themselves had experienced in their service to God and his People?

The Transfiguration not only revealed something about Jesus, but it also gave the disciples a glimpse into the Trinity. God the Father's voice was heard from the cloud, telling the disciples about the uniqueness of Jesus: he is not another prophet or Lawgiver; he is the Son of God, and they should listen to him. The cloud represented the Holy Spirit, as it had become a sign during Old Testament times of God's presence among his People.

The laws and prophets of the Old Testament had prepared the way for the coming of the Son of God. But now, Jesus is the chosen one, the One in whom we find the truth, the One who reveals God to the world. "I am the light of the world. Whoever follows me will not walk in darkness, but will have the light of life" (**John 8:12**).

## IDENTIFY

There are times when we do not listen to people's good advice. Identify a time when you did not listen to good advice and how it affected you.

_____

_____

_____

_____

_____

## God's Glory Revealed

**How does the Holy Spirit further God's work on Earth?**

No one can deny that life has its boring moments. But there are also glorious moments—exciting times that take your breath away:

- making the team
- going on the big class trip
- getting praise from someone you admire
- moments of understanding, discovery, or inspiration

In these moments, we have a glimpse of what glory feels like. It seems as if everything is coming together. We feel more deeply aware and alive. We realize, "Life is really worth it!" or "God is good!"

Just like a loving mother who takes time to point out things to her young children that they might otherwise miss, the Church helps us see and appreciate the glory of God just beneath the surface of life.

## The Holy Spirit Guides the Church

Jesus promised his Apostles that the Holy Spirit would come to them. The Holy Spirit would help them spread the Good News of Jesus' life to others once Jesus had ascended to his heavenly Father. The Holy Spirit would be their Advocate, guiding and comforting believers and strengthening them to know and live by Christ's truth.

The Church was fully revealed on **Pentecost**, fifty days after Jesus' Resurrection on Easter, when the Holy Spirit descended on those first Apostles and disciples so that all believers thereafter would have help like that of a loving parent, pointing out to them what is truly important in life.

### Catholic Faith Words

**Pentecost** the feast that celebrates the coming of the Holy Spirit upon the Apostles and first disciples fifty days after Easter

© Our Sunday Visitor

## CATHOLICS TODAY

Every year, Catholics end the Easter Season by celebrating the Feast of Pentecost, remembering the day the Holy Spirit came to the Apostles in the form of fire and wind, filling them with the courage to go out and spread the news of salvation in Jesus Christ. That day, no matter what language they spoke, everyone who heard the Apostles understood them!

On Pentecost, the Church celebrates the Gifts of the Holy Spirit given to us at Baptism and Confirmation. Those gifts help us build unity in the Catholic faith, grow in moral and spiritual well-being, and give us strength to witness to the Risen Lord in our lives. On Pentecost, the Church gives thanks by renewing her commitment to spread the Word.

The Church helps us recognize and give thanks for the many ways in which God reveals his glory. In the Church, the Holy Spirit prepares us to know and love Christ, to share his communion, and to transform us in Christ's saving work.

> Apart from religion class or a parish youth group, when was the last time you talked about Jesus to another person?

> If you're shy about talking about your faith, how can you show your faith to others?

## DESCRIBE

Make a list of your most glorious moments.

1. _____

2. _____

3. _____

Describe how the experiences brought you closer to your family, friends, or God.

_____

_____

_____

_____

_____

# Relating to God

**How do you respond to God's gifts?**

God does not leave it up to us to invent our relationship with him. He is always initiating a relationship with us, and waiting for us to respond. His Church helps us know and love him. God gives us the free, loving gift of his own life and help to do what he calls us to do. This gift is called **grace**, and it is participation in the life of the **Holy Trinity,** the mystery of one God in three Divine Persons.

We do not deserve God's grace. We cannot earn it. God offers us this gift in many ways, particularly in the Seven Sacraments. But the choice is always ours. We are free to accept and respond to this gift. When we do respond to grace, it strengthens and deepens our relationship to the Trinity.

## Knowing the Trinity

In the Sacrament of Baptism we are baptized in the name of the Father, and of the Son, and of the Holy Spirit. Baptism is our gateway to the other Sacraments, and our first share in God's life and help. It is so important that, if there is great need, anyone can baptize another person. But only in an emergency situation, such as when the person is in danger of dying without being baptized. The person performing the Baptism must do it for the same reasons that the Church does. Water must be used, poured three times on the person's head, while the following words are said: "I baptize you in the name of the Father, and of the Son, and of the Holy Spirit."

As we get older, we are introduced to different ways of speaking about God. At Mass, at home, and in religion classes, we pray to God using different titles that reflect the roles he has in our lives.

A favorite prayer addressed to Jesus is called the Jesus Prayer, which uses two of his many titles: "Lord Jesus Christ, Son of God, have mercy on me, a sinner." When you speak of Jesus as "Lord," you are saying that you believe he is God. When you proclaim the Nicene or Apostles' **Creed** at Mass, you also make a formal statement of this belief.

> ## Catholic Faith Words
>
> **grace** God's free, loving gift of his own life and help to do what he calls us to do. It is participation in the life of the Holy Trinity.
>
> **Holy Trinity** the mystery of one God in three Divine Persons: Father, Son, and Holy Spirit
>
> **Creed** a formal statement of what is believed about the Holy Trinity and the Church. The word *creed* comes from the Latin for "I believe." There are two main creeds of the Church: the Nicene Creed and the Apostles' Creed.

© Our Sunday Visitor

## To Whom We Pray

Prayer is usually addressed to the Father, although it can also be directed to Jesus and the Holy Spirit. The chart below shows titles we use to address God the Father, God the Son, and God the Holy Spirit.

Choose one title from each column and explain what it means to you to call God by that name.

| Titles Used in Prayer | | |
| --- | --- | --- |
| **The Father:** | **The Son:** | **The Holy Spirit:** |
| Lord God | Lord Jesus Christ | Lord, Giver of Life |
| Almighty God | Son of God | Spirit of Truth |
| Heavenly Father | Lamb of God | Come, Holy Spirit |
| _____ | _____ | _____ |
| _____ | _____ | _____ |

### REFLECT

Explain the consequence in this world, for ourselves, others, and even globally, for not accepting God's gift of grace.

_____

_____

_____

## IN SUMMARY    Catholics Believe

We relate to the Three Divine Persons of the Trinity in different ways. We are children of God the Father, brothers and sisters of Christ, and Temples of the Holy Spirit.

- Jesus' Transfiguration revealed his Divine glory as the Son of God, and shows us God the Father, Son, and Holy Spirit.

- The Holy Spirit is alive and active in the Church, who helps us recognize and give thanks for the many ways in which God reveals his glory.

- God gives us the free, loving gift of his own life and help to do what he calls us to do. This gift of grace is a participation in the life of the Holy Trinity.

## Our Catholic Life

During Mass, we often call on all three Divine Persons of the **Trinity** in one prayer. In our personal prayer we can call on the the Trinity, together or individually. We can open ourselves to their work by thinking about how we might need each of them—God the Father, God the Son, and God the Holy Spirit—right now and why:

God the Father, protector and provider, who …

God the Son, friend, Redeemer, and source of wisdom, who …

God the Holy Spirit, guide, comforter, source of strength, who …

> When did you last pray to a specific Person of the Trinity?

## People of Faith

### Saint Lucy, 283–304

Saint Lucy lived nearly two thousand years ago. When she was ordered to make a sacrifice to an image of the Roman emperor, Lucy refused, saying, "If you were to lift my hand to your idol and so make me offer against my will, I would still be guiltless in the sight of the true God, who judges according to the will and knows all things." Because of her refusal, she was killed. Today we remember her as one of seven women mentioned by name during Mass. The Church celebrates her feast day on **December 13**.

For more, go to **aliveinchrist.osv.com**

## IDENTIFY

Explain what place God has in your life.

_____

_____

_____

What do you need most from God right now or what can you offer him?

_____

_____

What is one thing God is calling you to do? How could you do it?

_____

_____

_____

## ♥ Profession of Faith

**Reader 1:**  I believe in one God,
the Father almighty,
maker of heaven and earth,
of all things visible and invisible.

**Reader 2:**  I believe in one Lord Jesus Christ,
the Only Begotten Son of God,
born of the Father before all ages.
God from God, Light from Light,
true God from true God,
begotten, not made, consubstantial with
    the Father;
through him all things were made.
For us men and for our salvation
he came down from heaven,
and by the Holy Spirit was incarnate of the
    Virgin Mary,
and became man.

**All:**  Yes, I believe.

**Reader 1:**  For our sake he was crucified
    under Pontius Pilate,
he suffered death and was buried,
and rose again on the third day
in accordance with the Scriptures.

He ascended into heaven
and is seated at the right hand of the Father.
He will come again in glory
to judge the living and the dead
and his kingdom will have no end.

**All:**  Yes, I believe.

**Reader 2:**  I believe in the Holy Spirit, the
    Lord, the giver of life,
who proceeds from the Father and the Son,
who with the Father and the Son is adored
    and glorified,
who has spoken through the prophets.

**Reader 3:**  I believe in one, holy, catholic and
    apostolic Church.
I confess one Baptism for the forgiveness
    of sins
and I look forward to the resurrection of
    the dead
and the life of the world to come.

**All:**  Amen.

▶ *Sing or play "I Believe"*

Go to **aliveinchrist.osv.com** for an interactive review.

**A** **Work with Words** Circle the letter of the choice that best completes the sentence.

1. The revelation of Jesus' Divine glory to his Apostles on a mountaintop is called the ____.
   a. Last Supper
   c. Sermon on the Mount
   b. Transfiguration
   d. Ascension

2. ____ is God's free, loving gift of his own life and help to do what he calls us to do.
   a. Courage
   c. Mercy
   b. Canon law
   d. Grace

3. The day the Holy Spirit descended upon the Apostles and first disciples is known as ____.
   a. Easter
   c. the Ascension
   b. Pentecost
   d. the Transfiguration

4. Jesus promised the Apostles that the ____ would help them spread the Good News after his Ascension.
   a. disciples
   c. Holy Spirit
   b. Bible
   d. Church

5. The Transfiguration gave the disciples a glimpse into ____.
   a. the Word
   c. salvation
   b. mercy
   d. the Holy Trinity

**B** **Check Understanding** Complete each sentence with the correct term(s) from the Word Bank. You may use some terms more than once.

| | |
|---|---|
| Father | Holy Spirit |
| Pentecost | Moses |
| Christmas | Creed |
| Holy Trinity | Son |
| Elijah | Abraham |

6. The two men who appeared with Jesus at the Transfiguration were

   _____ and

   _____.

7. A mission of Jesus in the Holy Trinity is to

   reveal God the _____

   to the world.

8. _____ is celebrated as the full revelation of the Church.

9. When we proclaim a

   _____ at Mass,

   we make a formal statement of belief.

10. In the Sacrament of Baptism, we are baptized in the name of the

   _____, the

   _____, and

   the _____.

**C** **Make Connections** On a separate sheet of paper, write a response to the questions: List two different titles by which we address the Father, Son, and Holy Spirit. Reflect on what those titles reveal about the various roles the Trinity has. How are their roles the same? How are they different?

# We Are Christ's People

## ♡ Let Us Pray

**Leader:** Wondrous Lord, how good it is to know that we are never alone. How good it is to know that we belong to you. May all that we do and all that we say be done in the name of Christ Jesus.

"O LORD, our Lord,
   how awesome is your name through all
      the earth!"   **Psalm 8:2**

**All:** O God, give us wisdom to know where we belong. Give us wisdom to go where you lead us.

### 📖 Scripture

"Jesus said to them, 'Did you never read in the scriptures:

"The stone that the builders rejected
   has become the cornerstone;

by the Lord has this been done,
   and it is wonderful in our eyes"?'"

**Matthew 21:42**

**Have you ever thought...**

- How is Jesus the cornerstone of the Church?
- What does it mean to belong to the Church?

© Our Sunday Visitor

# Getting Started

In this chapter, you will learn how Jesus accomplished what his Father set out for him to do, and understand how though Baptism, we share in his mission as Priest, Prophet, and King. You will also examine how the Church helps us develop our faith and brings us together through Baptism and belief in Christ.

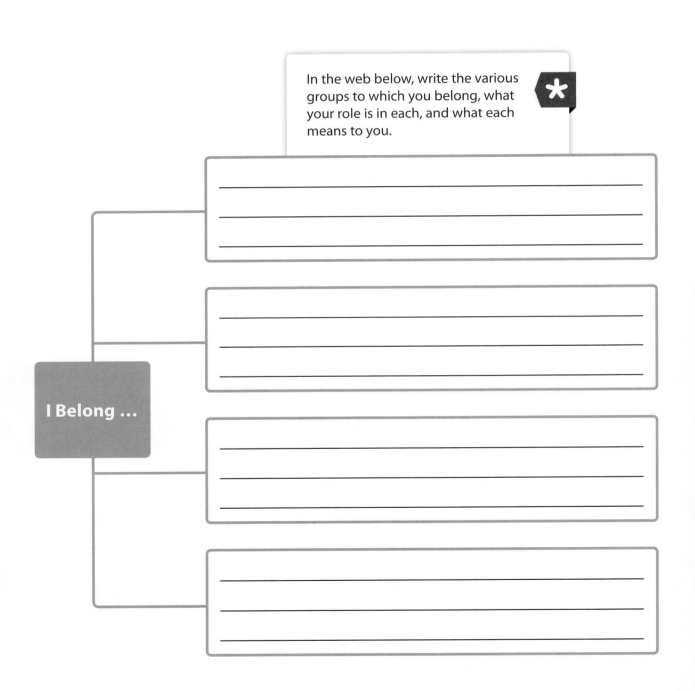

In the web below, write the various groups to which you belong, what your role is in each, and what each means to you.

I Belong ...

## Catholic Faith Words

- salvation
- *ekklesia*
- domestic Church
- offices of Christ

## IDENTIFY

**Jesus the Cornerstone**  Using the imagery of Jesus as the cornerstone, build a spiritual house. Label each of the stones with ways that your faith in Jesus has been built and grown to this point. You can include the names of people or groups who have supported you or created a sene of belonging.

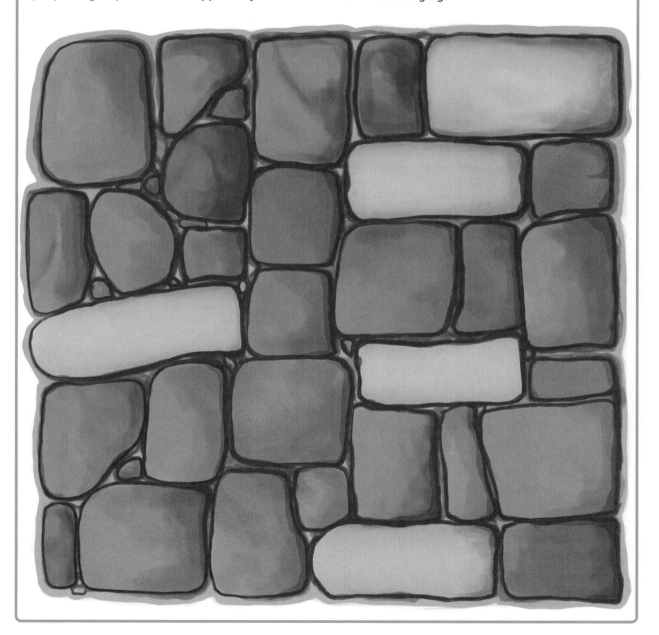

# We Belong to the Church

**How does the Church help us develop our faith?**

Throughout life, we belong to a variety of groups. We are part of a family, a class, a school, a parish, a team, a circle of friends. We are born into some communities. We choose to belong to others. And other groups choose us.

We can belong to many groups at one time, but some groups are more essential to who we are. For example, we don't stop being part of our family because we are part of a sports team or a community group. And, as Catholics, we are part of God's People, his Church.

## From "No People" to "God's People"

From the time of Abraham and Moses, God called the Israelites, later called the Jews, to be his Chosen People. He is their God; they are his People.

But with the coming of the Son of God, those who believed in him became part of the new People of God in Christ, his Church. We are Christ's Church because he is with us always, present among us as we pray and worship him, acting through us to continue his mission in the world.

No longer do you have to be Jewish to be part of God's People. What you need to have is faith in Jesus. You do not have to be born into God's Chosen People; you have to be born anew through Baptism. Peter tells us:

### 📖 Scripture

"But you are 'a chosen race, a royal priesthood, a holy nation, a people of his own, so that you may announce the praises of him who called you out of darkness into his wonderful light. Once you were 'no people,' but now you are God's people" **1 Peter 2:9–10**

If we are called to be part of God's People, how does that happen? Are some called and others not? No, God invites everyone to be a part of his family, and he does it through the Church herself.

> **What has God called you to do?**

## Faith and Baptism

The Church is the Bride of Christ: He loved her and gave himself for her. Jesus is in relationship and communion with her. He has purified her by his Death.

Through the work of the Church, the Good News of Jesus is brought to people everywhere. Those who have faith and choose to be baptized become members of God's People. In fact, the Church is like an international household of faith. Though members speak all different languages and represent many cultures, we are all united through Baptism. We form one family of faith, one People of God.

We cannot underestimate the importance of faith. Yes, it's a free gift from God, but it's also our choice. We don't have to have perfect faith to be baptized. In fact, faith before Baptism is a young faith that needs to mature and grow. Our faith grows as we learn and experience life, with the help of our family, the example of other Catholics, our teachers and catechists, prayer, and the Seven Sacraments.

**Procession and Mass of the Holy Cross at the Old City Church of Holy Sepulchre in Jerusalem**

## EXPLAIN

In 1 Corinthians 12:27, Saint Paul tells us, "Now you are Christ's body, and individually parts of it." When Paul says you are the Body of Christ, how is that different from membership in any of the groups you listed on page 104? Explain the differences on the lines below.

_____

_____

_____

_____

_____

In the Church's liturgy, the work of Christ's salvation is made present.

# God's Plan for the Church

**How does the Church bring us together?**

The Church exists to spread the Good News of Jesus Christ. The purpose of the Church is to reach out and let everyone know about **salvation**—the loving action of God's forgiveness of our sins and the restoration of our friendship with God through Christ.

God's plan is that all people come to know him. He uses the Church as a way to make this happen. As both the means and the goal of God's plan, the Church is a planned part of his good creation. She began in the Old Covenant, the promise given to Abraham and Moses by God. The Church is founded in the words and actions of Jesus Christ, fulfilled by Jesus' Death and Resurrection, and revealed at Pentecost in the outpouring of the Holy Spirit upon the Apostles. She is perfected in the glory of Heaven.

Together as the Church, we help one another. As diverse as we are, we are all in it together. The spiritually strong, the weak, those suffering in mind and body, young and old, the poor and the persecuted, are all the Church. The word *Church* is not used much in the Gospels. But when it is, it carries with it a great deal of weight. Jesus teaches his disciples that the Church has the authority to mediate between two members at odds with each other.

> ## Catholic Faith Words
>
> **salvation** the loving action of God's forgiveness of sins and the restoration of friendship with the Father brought by Jesus Christ
>
> **ekklesia** the original term for church in Scripture, meaning "convocation" or "those called together"
>
> **domestic Church** a term for the Catholic family, because it is the community of Christians in the home. God made the family to be the first place we learn about loving others and following Christ.

The original term for church in Scripture is *ekklesia*, which means "convocation" or "those called together." The Word of life in the Gospel gathers the People of God. Once gathered, they are nourished through the Body and Blood of Christ.

> **What is God's plan for the Church? What part do you think you have in God's plan?**

## We Are Family

The Catholic family is the center of faith, and we call the family the **domestic Church**. This means that your home is a smaller version of the larger Church. Parents and other family members carry the primary responsibility for being good examples in educating and bringing up their children in the faith of the Church, to know, love, and serve Jesus Christ.

Just like your family members come together, the Third Commandment tells us, the Church, to come together to observe the Lord's Day, Sunday. The most important way we do this is by participating in the Mass.

Why is it so important to take part in the celebration of the Mass every week? We are nourished by the Word of God and by the Eucharist when we gather together.

We need this spiritual food often, just as a person needs physical food. Otherwise, we will starve and our faith will become weaker. We won't be growing strong because we will have separated ourselves from the Church and Christ's gift of himself in the Eucharist. In the Body of Christ, the Church, we receive the fullness of God's life and love in Holy Communion.

> **What do you think it means that we call the family the domestic Church?**

> **Why do we compare the Church to a family? How is the Church like a family? How is she different?**

## READ AND DISCUSS

Look up and read the following Scripture passages about the Church. Place a check mark next to your favorite and compare your answer with a classmate. Explain what the passage means to you in terms of the Church.

○ 1 Corinthians 12:12–26      ○ 1 Peter 2:9–10      ○ Ephesians 2:19–22

Detail of a ceiling fresco in the Sacristy of San Marco, Italy, depicts the prophet Jeremiah

# His Work Is Ours

**How does Jesus accomplish what his Father set out for him?**

When you hear the word *office*, you probably think of a place where someone works. The word has other meanings, too. For example, the office of president would refer to a position of authority, trust, or duty given to someone. An office is also a function or role given to someone.

During the time of the Israelites and Jews before Jesus' time, men were appointed to be priests to offer sacrifices to God to keep the covenant, prophets to speak God's Word and call the people to live faithfully, and kings to rule God's people. These were their offices, and they were anointed and sent by God to do his work.

## Catholic Faith Words

**offices of Christ** the three roles of Jesus (Priest, Prophet, and King) that describe his mission and work among God's people; all those baptized share in these three roles

Then God the Father sent his own Son to us. The Father anointed Jesus with the Holy Spirit as shown at his Baptism and established him as the Priest, the Prophet, and the King. These roles are called the three **offices of Christ**. They describe his mission and work among God's People.

## We Share in Jesus' Mission

When we were baptized, we were united with Christ and his mission. We, too, were anointed to share in Christ's role of priest, prophet, and king to the world. We live out these offices, or roles, in our daily lives at school, at home, in sports practice, at work. We can show others what it means to follow Christ and to live for God's Kingdom. "But Jesus answered them, 'My Father is at work until now, so I am at work'" (**John 5:17**).

### The Offices of Christ

As **priest**, Jesus offers the most amazing sacrifice, doing something no other can do. He gave his life so that we all can be reconciled with the Father. He intercedes with the Father for us.

As **prophet**, Jesus completes the Law and prophecy that had come before him. He gives us the words of truth and life that no one else can.

As servant **king**, Jesus leads by example, teaching his people to give God honor and praise and give of themselves for the needs of others. Jesus was not the ruler the people had expected. He was not concerned with earthly kingdoms or politics, but with God's Kingdom.

## Participating in Jesus' Mission

○ **Priest:** We can offer our daily work to God, our studies, our time in prayer, difficult times and fun times, the ways we take care of others—all can be a spiritual gift to God.

○ **Prophet:** We can tell others about Jesus' message, the way to live as a disciple, and stick up for what is right and for those who can't stand up for themselves. We can ask questions and learn more about our faith, and teach others about Jesus by acting as he did.

○ **King:** We can serve others as leaders in classes, on teams, in clubs, around our neighborhoods. We can make the needs of others our needs too. We can participate in parish activities and lead others by our example of acting fairly and working for peace.

1. Place a check mark next to the role that is easiest for you.
2. Explain your answer in the space below.

_____
_____
_____
_____

## INTERVIEW

Meet with one leader in your school and ask about his or her role. Ask him or her which of the offices he or she feels called to perform most often in his or her work: priest, prophet, or king? What does performing that role involve? Take notes and share your results in class.

## IN SUMMARY    Catholics Believe

As the People of God, all the Church's members have an important relationship with God and a role in spreading his message.

- We belong to the People of God through Baptism and belief in Christ, which matures as we grow and experience more.

- The Church is part of God's plan for all people to come to know him and love him, and the Catholic family has a special role in this plan as the domestic Church.

- Through Baptism, each of us shares in Christ's mission as Priest, Prophet, and King. We offer our lives and prayer to God, and we show others the Good News through our words and actions, and through how we serve and lead others.

## Our Catholic Life

Our life in the Church includes participating in the mission of Jesus as priest, prophet, and king. One way we do this is by offering our lives and prayers to God, both in Church and out in the world. Another way is by sharing the message of the Good News in our words and actions. One of the **Precepts of the Church** is to take part in Mass on Sundays and holy days and to keep these days holy, avoiding unnecessary work. On Sundays, Catholics can spend time in prayer and thought on how they could serve and lead others over the next week, acting as priest, prophet, and king in their homes, school, and workplaces. Spend some time this weekend considering what you can personally do.

> **What is one way you can live as priest, prophet, or king this week?**

## People of Faith

### Saint Angela Merici, 1474–1540

Saint Angela was a very devout child. As she grew up, she saw that many poor young women were not able to get a good education, so when she was 20 she began teaching girls in her home. When she was 61 years old, she founded the Company of St. Ursula, an order of nuns, with twelve other women. The Ursulines were the first Catholic sisters to come to the new world. In 1639, they built a mission in Canada to teach the native people. The Ursulines still operate schools in the United States and Canada. The Church celebrates her feast day on **January 27.**

For more, go to
**aliveinchrist.osv.com**

## IDENTIFY

Imagine you are a reporter interviewing a Catholic person. This person spoke about being part of God's family and the Church, reasons it is important to attend Mass regularly, and how each Catholic is called to act as priest, prophet, and king. Choose one of these topics and reread the section on it in this chapter.

**Your topic:**

_____

Write an article based on your "interview," on your chosen topic. Write a headline and an opening sentence for your article here.

_____

_____

_____

## ♥ Celebration of the Word

**Leader:** We gather here this day
in the name of the Father,
and of the Son,
and of the Holy Spirit.

**All:** Amen.

**Leader:** Let us be attentive to the wisdom of Saint Paul's first letter to the Corinthians.

*Read 1 Corinthians 12:12–14, 27–31.*

The word of the Lord.

**All:** Thanks be to God.

**Leader:** O God of all,
before we were even born you formed us
and shaped us as one like you.

On the day of our birth, you claimed us as your own.

On the day of our Baptism, your Church welcomed us
into the family of believers,
who claim Christ, your Son, as Lord.

How good it is to know that we have
always belonged,
that we are never alone,
that there are others out there just like us,
that we are chosen members of something
greater than ourselves!

Help us to understand what a gift it is to
be members of a community
that chooses Christ in times of trouble,
that chooses Christ in times of joy and
excitement,
that chooses Christ in times of worry and
decision making,
that chooses Christ to lead us each and
every day.

May all that we do
and all that we say
be done in the name of Christ Jesus.

**All:** Amen.

▶ *Sing or play "Healing Waters"*

Go to **aliveinchrist.osv.com** for an interactive review.

**A** **Work with Words** **Circle the letter of the choice that best completes the sentence.**

1. Each Catholic family is called to be a(n) ____.
   a. domestic office
   c. domestic Church
   b. *ekklesia*
   d. parish

2. The loving action of God's forgiveness of sins and the restoration of our friendship with God is called ____.
   a. salvation
   c. Heaven
   b. abba
   d. prudence

3. In Scripture, the word for Church, *ekklesia*, means ____.
   a. chosen People
   c. People of God
   b. those called together
   d. people of the Word

4. Jesus' mission as Priest, Prophet, and King is known as the ____.
   a. new covenant offices
   c. Old Testament offices
   b. fulfillment of God's law
   d. three offices of Christ

**B** **Check Understanding** **Indicate whether the following statements are true or false. Then rewrite false statements to make them true.**

5. The Church is like an international household of faith, all united through Baptism. **True/False**

_____

_____

6. The Church exists to spread the Good News of Jesus Christ. **True/False**

_____

_____

7. From the time of Abraham and Moses, God called the Israelites to be his Chosen People. **True/False**

_____

_____

8. Through the Sacrament of Reconciliation, we share in Jesus' mission as priest, prophet, and king. **True/False**

_____

_____

9. The First Commandment requires us to come together on Sunday to observe the Lord's Day. **True/False**

_____

_____

10. Jesus showed us that the true meaning of leadership is service. **True/False**

_____

_____

**C** **Make Connections** **Write a one-paragraph response to the question: As a baptized member of the Church, how can you more fully live out your role as a prophet, a priest, or a king?**

_____

_____

_____

_____

_____

_____

_____

_____

# Temple of the Holy Spirit

## ♡ Let Us Pray

**Leader:** Holy Spirit, open our eyes to see your wonders around us. Open our ears to hear the Gospel message of Jesus Christ. Open our hearts to receive the love you offer.

"Where can I go from your spirit?
From your presence where can I flee?"  **Psalm 139:7**

**All:** Holy God, may your Spirit be our guide. Help us hear what you are telling us to do.

### 📖 Scripture

"The word you hear is not mine but that of the Father who sent me. I have told you this while I am with you. The Advocate, the holy Spirit that the Father will send in my name—he will teach you everything and remind you of all that [I] told you. Peace I leave with you; my peace I give to you."  **John 14:24–27**

**Have you ever thought...**

- How is the Holy Spirit leading you?
- How do the Gifts of the Holy Spirit help you live a faith-filled life?

# Getting Started

In this chapter, you will learn how the body and soul united make us who we are and how this unity is part of God's plan. You will also learn about the Gifts and Fruits of the Holy Spirit, and discover the Holy Spirit's plan for the Church.

## Catholic Faith Words

- Temple of the Holy Spirit
- character
- Gifts of the Holy Spirit
- Fruits of the Holy Spirit
- Mystical Body of Christ

1. Fill in the chart below with things that humans need to live.

2. Place a check mark next to the things that are physical needs, and fill in the circle next to those that are spiritual.

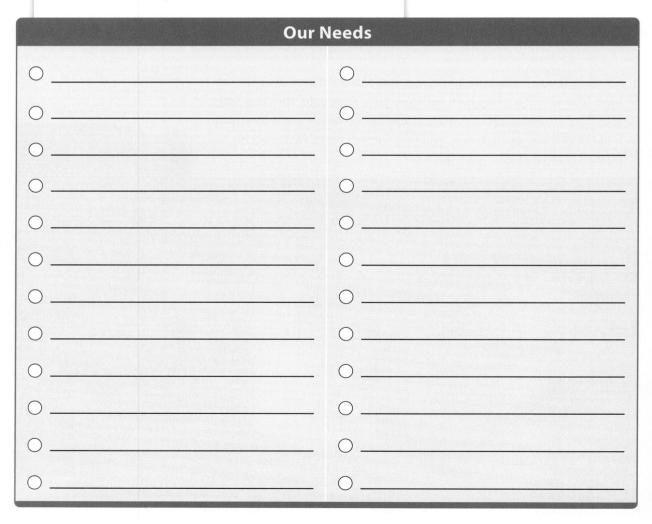

## Our Needs

## IDENTIFY

**Gifts to Offer** Think about the gifts that God has given you. They don't have to be big and extraordinary. What are some of the gifts you have? How can your gifts help meet the needs of others?

**Gifts I Have**

_____

_____

_____

_____

_____

_____

_____

_____

_____

_____

**How These Gifts Can Help**

_____

_____

_____

_____

_____

_____

_____

_____

_____

_____

_____

# Something More

**How do the body and the soul work together in God's plan?**

We are given our bodies by God. We care for and nourish them by eating and drinking properly. We also care for our bodies by exercising and keeping our bodies strong. Souls are similar. Just as a body can be undernourished or weak, a soul can be malnourished and weak.

Everyone has a soul, a spiritual principle which God created in them. You cannot examine your soul like the parts of your body. But it is there, inside, individual, spiritual and everlasting. Your soul is an essential part of who you are—your body and soul together make you who you are.

In his letters to the people of Corinth, Saint Paul describes how the Holy Spirit resides within the body. He uses the image of a temple and applies it to our body and soul, as the **Temple of the Holy Spirit**.

## Scripture

"Do you not know that your body is a temple of the holy Spirit within you, whom you have from God, and that you are not your own? For you have been purchased at a price. Therefore, glorify God in your body."

1 Corinthians 6:19–20

Faithful people pay attention to their souls. Caring for and paying attention to your soul is the flip side of caring for and paying attention to your body. Care of your soul and care of your body are two sides of the same coin of nourishing yourself. In his *Theology of the Body*, Pope Saint John Paul II pointed out that our bodies and souls are united within us. Whatever we do with our bodies, we also do with our souls. That's why it is so important to care for our bodies and use them only as God intended.

You can't take care of the world around you unless you first take care of yourself. Nourishing and building your soul are important tasks if you are going to grow and mature.

> **What are some of the ways you already nourish your soul?**

## Catholic Faith Words

**Temple of the Holy Spirit** the way Saint Paul describes how the Holy Spirit resides within the body

© Our Sunday Visitor

*Deposition of Christ (depicting the Temple)*, 1435, by Fra Angelico

## The Temple in Jesus' Day

In Jesus' time, and for about forty years after his Crucifixion (before Paul's letter to the Corinthians was written), the Temple in Jerusalem was the main focus for Jewish religion. Paul was Jewish before he was baptized as a Christian.

The Temple was where devout Jews offered sacrifices to God. This was the third Temple to stand on this spot, which was a sign of God's presence among his Chosen People. It was the place that symbolized their entire religious practice. It was so significant that every male Jew was required to visit the Temple once a year to make a sacrifice to God of a dove, a sheep, or an ox. This understanding of the Temple may have influenced Saint Paul when he wrote that each of us is a temple of the Holy Spirit meant to give glory to God. (See 1 Corinthians 6:19.)

## REFLECT AND WRITE

Reread the Scripture from 1 Corinthians. Spend a few minutes reflecting on it. Then write a short prayer giving thanks to God for the gift of your body and asking for help in respecting that gift.

_____

_____

_____

_____

_____

_____

_____

# Food for the Soul

**What gifts does the Holy Spirit give us?**

You need to eat right to feel right. The right kinds of food promote healthy growth in our bodies. Balanced meals include all the vitamins, minerals, and other nutrients our bodies need.

Our souls are nourished by God's grace. Grace comes to us in a variety of ways, most importantly in Baptism, the Eucharist, and the other Sacraments. Baptism is the gateway into the life of the Holy Spirit. In Baptism, we are set apart as belonging to Jesus Christ by being marked with a permanent spiritual seal called a **character**. This seal strengthens us to be Christ's witnesses in the world. Other Sacraments that confer a lasting seal are Confirmation and Holy Orders.

© Our Sunday Visitor

## Catholic Faith Words

**character** a permanent, sacramental, spiritual seal that strengthens us to do God's work. A seal is given in the Sacraments of Baptism, Confirmation, or Holy Orders.

**Gifts of the Holy Spirit** seven powerful gifts God gives us to follow the guidance of the Holy Spirit and live the Christian life. We are sealed with the Gifts of the Holy Spirit at Confirmation.

**Fruits of the Holy Spirit** the qualities that can be seen in us when we allow the Holy Spirit to work in our hearts

## The Gifts of the Holy Spirit

Who helps us to be witnesses of the Good News? The Holy Spirit does.

In Baptism, throughout life, and most especially in Confirmation, he gives us gifts to guide us. The Sacrament of Confirmation

---

In the space provided write one way you could use each Gift of the Holy Spirit in your life right now.

| Using the Gifts | |
|---|---|
| **Wisdom**: to develop a deep understanding of God and life | _____ |
| **Understanding**: to see truth and live faithfully | _____ |
| **Counsel** (Right Judgment): to judge good and evil and avoid sin | _____ |
| **Fortitude** (Courage): to act with confidence, strength, and courage | _____ |
| **Knowledge**: to understand the Word of God | _____ |
| **Piety** (Reverence): to worship and respect the Lord | _____ |
| **Fear of the Lord** (Wonder and Awe): to love and honor God | _____ |

seals us with a special outpouring of the seven **Gifts of the Holy Spirit**, which give us guidance on how to live a holy life. Confirmation also deepens the grace of Baptism, and strengthens us to give witness to Christ in the world. The Gifts help us follow the guidance of the Holy Spirit and live the Christian life. They are referenced in Isaiah 11:1–5.

## Fullness of the Spirit

Ever since our Baptism, we have received many gifts from God. We have been growing in faith, hope, and love. At Confirmation, we are again anointed with the Holy Spirit, who first entered our lives in Baptism. Through Confirmation, our relationship with God is strengthened and deepened.

Why does your relationship with God need to deepen? Because your world expands as you grow older. You will meet new people, and go beyond your family and household. Every day you will meet new challenges.

Therefore, you need the Holy Spirit and his gifts so that you can

- connect on a deeper level to Jesus
- grow as a member of the Church
- become more involved with the activity, ministry, and mission of the Church
- be strengthened to witness to the faith by the things you say and do

In many ways, the Gifts of the Holy Spirit play an important role in maturing you as a Catholic. We all need to use these Gifts, just as we use other things we learn as we grow, for them to have a lasting impact on our lives. All Christians should strive to put into practice the example of Christ's life and his teaching. The Church also names twelve

ways in which a mature Christian shows that he or she is bearing fruit in the Spirit—the **Fruits of the Holy Spirit**. These qualities can be seen in us when we allow the Holy Spirit to work in our hearts (see Galatians 5:22–23).

Each person, cooperating with the Holy Spirit, shows Christian maturity in unique ways. These Fruits of the Holy Spirit all contribute to how you can grow as a person, and as a Catholic. For more on the Fruits of the Holy Spirit, see page 375 of the Our Catholic Tradition section of your book.

> **What are some ways you can become more involved in the work of the Church?**

### ROLE-PLAY

With a classmate, choose two or three Gifts of the Holy Spirit. Discuss situations in which people your age could rely on these gifts. Then role-play the situations with two different outcomes: one in which the person relied on the gift, and one in which the gift did not seem present.

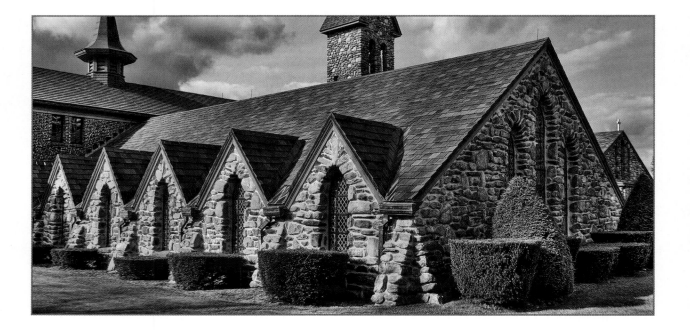

# A Temple Not Built by Human Hands

**What plan does the Holy Spirit have for the Church?**

The Church is truly a mystery, visible and spiritual at the same time. The Church is both a structured organization of members with a variety of roles, and the Body of Christ. The Church is a visible community and a spiritual one. This visible organization needs buildings and structures. Parish churches, along with schools, hospitals, monasteries, convents, shelters, centers, halls, and office buildings, make up the bulk of our buildings.

But just as we are more than our bodies, the Church is more than just the visible organization or her property.

## Catholic Faith Words

**Mystical Body of Christ** a name for the Church, whose baptized members are all united to Christ and one another through the Holy Spirit, forming one holy people with Christ as her head

## What the Church Is

The Church is the **Mystical Body of Christ**. The Church unites all believers through the Holy Spirit into one holy people, with Christ as their head and themselves as the body, or members. The same Spirit unites members to one another as brothers and sisters in the faith.

The Holy Spirit is like a "soul" for the Church. In other words, the Mystical Body is not just a collection of human beings who happen to believe the same thing or belong to the same community. Together they are the Church because the Holy Spirit lives in them, giving them energy and life, helping them live as the People of God.

## Scripture

"For we are the temple of the living God; as God said:

'I will live in them and move among them, and I will be their God and they shall be my people . . .

> and I will be a father to you,
>> and you shall be sons and daughters to me,
>
> says the Lord Almighty.'"
>
> 2 Corinthians 6:16–18

The Holy Spirit makes this promise real and builds up this true spiritual Temple, giving life to the Church and making her holy. He helps us relate to God in this world.

## The Spirit Leads Us Where We Would Not Go

Everyone seeks to be comfortable, protected from the dangers of the world. No one wants to be hungry, homeless, and hurting. The Church, urged on by the Holy Spirit, follows Christ in his mission of outreach to those who are poor and in need. The Church goes to every part of the world where healing and hope are needed. The Holy Spirit leads us, and we go!

## CONSIDER

Who or what in your neighborhood or city could use help or healing? Describe some ways that you and your classmates could help.

_____

_____

_____

_____

_____

_____

_____

## IN SUMMARY    Catholics Believe

God the Holy Spirit lives within each of us as individuals and in the Church as a community. We are Temples of the Holy Spirit, as is the Church.

- Our souls and bodies united make us who we are, and we need to take care of our souls like we take care of our bodies.

- The Gifts of the Holy Spirit help us to give witness to Christ and live faithful lives, and the Fruits of the Holy Spirit are the results of those gifts working in our lives.

- The Church is both a visible, structured organization and the Mystical Body of Christ, in which the Holy Spirit lives uniting the Church, guiding her, and giving her life.

## Our Catholic Life

We know we need to keep our bodies healthy so we can live a long life and act as examples to others. Some of the ways we do this include getting the right amount of exercise, sleep, and good nutrition, practicing good personal hygiene, and controlling anger and other emotions that cause stress. Part of our work as Catholics is keeping the **Body of Christ** healthy, too, by praying for her work in our communities and around the world, offering our time, talents, and money to continue that work and celebrate God's gifts to us, and supporting the work of priests, deacons, and those in conscerated religious life, who have dedicated their lives to the Church. When a Catholic community is in good health, it shows in the Church as a whole.

> What do you do to stay healthy? In what ways can you help keep the Church healthy, too?

## People of Faith

**Blessed Cyprian Michael Iwene Tansi, 1903–1964**

From the tropical rain forests of his native Nigeria to his final home at a monastery in England, Father Tansi shared the love of the Holy Spirit with everyone. Many of the villages in which Father Tansi preached didn't have churches. He taught the Word of God and labored alongside the villagers to build churches. Later he became a Trappist monk and took the name Cyprian. During a visit to Nigeria in 1998, Pope Saint John Paul II praised his work and beatified him. The Church celebrates his feast day on **January 20.**

For more, go to
**aliveinchrist.osv.com**

## IDENTIFY

Identify one item from each of the ways to keep the Church healthy that you want to work on further. Write down three action steps in pursuing these goals.

1. _____

2. _____

3. _____

## ♥ Prayer to the Holy Spirit

**Leader:** Together, let us pray a prayer to the Holy Spirit.

**All:** Come, Holy Spirit,
fill the hearts of your faithful.
And kindle in them the fire of your love.

**Reader 1:** God, You have always sent your spirit to fill and enliven those who are open to your great love and gifts. These small flames we hold have come from one lit candle.

We know that there is one Holy Spirit who has filled individual hearts and souls from the beginning of creation.

This Holy Spirit, the Spirit of God, nourishes us, especially through the Word of God and through the Seven Sacraments.

Although these burning lights will go out, your light burns eternally in the Church.

**All:** Send forth your Spirit
and they shall be created.
And you will renew
the face of the earth.

**Reader 2:** Holy Spirit, all things are created and renewed through your loving work. We hope to bear in our lives the Fruits of the Spirit: love, joy, peace, patience, kindness, goodness, faithfulness, gentleness, self-control. Let us pray:

**All:** O God, who instructs the hearts
Of your faithful
By the light of you, Holy Spirit,
Grant us by the same Holy Spirit
To be truly wise
And ever to rejoice in his consolation.
Through Christ, our Lord.
Amen.

*Pause for reflective silence.*

▶ *Sing or play "Come, Holy Spirit"*

Go to **aliveinchrist.osv.com** for an interactive review.

**A** **Work with Words** Circle the letter of the choice that best completes the sentence.

1. Your ____ is the spiritual principle of a person that is created by God, individual, and everlasting.
   a. intellect
   b. body
   c. character
   d. soul

2. In Baptism, we are marked with a permanent spiritual seal called a ____.
   a. soul
   b. Confirmation
   c. character
   d. mystery

3. In ____, we are again anointed with the Holy Spirit, who first entered our lives in Baptism.
   a. Confirmation
   b. Holy Orders
   c. Mass
   d. Church

4. The Church is the Mystical Body of Christ because in her the Holy Spirit ____ to Christ as one holy people.
   a. gives honor
   b. unites believers
   c. gives hope
   d. offers believers

**B** **Check Understanding** Complete each sentence with the correct term(s) from the Word Bank. You may use some terms more than once.

| | |
|---|---|
| law | Seven Sacraments |
| Fruits | Baptism |
| priesthood | Body of Christ |
| Holy Spirit | Trinity |

5. According to Paul, our bodies are Temples of the _____.

6. Through the _____ our souls are nourished by God's grace.

7. _____ is the gateway into the life of the Holy Spirit.

8. The Church is both a structured organization of members and the _____.

9. The _____ guides the Church in her mission to help those who are poor and in need.

10. Charity, joy, and peace are examples of the _____ of the Holy Spirit.

**C** **Make Connections** Write a short response to the question: Imagine a spiritual food pyramid of things that would nourish your soul. Based on your pyramid, how healthy is your soul today?

_____

_____

_____

_____

**A** Work with Words  **Match the words on the left with the correct definitions or descriptions on the right.**

____ **1.** Transfiguration

____ **2.** grace

____ **3.** Pentecost

____ **4.** salvation

____ **5.** domestic Church

____ **6.** *ekklesia*

____ **7.** soul

____ **8.** Mystical Body of Christ

____ **9.** Fruits of the Holy Spirit

____ **10.** Creed

**a.** the revelation of Jesus' Divine glory to Peter, James, and John

**b.** Christian families are called to be this

**c.** God's forgiveness of our sins and restoration of our friendship with him

**d.** qualities that can be seen in us when we allow the Holy Spirit to work in our hearts

**e.** word for Church that means "those called together"

**f.** a spiritual principle that is created by God

**g.** believers united by the Holy Spirit as one holy People

**h.** free, loving gift of God's own life and help to do what he calls us to do

**i.** a formal statement that means "I believe"

**j.** the coming of the Holy Spirit upon the disciples fifty days after Jesus' Resurrection

**B** Check Understanding  **Indicate whether the following statements are true or false. Then rewrite false statements to make them true.**

**11.** The Sermon on the Mount gave the disciples a glimpse into the divinity of Christ.
**True/False**

_____

_____

**12.** The Holy Spirit prepares us to love Christ and share in his communion.  **True/False**

_____

_____

**13.** The Paschal Feast celebrates the revelation of the Church.  **True/False**

_____

_____

**14.** Jesus reveals God the Father to the world.  **True/False**

_____

_____

**15.** People who have faith and are baptized become members of God's People.  **True/False**

_____

_____

**16.** From the time of Peter and Paul, God called the Israelites to be his Chosen People.
**True/False**

_____

_____

**17.** We are sealed with the four Gifts of the Holy Spirit at Confirmation.  **True/False**

_____

_____

**18.** According to Paul, our bodies are Temples of the Holy Spirit.  **True/False**

_____

_____

**19.** Prayer is the gateway into the life of the Holy Spirit.  **True/False**

_____

_____

**20.** Charity, joy, and peace are examples of the Fruits of the Holy Spirit.  **True/False**

_____

_____

**21.** When we are confirmed, we are anointed to share in Christ's role as priest, prophet, and king.  **True/False**

_____

_____

**22.** The Seven Sacraments nourish us to share in God's grace.  **True/False**

_____

_____

**Make Connections** **Write a short answer to these questions.**

**23.** How does the Holy Spirit prepare us to love Christ and to share in his communion?

_____

_____

_____

_____

_____

_____

_____

**24.** Think about the roles of each Person of the Trinity. Which Person of the Trinity do you tend to relate to the most? Which do you relate to the least? What do your answers show about your view of God?

_____

_____

_____

_____

_____

_____

_____

**25.** Your body is a Temple of the Holy Spirit. Use this analogy of a temple or house where God lives to describe the condition of your heart. What would God see as he walks through your Temple? What might he ask you to move or change?

_____

_____

_____

_____

_____

_____

_____

# JESUS CHRIST

*How does Jesus forgive our sin and call us to conversion through his Body, the Catholic Church?*

## CHURCH HISTORY TIMELINE

| | |
|---|---|
| **680** | Third Ecumenical Council of Constantinople convenes |
| **1054** | The Great East-West Schism |
| **1215** | The Fourth Ecumenical Lateran Council ends |
| **1517** | Martin Luther posts his 95 Theses |

Go to page 348 for more

## Our Catholic Tradition

- As Church members, we look to Jesus as an example of friendship and respect for others. The first Christians demonstrated friendship in how they worshipped together, followed Jesus' example, and cared for each other. (CCC, 949)

- God offers forgiveness and eternal life to those who accept his grace by following his Son, Jesus, in faith. The Holy Spirit helps us recognize our past sinfulness and helps us overcome sin in the future. (CCC, 2009–2010)

- The Church is made up of Catholics united by a common creed, the Seven Sacraments, and the Pope's leadership. She is made up of people from different cultures who express their common faith in different ways. (CCC, 866, 868)

## Our Catholic Life

- Jesus met many people in different circumstances. Even though his interaction with them varied, he welcomed them all, urged them to believe, and encouraged them to change their lives. (CCC, 543–545)

- We are justified by Jesus. We are forgiven and made whole again. We don't earn our own righteousness; it is God's free gift. (CCC, 2007–2009)

- A unity exists among all baptized Christians, and we pray and work toward the full unity that Christ desires for all his followers. (CCC, 855)

# Encountering Christ

## ❤ Let Us Pray

**Leader:** God our Father, through your Son, Jesus, we come to
know about the relationship of love and friendship you
want to have with us. May the example of Jesus teach
us what it means to be accepting of others and to love
them unconditionally.

"Blessed those whose way is blameless,
who walk by the law of the LORD." **Psalm 119:1**

**All:** Jesus, may we be one in you.

## 📖 Scripture

"I pray not only for them, but also for those who will believe in me through their word, so that they may all be one, as you, Father, are in me and I in you, that they also may be in us, that the world may believe that you sent me. And I have given them the glory you gave me, so that they may be one, as we are one, I in them and you in me, that they may be brought to perfection as one, that the world may know that you sent me, and that you loved them even as you loved me. Father, they are your gift to me." **John 17:20–24**

### Have you ever thought...

- What is Jesus' relationship with his Father like?

- Did Jesus have friends? If so, what did he expect from them?

# Getting Started

In this chapter, you will learn about Jesus' closest friends, including the Twelve Apostles and his other disciples, and explore the ways that Jesus treated them, his family, and other people. You will also discover how the early Christians interacted with each other and spread Jesus' message.

## Catholic Faith Words

- disciple
- Apostles
- Ascension

In the chart below, record some things you know about Jesus' family, his disciples, and the people he helped.

| Jesus and His Relationships | |
|---|---|
| **Jesus' Family** | |
| **Jesus' Disciples** | |
| **People Jesus Helped** | |

© Our Sunday Visitor

**Take a Closer Look** It can be easy to take our friendships for granted. Take a close look at two of your good friendships. Write words and phrases that describe these friendships.

_____

_____

_____

_____

_____

_____

_____

What do you value most about these friendships?

_____

_____

_____

_____

_____

_____

_____

_____

_____

_____

How are your friendships a reflection of God's love for you?

_____

_____

_____

_____

_____

_____

_____

_____

_____

_____

_____

## The People Jesus Met

**How did Jesus treat people?**

Jesus was sometimes criticized for the kinds of people he spent time with. Being judged and facing the pressure not to be with a certain kind of person is not fun. Jesus is an example of how to rise above that kind of thinking.

Think of these words, found in the middle of the Lord's Prayer: "thy kingdom come, thy will be done on earth as it is in heaven." Bringing the ways of the Kingdom from Heaven to Earth is exactly what Jesus did. In Heaven, everything is perfect. All are in complete happiness, and no one is left out. When we

take care not to leave anyone out, that's one way of living the Kingdom here on Earth.

Jesus encountered many different people in his ministry. He saw their need and called them to have faith. He called out the names of some, not caring how other people treated them or labeled them. He spent time teaching and eating with them, asking them to believe and to change their lives. Those

### Catholic Faith Words

**disciple** one who learns from and follows the example of a teacher. The disciples of Jesus are those who believe in him, follow his teachings, and put them into practice.

**Apostles** the twelve men Jesus chose to be his closest followers and to share in his work and mission in a special way

### 📖 Scripture

"Why does he eat with tax collectors and sinners?" **Mark 2:16**

Bartimaeus ... sat by the road begging "Master, I want to see." **Mark 10:51**

A woman known as a sinner wept on Jesus' feet, dried them with her hair, and anointed them ... Jesus [said] "So I tell you, her many sins have been forgiven; hence, she has shown great love." **Luke 7:47**

### 📖 Go to the Source

For more on these stories, read *Mark 10:46–52, Matthew 12:9–14,* or *Luke 7:36–50.*

who did became his disciples. A **disciple** is one who learns from and follows the example of a teacher. Disciples of Jesus, both then and now, believe in him, follow his teachings, and put them into practice.

Jesus called some disciples to be his **Apostles**, his closest followers. These twelve men traveled with him and shared in his work of preaching the Good News and the coming Kingdom. After the coming of the Holy Spirit, the Apostles continued Christ's work and mission in a special way.

Still others were his friends who did not go on the road, but were with him when he traveled through their towns. They, too, were his disciples, and welcomed him and the Apostles in their homes and at their tables.

What connects all of these different people who were part of Jesus' life? Jesus met each of these people where they were in life. Many ordinary people loved Jesus for his open heart—not only because he made them better physically or emotionally, or brought them the peace of forgiveness. They also loved him because he cared about them. He took the time to acknowledge them and show them God's love. To Jesus, they mattered. They were important.

| The Twelve Apostles | |
| --- | --- |
| Simon (Peter) | Thomas |
| Andrew | Matthew |
| James | James |
| John | Thaddeus |
| Philip | Simon the Cananaean |
| Bartholomew | Judas Iscariot |

For more information on the Apostles, go to page 363 of the Our Catholic Tradition section of your book.

## COMPARE

Think about the different people in your life: acquaintances, close friends, or classmates. How are you different from them? How are you the same?

_____

_____

_____

_____

What are some ways you could be more open and accepting of them all, like Jesus?

_____

_____

_____

© Our Sunday Visitor

# Jesus' Closest Friends

**How did people become friends with Jesus?**

Close friends are the people we feel most comfortable with—people we love like family, and people we can pour our hearts out to. We learn from the Gospels that Jesus had such friends.

The Apostles Peter, James, and John were Jesus' closest friends. They were the only ones who

- saw Jesus' Transfiguration. (See Mark 9:2–8.)
- entered Jairus' home when Jesus raised his daughter from the dead. (See Luke 8:40–56.)
- came with Jesus when he went off to pray alone on the night before he was arrested. (See Mark 14:32–42.)

Mary Magdalene also was a close friend to Jesus. She was

- at the Cross when Jesus died. (See Matthew 27:55–56.)
- the first person Jesus appeared to after he rose from the dead. (See John 20:11–18.)

**The Apostle Peter**

**Mary Magdalene**

© Our Sunday Visitor

## Peter and Mary Magdalene's Actions

_____ When they arrested Jesus, I ran and told people I didn't know who he was.

_____ I was there at the foot of the Cross when Jesus died.

_____ Three times I denied being Jesus' friend.

_____ I was the first to whom Jesus appeared at the Resurrection.

_____ Jesus gave me the keys to the Kingdom.

1. Write the letter P next to Peter's actions and the letter M next to Mary's.

2. In the space below, write one question you would ask Peter or Mary about Jesus.

_____

_____

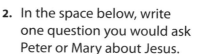

## Friends from Bethany

Lazarus, Martha, and Mary were a brother and two sisters who lived in Bethany. They were also close friends of Jesus.

Jesus settled an argument between them when Martha was busy doing housework while Mary just sat at Jesus' feet, listening to him and not helping her sister. (See Luke 10:38–42.) Jesus brought Lazarus back to life after he had been in the tomb for four days. (See John 11:1–44.)

There were other women, besides Martha and Mary of Bethany and Mary Magdalene, who followed Jesus and provided for him out of their own resources. Joanna and Susanna are also named (see Luke 8:3), as well as the mother of James and John (see Matthew 27:56).

## CONSIDER

If Jesus asked you to pick three of your friends to be his Apostles, which of your friends would you pick? Write down the initials of each friend and the reason(s) why you selected him or her.

1. _____

_____

2. _____

_____

3. _____

_____

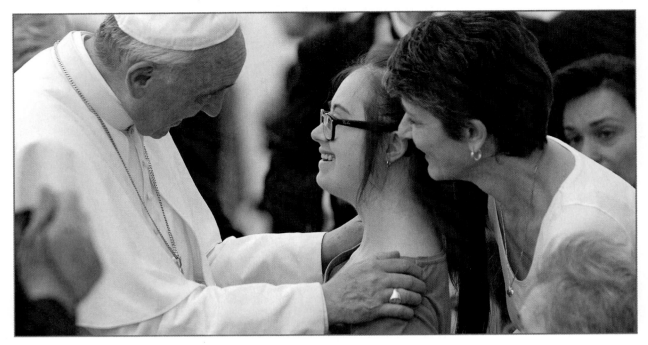

"Wherever we go ... we are at home, we are with our family, we are brothers and sisters." —Pope Francis

# The First Church Members

**What can we learn from the early Christians?**

Have you ever had to say goodbye to a close friend whom you will probably never see again? If so, then you know that it is a very sad, lonely feeling.

That's how Jesus' followers and friends must have felt after his **Ascension**, when the Risen Christ was taken up in glory to his Father in Heaven. They watched him ascend into Heaven.

Jesus had promised that they would not be alone, that the Holy Spirit would come upon them. They would be strengthened to be Jesus' witnesses throughout the world. But they probably felt lost, not knowing how they could possibly keep his message alive.

Then the Holy Spirit came to them on Pentecost. Wind, tongues of fire, and an inner strength came from God and made them a changed group of people, filled with courage and understanding.

- They became a united community.
- They looked after each other.
- They opened their homes to each other; they discussed Jesus' teachings together and motivated one another to tell others about him and his message.
- They broke bread together as Jesus commanded at the Last Supper.
- They shared their money, their food, and their possessions.

In short, they helped each other out in every way possible. Their community showed us what solidarity looks like, sharing more than material things by providing

## Catholic Faith Words

**Ascension** the event of the Risen Christ being taken up into Heaven forty days after his Resurrection

for one another's spiritual needs, too. These women and men demonstrated true Christian friendship: trust, loyalty, generosity, hospitality, concern, joy, and hope. If we follow their example, we will embrace everyone as part of God's family, no matter whether they have different backgrounds or different kinds of personalities.

| Who Were They? | |
|---|---|
| Peter | • the first to speak after receiving the Holy Spirit (See Acts Chapters 2 and 3.)<br>• was imprisoned, but escaped when an angel caused the doors to open and his chains to fall off (See Acts 12:1–19.) |
| Stephen | • one of the first seven deacons to the Apostles (See Acts 6:1–7.)<br>• the first martyr, giving up his life for believing in Jesus (See Acts 7:55–60.) |
| Saul, also known as Paul | • persecuted the disciples and was present when Stephen was stoned to death (See Acts 7:58 and 8:1.)<br>• changed his life after he was temporarily struck blind and heard the voice of Jesus asking him why he persecuted Jesus (See Acts 9:4–5.)<br>• wrote many of the letters of the New Testament and was a great leader |
| Lydia | • was a businesswoman, a dealer of purple cloth, in Philippi (See Acts 16:14.)<br>• offered her home to Paul and Silas; when they left prison, they returned to her home (See Acts 16:40.) |
| Prisca and her husband Aquila | • were tentmakers, as was Paul; they spent time working together, while Paul stayed with them at their home in Corinth (See Acts 18:1—3.)<br>• used their home as a Church center for the faith community (See 1 Corinthians 16:19.) |
| Phoebe | • a woman who served the Church at Cenchrae (See Romans 16:1.)<br>• was a friend of Paul; he recommended that she be received "in a manner worthy of the holy ones" (See Romans 16:2.) |

Saint Paul

# IN SUMMARY   Catholics Believe

As members of the Church, we look to Jesus as an example of friendship and respect for others.

• Jesus met many people in different circumstances. Even though his interaction with them varied, he welcomed them all, urged them to believe, and encouraged them to change their lives.

• Jesus called some disciples to be his Apostles, his closest followers. These twelve men traveled with him and shared in his work of preaching the Good News and the coming Kingdom.

• The first Church members demonstrated true Christian friendship by the way they worshipped together, followed the example of Jesus, and took care of one another.

## Our Catholic Life

Friendship is a gift. When we become friends with people, we share in their happiness and their sadness, and we support them as they support us. Jesus' friendships shared these traits, but they were different in one important way: **Jesus' friendship and love were given unconditionally.** He didn't need friends, but he chose to have them and enjoyed their company, just like they enjoyed his. His friends learned from him, ate with him, traveled with him, and extended his friendship and messages to others they met both before and after Jesus' Death. Jesus' friendship and love transformed the lives of his friends. We, too, can have that kind of impact on the friends we make, by acting as good examples of Christian love to those we meet.

> How has friendship with Jesus changed you? How do you share his friendship with others?

## People of Faith

### Prisca and Aquila, first century

Prisca and Aquila lived in Corinth, Greece. They were Roman Jews who had been banished by the Emperor Claudius because of their faith. Aquila and Saint Paul were tentmakers by trade and worked together while Paul stayed in Corinth. In the spirit of Jesus, Prisca and Aquila opened their hearts to Saint Paul in friendship. He expressed his thankfulness in letters he sent to his followers. Paul stayed with Prisca and Aquila in Corinth for about a year and a half, making many converts among the Jews there. The Church celebrates Prisca and Aquila's feast day on **July 8.**

For more, go to
**aliveinchrist.osv.com**

## RANK

What is your "Top Five" list of qualities needed for friendship? Begin with five and work your way up to the most important characteristic of friendship at number one. Then rank them in the order of importance you think Jesus would place on each.

_____

_____

_____

_____

_____

_____

_____

_____

_____

_____

## ♥ Celebration of the Word

**Leader:** We know and believe that when two or more gather, Christ is with us.

Let us take this time to listen to all he has to say to us through the Scripture reading.

**Reader 1:** A reading from the holy Gospel according to Luke.

*Read Luke 19:1–10.*

The Gospel of the Lord.

**All:** Praise to you, Lord Jesus Christ.

**Reader 2:** As Jesus welcomed and called Zacchaeus down from the tree, help us to welcome and seek out all those among us who sit on the outside of our circle of friends, who are different, and who are in need of comfort and friendship.

**Reader 3:** As Jesus welcomed and healed the man who was born blind, help us to welcome and comfort all those among us who have illness or disability and are in need of a friend.

**Reader 4:** As Jesus, who on the day of his Death welcomed the criminal into paradise with him, help us welcome and forgive all who have hurt us.

**Leader:** Gracious Father, send the Holy Spirit to walk with us and guide us in all our choices.

Be with us in the times when it is easy to serve you and in the times when the pressures around us make it seem almost impossible.

Help us to know that you love us.

Remind us always and often that you are the God who welcomes all.

We ask this prayer in the name of Jesus, our brother and friend.

**All:** Amen.

▶ *Sing or play "You Stand Knocking"*

Go to **aliveinchrist.osv.com** for an interactive review.

**A  Work with Words** Circle the letter of the choice that best completes the sentence.

1. A person who learns from and follows the example of a teacher is called a(n) ____.
   a. Apostle          c. assistant
   b. disciple         d. lieutenant

2. Jesus brought ____ to life, after being in the tomb for four days.
   a. Mary             c. Jairus
   b. Martha           d. Lazarus

3. Jesus' ____ were the twelve men who shared in his work and ministry in a special way.
   a. friends          c. Apostles
   b. disciples        d. companions

4. The event of the Risen Christ being taken up into Heaven is called the ____.
   a. Annunciation     c. Assumption
   b. Absolution       d. Ascension

5. ____ was the first martyr, the first person to be killed for believing in Jesus.
   a. Stephen          c. Paul
   b. Peter            d. Timothy

**B  Check Understanding** Indicate whether the following statements are true or false. Then rewrite false statements to make them true.

6. Matthew, James, and John were the only disciples who came with Jesus when he went off to pray on the night before he was arrested. **True/False**

_____

_____

7. Peter was the first person Jesus appeared to after he rose from the dead. **True/False**

_____

_____

8. The Holy Spirit came as tongues of fire and made the disciples a united community. **True/False**

_____

_____

9. The disciples shared their money, their food, and their possessions. **True/False**

_____

_____

10. Priscilla was a businesswoman in Philippi, who offered her home to Paul and Silas. **True/False**

_____

_____

**C  Make Connections** Write a one-paragraph response to the question. Think about someone you know who might feel left out—someone at school, at church, or in your community. How would Jesus respond to that person and what can you learn from his example?

_____

_____

_____

_____

_____

_____

_____

# Life in Christ

## ♡ Let Us Pray

**Leader:** God Almighty, we gather in the name of your Son, Jesus Christ. Help us make choices that will bring the light of Christ to the world.

"The LORD is my shepherd;
    there is nothing I lack." **Psalm 23:1**

**All:** Dear Lord, help us make good choices!

### 📖 Scripture

"The Spirit of the Lord is upon me,
    because he has anointed me
    to bring glad tidings to the poor.
He has sent me to proclaim liberty to captives and
    recovery of sight to the blind,
    to let the oppressed go free,
and to proclaim a year acceptable to the Lord."

Luke 4:18–19

### Have you ever thought...

- What does Jesus' mission mean to you?

- What difference can believing in Jesus make in how you live?

# Getting Started

In this chapter, you will discover the ways our belief in Jesus affects our lives, learn about justification and righteousness, and consider the role of conversion in our lives.

Below are some titles for Jesus that come from the Gospel according to John. Jesus used these words to describe himself and how he provides for us.

1. Add the missing words to complete the titles.

2. Then choose one and describe what it means and how it connects to the new life Jesus offers us.

## Titles of Jesus

I am the _____ Shepherd.

I am the _____ and you are the branches.

I am the _____ of the world.

I am the Bread of _____ .

Title you chose: _____

_____

What does it mean? _____

How does it connect to the new life Jesus offers us? _____

_____

_____

_____

- justification
- eternal life
- righteous
- conversion

## WRITE

**Who Are You?** You have different roles and titles, and each tells something about you and the people or activities that are a part of your life. For instance, you are a son or daughter, a student, a friend, possibly a sibling or cousin, perhaps a soccer player or a pianist, and so on. List five of the roles you have and name one way your life is affected because of each role.

1. _____
   _____

2. _____
   _____

3. _____
   _____

4. _____
   _____

5. _____
   _____

Now choose two roles and describe how you make a difference in the lives of others through those roles.

_____
_____
_____
_____
_____
_____
_____
_____
_____
_____
_____

**Pope Saint John Paul II speaks with his would-be assassin Mehmet Ali Ağca in his jail cell in 1983.**

# The Promise of Life

### How do we know who Jesus is?

How do we get to know Jesus? In the Gospels according to Matthew, Mark, Luke, and John, we find out a lot about who Jesus is. We discover what he says about his relationship with the Father and with us. The Gospels tell us about Jesus' teachings and remind us that Jesus loves and understands us, knows our needs, and wants to give us what only God can give: life.

In his letters, Saint Paul reminds us of the power our relationship with Christ brings us:

> ## 📖 Scripture
>
> "For you were once darkness, but now you are light in the Lord. Live as children of light, for light produces every kind of goodness and righteousness and truth."
>
> Ephesians 5:8–9

Pope Saint John Paul II labeled the violence, hatred, fear, and anger in society as part of the "culture of death." He challenged Catholics to live in and create a "culture of life"—to live as "children of light" and to bring about a transformation of our culture.

While Pope Saint John Paul II was speaking about broad social issues such as the violence of poverty and unjust distribution of resources, he also advocated smaller, personal changes. For example, instead of seeking revenge, we can show forgiveness whenever we are wronged. Pope Saint John Paul II made a point to visit his would-be assassin in his jail cell, where they spoke and the Pope forgave the man. Instead of accepting violence in movies or video games, we can turn away from it and choose other entertainment. Instead of being afraid of people who are different, we can look for ways to appreciate those differences.

## Jesus' I Am Statements

| Jesus Tells Us | What It Means for Us |
|---|---|
| "I am the vine, you are the branches" (John 15:5). | • Jesus is the source of life. Think of yourself as bringing good and healthy fruit to others through your actions.<br><br>• _____ |
| "I am the good shepherd, and I know mine and mine know me" (John 10:14). | • Jesus is the caring shepherd who knows what you need and takes care of you.<br><br>• Think about some things you might do that would show your care and concern for family, friends, or neighbors. |
| "I am the bread of life; whoever comes to me will never hunger, and whoever believes in me will never thirst" (John 6:35). | • Jesus gives us spiritual life the way food and drink nourish our bodies.<br><br>• Think of what you can do to increase your spiritual life, to nourish your soul. |
| "I am the light of the world. Whoever follows me will not walk in darkness but will have the light of life" (John 8:12). | • Jesus is your companion in life, shining a light on the path so you know where to walk.<br><br>• If you follow his teachings, they will show you the way to respect the dignity of life—yours, and that of everyone else you meet.<br><br>• _____ |

> ★ In the spaces provided, write ways you can live by Jesus' teaching.

## INTERVIEW

In groups of two or three, imagine that you are talking with Pope Saint John Paul II. Write six questions that you would ask him about our world, his idea of the "culture of death," and how a "culture of life" can change things.

_____

_____

_____

_____

_____

_____

_____

_____

# Made Just and Right

**How does Jesus affect your life?**

If Jesus is the Light of the World, the Bread of Life, and the Vine, what are we? We are his followers who sometimes stumble in darkness. We are the spiritually hungry and needy. We are the branches that are connected to Jesus and give witness to him by all that we say and do. And as the Church, we are all in this together.

These images of Jesus remind us that Jesus offers life, but how do we respond? How are we to live now so that we can know the happiness of living forever with God? We learn from the New Testament letters that doing what is just and right, and standing up for what is good, are a big part of our response: "But if Christ is in you, although the body is dead because of sin, the spirit is alive because of righteousness" (Romans 8:10).

## Justification and Righteousness

"Just" and "right" are good qualities. We say someone is "just" if he or she acts fairly. We say something is "right" if it is correct.

Our spiritual life needs to be just and right. Justification and righteousness are words that try to capture concepts that have to do with God's action and our response. They help us understand our need for Jesus in our lives.

**Justification** is the forgiveness of sins and the return to the goodness for which humans were first created. Justification goes beyond our sins being pardoned. It involves being made holy and being renewed spiritually. Jesus has "justified" humans by giving his very self in love for us.

What does it mean to be justified? The word *justify* means "to demonstrate or prove to be just or right," and "to declare free of blame or to absolve." By the act of his becoming human, dying, and rising to new life, the Son of God has made it possible for people to be just and right once again with God. All we

### Catholic Faith Words

**justification** the forgiveness of sins and the return to the goodness for which humans were first created

**eternal life** life forever with God for all who die in his friendship

**righteous** to act in accordance with God's will, being in his friendship, free from guilt or sin

need to do is accept God's grace by following Jesus in faith. When we are justified, we

- are motivated by the Holy Spirit to see what is sinful in our lives and to turn away from the things, people, and actions that keep us from God
- grow in our love for God, by the choices we make, the people we spend time with, and the ways we pray
- accept forgiveness and live righteous lives, living in accordance with God's will, free from guilt or sin
- desire to avoid sin and strive to strengthen our relationship with Jesus
- receive grace (God's free and loving gift of his own life and help) and grow in holiness
- are replenished and made like new

## Free to Us

Justification was earned for us by the Passion of Christ and is given to us when we are baptized. God makes us just by the power of his mercy. Being justified brings us to praise and give glory to God for the gift of **eternal life**—life forever with God for all who die in his friendship.

© Our Sunday Visitor

Eternal life is God's free gift! We cannot buy it, and we do not earn it. God rewards us with eternal life because he freely chooses to share it with us.

To gain this free gift of eternal life, we must respond to God's grace and cooperate with his ways. We live in "right" relationship with God because, through the sacrifice of Jesus and the power of the Holy Spirit, we have been given Divine life in Baptism.

We are **righteous** when we live as disciples of the Lord, acting in accordance with his will and being free from guilt and sin. After this initial turn toward God prompted by the Holy Spirit, we can achieve eternal happiness if we follow Jesus and continue to live in God's friendship. The Holy Spirit inspires us and moves us to live as Jesus' followers. He lives within us and influences us to live right and just lives.

## REFLECT

Write about a part of your life that is going well. What are you grateful for?

_____

_____

Think of something in your life that is not going so well. Write about how following Jesus more closely could help you improve things so they become more "just" and "right."

_____

_____

# Making a Change

**What is conversion?**

The world is full of stories about people who used to perform sinful actions, but changed their lives around and now do good. Perhaps you have heard or read about

- someone who used to be in a gang that injured people and destroyed property, but now spends time helping other gang members get out and find support
- someone who used to be a computer hacker, illegally accessing people's personal information, who now volunteers with nonprofit agencies making their networks more secure
- someone who used to be very prejudiced against certain groups of people, who now speaks out whenever he or she hears a racial joke or comment

In their own ways, each of these people experienced a conversion.

Conversion means change. From a faith perspective, **conversion** is a sincere change of mind, heart, and desire to turn away from sin and what keeps us from growing in God's love. It includes turning away from evil, wanting to change one's life, following the path of renewal, and being moved by God's grace to turn back toward him.

Sometimes we have big conversions, and sometimes we have smaller ones. Conversion doesn't happen overnight or just once in our lives. It's ongoing, a continual process of becoming the people God intends us to be. As we are exposed to new and different challenges, sometimes we don't make the best choices or do the right things. But our faith really is Good News because God is merciful and forgiving! The Holy Spirit works in us, helping us appreciate that conversion must be part of our lives. It is a response to God's love and forgiveness, and it is sustained through life by our cooperation with God's grace.

A sin always involves failure. If we recognize what we did wrong, and ask for forgiveness, we can learn from it and change our ways. Our sins may get more serious if we keep doing them over and over again without improving or growing spiritually.

## Catholic Faith Words

**conversion** a sincere change of mind, heart, and desire to turn away from sin and evil and turn toward God

Former gang members and drug addicts pray with religious sisters from a Catholic shelter

## Conversion in Action

Once we recognize that something we have been doing is sinful, then we need to

- be sorry for that sin
- reject our past sinful ways
- seek God's forgiveness in the Sacrament of Penance and Reconciliation and his grace to strengthen us against future sin
- commit to trying to avoid sin in the future

We know that God is merciful and forgiving, and he gives us hope and a share in his life. The grace that leads us to conversion is a free gift from God. We cannot buy it, and we didn't earn it. The Holy Spirit moves and inspires us, and participation in the Sacrament of Penance and Reconciliation brings us closer to eternal life.

### WRITE

Recall a conversion story that you have heard or were a part of—a story about a person who overcame a particular sin and turned into someone who "lived in the Light" of what was just and right.

Write out that story in your own words. You could also write a personal story about one of your own conversions, or create a fictional story of someone who experiences a conversion in a surprising way and how the person's change affected others.

## IN SUMMARY | Catholics Believe

Through Jesus' saving act on the Cross, God offers us forgiveness and eternal life.

- Jesus is the Vine, the Bread of Life, the Light of the World who offers eternal life to those who accept God's grace by following Jesus in faith.

- We are justified by Jesus. We are forgiven and made whole again. We don't earn our own righteousness; it is God's free gift.

- Conversion is a continuing process. The Holy Spirit helps us recognize our past sinfulness and helps us overcome sin in the future.

## Our Catholic Life

Young people spend a lot of time thinking about their relationships with friends, family, team members, and people they get to know at Church. We wonder how our friendships are going, what people think of us and our decisions, and whether we are showing our best to everyone we know. But our most important **relationship** is with God. There are ways we can make this relationship better and stronger. These steps include spending time in prayer and reading the Bible, getting to know Jesus and his teachings better, paying attention to the way the Holy Spirit might be calling us to act, and finding people—friends and trustworthy adults—who can help us grow spiritually, and asking for their help.

> What is one thing you can do this week to make your relationship with God stronger?

## People of Faith

### Blessed Victoria Rasoamanarivo, 1848–1894

Victoria Rasoamanarivo founded the Catholic Action movement in Madagascar. This organization focuses on improving the conditions of the people in different nations. There were few priests on the island, so Victoria taught the people about the blessings they would receive through acceptance of Jesus as Lord. She helped the poor and promoted the rights of women. During his visit to Madagascar in 1989, Pope Saint John Paul II beatified Victoria Rasoamanarivo. The Church celebrates her feast day on **August 21**.

For more, go to
**aliveinchrist.osv.com**

## CONSIDER

Remember a few times during your life when you recognized your sinfulness and changed your way of acting. How have you grown and matured in your ability to recognize sinfulness, make good decisions, and follow through?

_____
_____
_____
_____
_____
_____
_____
_____
_____
_____

## Reflection on Jesus

**Leader:** The reading from Philippians tells us there will be a time when every nation will praise the name of Jesus. But Jesus did not come to Earth to force us to praise him. Jesus came with gentle power, humility and selflessness. Jesus is God. It is right, as Saint Paul says, to offer him our praise and worship without hesitation.

**Reader 1:** A reading from Saint Paul's Letter to the Christians at Philippi:

"Do nothing out of selfishness or out of vainglory; rather, humbly regard others as more important than yourselves, each looking out not for his own interests, but [also] everyone for those of others. Have among yourselves the same attitude that is also yours in Christ Jesus,

Who, though he was in the form of God, did not regard equality with God
   something to be grasped.
Rather, he emptied himself,
taking the form of a slave,
coming in human likeness;
and found human in appearance,
he humbled himself,
becoming obedient to death,
   even death on a cross."

**Leader:** Jesus, you must show us how to follow. In our own ways, we must learn how to empty ourselves of pride and selfishness. We too must learn how to be obedient and to do our Father's will.

**Reader 2:** A continuation of the reading from Saint Paul:

"Because of this, God greatly exalted him
and bestowed on him the name
that is above every name,
that at the name of Jesus
every knee should bend,
of those in heaven and on earth and under
   the earth,
and every tongue confess that
Jesus Christ is Lord,
to the glory of God the Father."
Philippians 2:3–11

**Leader:** God, our Father, we often fail to honor Jesus' name. The angel Gabriel told Mary to name her son "Jesus," which means "Savior," or "Redeemer." Jesus is our Savior. We should honor his name always.

**Side 1:** Jesus Christ, you are our Lord. Let our tongues always "confess" or proclaim it. "Praise you, Lord Jesus Christ."

**Side 2:** Jesus Christ, you are our Lord. Let us always remember to always show that we honor you.

**Leader:** Please mention any intentions you would like everyone to pray for.

**All:** (after each petition) We praise and honor you, Jesus.

▶ *Sing or play "Christ Is Lord"*

Go to **aliveinchrist.osv.com** for an interactive review.

**A** **Work with Words** Complete each sentence with the correct term from the Word Bank.

| | |
|---|---|
| conversion | justification |
| disciples | holiness |
| Christmas | culture of life |
| righteous | Lent |
| Pentecost | |

1. _____ is the forgiveness of sins and the return to the goodness for which humans were first created.

2. When we are _____, we want to live in accordance with God's will, in his friendship, free from guilt or sin.

3. _____ means turning away from what keeps us from God and turning back to him.

4. The season of _____ helps us focus on what would make our lives more just and right.

5. By showing forgiveness, we can help create a _____.

**B** **Check Understanding** Indicate whether the following statements are true or false. Then rewrite false statements to make them true.

6. Jesus is the Light of the World and the Bread of Life. **True/False**

_____

_____

7. The word *justify* means "to declare free of blame or to absolve." **True/False**

_____

_____

8. When we are baptized, we are joined to the righteousness of Christ who justifies us. **True/False**

_____

_____

9. Conversion is a change that happens once in our lives when we are baptized. **True/False**

_____

_____

10. Being justified brings us to praise and give glory to God for the gift of eternal life. **True/False**

_____

_____

**C** **Make Connections** Write a one-paragraph response to the following: Name and explain one of Jesus' "I Am" statements presented in this chapter. Create one modern "I Am" statement to describe who Jesus is to you right now.

_____

_____

_____

_____

_____

_____

_____

_____

# One in Christ

## ♥ Let Us Pray

**Leader:** God of all unity, Jesus prayed that we would all be one in him. As Catholics, we are a part of the Body of Christ. Teach us what this means.

> "Blessed are those who dwell in your house!
>   They never cease to praise you." **Psalm 84:5**

**All:** Father, unite us in your heart, we pray.

### 📖 Scripture

"There are different kinds of spiritual gifts but the same Spirit; there are different forms of service but the same Lord; there are different workings but the same God who produces all of them in everyone.... To one is given through the Spirit the expression of wisdom; to another the expression of knowledge according to the same Spirit; to another faith by the same Spirit; to another gifts of healing by the one Spirit; to another mighty deeds; to another prophecy; to another discernment of spirits; to another varieties of tongues; to another interpretation of tongues. But one and the same Spirit produces all of these, distributing them individually to each person as he wishes."

**1 Corinthians 12: 4–11**

### Have you ever thought...

- How do all Christians have different gifts yet one belief?
- What does it mean to be different but to share one faith?

# Getting Started

In this chapter, you will explore the core truths of our faith, learn how Eastern Catholic and Roman Catholic beliefs are similar and different and learn about how we are unified with other Christian churches.

In the web below, provide four examples of things that unite the Catholic Church no matter where she is, such as beliefs, practices, or prayers that we hold in common.

Examples of Our Unity

**The Same, but Different** How are you the same as a good friend of yours? How are you different from them? Brainstorm a list of similarities you share with a close friend, and then identify the differences between the two of you. What keeps you together as friends?

## My Friend and I

| How We Are Similar | How We Are Different |
|---|---|
| _____ | _____ |
| _____ | _____ |
| _____ | _____ |
| _____ | _____ |
| _____ | _____ |
| _____ | _____ |
| _____ | _____ |
| _____ | _____ |
| _____ | _____ |

Cholula, Puebla, Mexico

Ninh Binh, Vietnam

# Different But the Same

**What unites the Catholic Church?**

We all want to belong. We all like to feel comfortable with the people around us. Most of the time our friends like the same things we do. But sometimes you wind up in a group of people you don't know. What we often find is although new acquaintances may be different from us, there are things we share in common. The more we get to know new people, the better chance we have of discovering that we have more in common than we first thought.

## Expressing the Same Beliefs

The first disciples were from different backgrounds, but their faith in Jesus brought them together. At his Last Supper, Christ

> **Go to the Source**
>
> "... so that they may all be one ..." Jesus was praying these words about his Apostles, but this is a prayer for all of us. Read the rest of *John 17:20–26* to see what else Jesus said at the Last Supper, the night he was arrested.

prayed for all of his followers to be one. (See John 17:20–26.) He wanted them to put aside their differences, to know that they all belonged to God and were loved by God.

We proclaim one Lord, Jesus, and profess the same creed. A creed is a statement of the Church's belief and summary of the Christian faith. The word *creed* means "I believe." We all believe what's contained in the Nicene Creed and the **Apostles' Creed**, which is one of the Church's oldest creeds, taught since the time of the Apostles and used now also in the celebration of Baptism (see page 366 in the Our Catholic Tradition section of your book).

We celebrate the Seven Sacraments. The details of how we celebrate might be different, but we all baptize in the name of the Father, Son, and Holy Spirit. Through the Eucharist we are given life and are united by the same Holy Spirit. We become the one Body of Christ, the Church.

We are **apostolic**. We are led by the same Church hierarchy and teaching authority led by the Pope. Through the unbroken line of

© Our Sunday Visitor

Pristina, Montenegro

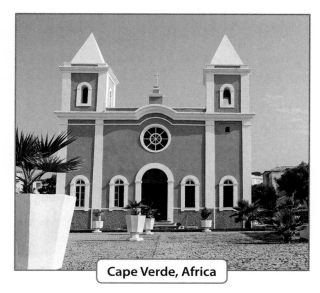

Cape Verde, Africa

## Catholic Faith Words

**Apostles' Creed** one of the Church's oldest creeds. It is a summary of Christian beliefs taught since the time of the Apostles.

**apostolic** a Mark of the Church. The Church is apostolic because her teaching authority comes directly from Jesus and his chosen Apostles, handed down through the bishops of the Church, who are direct successors of the Apostles.

**one** a Mark of the Church. The Church is one because the power of the Holy Spirit unites all the members through one faith and one Baptism.

bishops and Popes, direct successors of the Apostles, we can trace our history back to the Apostles. We are served by the ordained ministry of bishops, priests, and deacons.

We are committed to justice. Serving the poor and standing up against injustice have always been characteristics of Catholicism.

The Church has diverse people from many different cultures and with a variety of gifts. That diversity makes our customs and experiences richer and deeper. This unity is one of the four Marks of the Church. The

Church is **one** because the power of the Holy Spirit unites all the members through one faith and one Baptism. Even though different Catholic parishes have their own styles, Catholics are united by certain beliefs and practices. And all kinds of different people, with all their favorite ways of praying, are welcomed.

## COMPARE AND CONTRAST

Look at the pictures of the various churches. On the lines below, write three things they all have in common and then three differences you see.

**Similarities**

_____

_____

_____

**Differences**

_____

_____

_____

## United but Unique

**How are Eastern and Roman Catholics alike and different?**

You might have heard someone say she was Roman Catholic and wondered what that meant. Isn't it enough to say "I'm Catholic"?

There is one Catholic Church, but as she grew and spread during her early history, the people in different places expressed their Catholic belief in their unique customs, language, and favorite ways of praying. That's why there is more than one Church in the Catholic Church. The different Churches developed under the leadership of the Pope, the Bishop of Rome, and continue under his authority.

There are two overarching Churches: the Latin, or Roman, Catholic Church and the Eastern Catholic Church.

Roman Catholics and Eastern Catholics have different ways of worshipping, but their worship is a sign of the same mystery of Christ. Their Sacraments may be celebrated differently, but they share the same grace with those who receive them. What the Churches have in common (creed, Sacraments, and leadership under the Pope) and what they hold unique, show the true nature of the universal Church. The universal Church is one Catholic Church. We all worship the one Triune God. Our unity comes from the unity of the Holy Trinity: Father, Son, and Holy Spirit are three Divine and distinct Persons, but are one God.

> Have you ever worshipped in a Catholic Church that follows a different Rite from your own?

> If so, what did you see there that was new to you?

**Morning Mass celebration at Iviv Theological Seminary, Ukraine**

**Holy Communion during an Advent Mass at Iona Catholic High School in Ontario, Canada**

## The Catholic Church

The one universal Catholic Church is a communion of Churches. There are five main branches of the Eastern Catholic Church, with several particular Churches within each. Each particular Church has unique theology, laws, spirituality, and language, but they are all under the authority of the Pope and in communion with the Church in Rome.

**Baptism of a newborn baby**

## CATHOLICS TODAY

In the Eastern Catholic Church, babies are baptized, then confirmed, and then given Eucharist by the priest all during the same celebration. This emphasizes the unity of all three Sacraments of Initiation—Baptism, Confirmation, and Eucharist.

In the Roman Catholic or Latin Church, priests baptize babies, but Confirmation always comes later. The local bishop administers the Sacrament. This shows that Confirmation makes the recipient's bond to the Church stronger.

The celebration of Confirmation is one example of how the Eastern and Roman Churches celebrate the same beliefs but in different ways. At the Sacrament of Confirmation, the minister lays hands on the person and anoints the forehead with oil. In the Byzantine Tradition, other parts of the body like the eyes, ears, and hands are anointed as well. The words spoken are similar: "The seal of the gift that is the Holy Spirit" (Byzantine Tradition of the Eastern Church) and "Be sealed with the gift of the Holy Spirit" (Roman Church).

## DESCRIBE

Write down how you might describe one of the Sacraments of Initiation (Baptism, Confirmation, or Eucharist) to a person who has never seen any of the Seven Sacraments take place.

_____

_____

_____

_____

# Brothers and Sisters in Christ

### How do we come together?

All Catholics are Christians, but not all Christians are Catholic. Christians are people who believe in and follow Jesus Christ, the Second Person of the Holy Trinity. Some Christians are Baptist, some are Presbyterian, Lutheran, Methodist, Episcopalian, Pentecostal, or Disciples of Christ.

Some Christian communities call their leaders "bishops" and "priests"; others do not. Some have worship services that include Communion; others do not. Some have married male and female ministers; others do not.

> **Have you ever visited a Christian church that is not Catholic? If so, what was it like?**

---

**Catholic** Faith Words

**ecumenism** an organized effort to bring Christians together in cooperation as they look forward in hope to the restoration of the unity of the Christian Church

---

## The Christian Family History

Right now, all of these are separate Christian communities. The Christian churches of the world can be spoken of as a world Christian family. But how did all of these groups come to be?

For the first millennium, Christians were, for the most part, united as one Church under the leadership of the bishop of Rome, the Pope. Then, in A.D. 1054, because of arguments among Church leaders about Church authority, practices, and teaching, many in the Eastern Church split from the Western (Roman) Church. This is known as the Great Schism. The word *schism* means "division" or "cutting." Many Eastern Churches in Eastern Europe, the Middle East, and in Asia became known as the Eastern Orthodox Church. Those Eastern Churches who remained in communion with Rome were, and are still, known as the Eastern Catholic Church.

Then, in the 1500s, the Western Church experienced another split. In A.D. 1517, a priest named Martin Luther spoke out, or protested, against what he saw as abuses and errors in the Church. Although he began by calling for reforms, his actions led to the Protestant Reformation, in which Luther and several other Christian leaders and groups separated from the Catholic Church and the authority of the Pope. The unity, or full communion, of the Western Church was broken. Those who left the communion of the Catholic Church became known as Protestants.

## Christians Today

The Catholic Church (Roman and Eastern) is the one that is governed by the successor of Peter (the Pope), and all the bishops in communion with him. The Church of Christ subsists in the Catholic Church; through her alone can the fullness of the means of salvation be found. However, in many ways, all baptized Christians are joined together, even though they do not share all the beliefs of the Catholic faith, and their churches are not in perfect communion with the Pope.

This separation of Catholic and Protestant was a tragedy from many centuries ago. No one group was totally responsible for this. In spite of the separation, much holiness and truth can be found in other communities outside of the Catholic Church. We hope some day that all Christians can be united together, as Jesus hoped for: "I have given them the glory you gave me, so that they may be one, as we are one" (John 17:22).

But we do more than look forward in hope for the restoration of the unity of the Christian Church. We work toward building community with all Christians. The organized effort to bring Christians together in cooperation is called **ecumenism**. Ecumenism requires a lot of communication and cooperation among all Christians. We do this by praying together, discussing what we have in common, respecting one another, and learning more about what others believe.

**Leaders from different religious traditions perform an ecumenical service in Oberammergau, Germany.**

## IN SUMMARY    Catholics Believe

The universal Catholic Church is united by common beliefs and practices.

- The Church is made up of diverse people from different cultures that express their common faith in different ways.

- The Catholic Church is made up of Eastern Catholics and Roman Catholics who are united by a common creed, the Seven Sacraments, and the leadership of the Pope.

- A unity exists among all baptized Christians, and we pray and work toward the full unity that Christ desires for all his followers.

## Our Catholic Life

Learning about the history of the Church and how Christianity spread can inspire you to learn more about ways to live out the **Catholic faith**. We respect all people and their religious customs, we understand what our own faith brings us, and appreciate the specific things that make us Catholic (including the Marks of the Church, the Seven Sacraments, our Holy Days of Obligation, sacramentals, and more). We can share what we know and love about our Church with people who may not know much about her, or who share different faith traditions but are Christian and wonder what we all have in common.

> **What is one thing about your Catholic faith that interests you most?**

## People of Faith

### Saint Peregrine Laziosi, 1260–1345

Peregrine Laziosi was so ashamed of his anti-Catholic actions as a teenager that he began to pray and eventually became a Catholic. Soon after, he decided to become a priest, and joined the Servants of Mary. Later in life, Peregrine developed cancer. Doctors told him he would need his foot amputated. Peregrine spent the night before the surgery praying. He had a vision of Jesus reaching out and touching him. In the morning, his foot was healed. Peregrine was known for his ability to tell people about Jesus and encourage them to confess their sins. The Church celebrates his feast day on **May 1**.

For more, go to
**aliveinchrist.osv.com**

### LIST

On the lines below list four ways you show you are Catholic.

1. _____

2. _____

3. _____

4. _____

Then tell four ways you can share what it means to be a Catholic to someone who does not know about your faith.

1. _____

2. _____

3. _____

4. _____

## ♥ Prayer for Unity

**Leader:** Let us be attentive to the wisdom of Saint Paul's letter to the Ephesians.

**Reader 1:** Lead a life worthy of the calling to which you were called,

**Reader 2:** With all humility,

**Reader 3:** With gentleness and patience,

**All three:** Bearing with one another in love, making every effort to maintain the unity of the Spirit, in the bond of peace.

**Reader 1:** There is one Body,

**Reader 2:** There is one Spirit,

**Reader 3:** There is one Baptism,

**All three:** There is one God and Father of all.

**Reader 1:** Who is above all, through all, and in all.

**Reader 2:** Living the truth in love,

**Reader 3:** We should grow in every way into him who is the head, Christ.

**Reader 1:** So be imitators of God,

**Reader 2:** As beloved children,

**Reader 3:** And live in love

**All three:** As Christ loved us. **Based on Ephesians 4:1–7, 15, 5:1–2**

**Leader:** Guide us, O God, in your ways, so that we will learn to love others. We seek to live in the love Your Son showed us. We ask this in Christ, our Lord.

**All:** Amen.

▶ *Sing or play "One Bread, One Body"*

Go to **aliveinchrist.osv.com** for an interactive review.

**A** Work with Words **Complete each sentence with the correct term from the Word Bank.**

| | |
|---|---|
| Pope | Eastern |
| ecumenism | reformation |
| apostolic | Martin Luther |
| just | Latin |
| Creed | Doctrine |

1. The Catholic Church is

   _____ because, through the unbroken line of bishops and popes, we can trace her history back to the Apostles.

2. The Apostles'_____ is one of our oldest creeds and is professed in the celebration of Baptism.

3. The _____ Catholic Churches celebrate all three Sacraments of Initiation at the same time.

4. The different Churches within the one Catholic Church formed under the leadership of the

   _____.

5. The movement toward building unity and community among all Christian people is

   called _____.

**B** Check Understanding **Circle the letter of the choice that best completes the sentence.**

6. At the Last Supper Christ prayed for all of his followers to be ____.
   a. happy          c. one
   b. priests        d. perfect

7. As Catholics, we are united by our creeds, the Seven Sacraments, and our ____ ministry.
   a. ordained       c. long
   b. traditional    d. Latin

8. The two main Churches are the Latin or Roman and the ____.
   a. Armenian       c. Eastern
   b. Byzantine      d. Chaldean

9. The split between many in the Eastern Church and the Western Church in 1054 is known as the Great ____.
   a. Movement       c. Divide
   b. Reformation    d. Schism

10. Martin Luther called for reforms in the Church that led to the ____ Reformation.
    a. Ecumenical     c. Canon
    b. Protestant     d. Evangelical

**C** Make Connections **On a separate sheet of paper, write a one-paragraph response to the question: Think about someone you know who is a Christian but not a Catholic. What parts of your faith do you have in common? What beliefs are different?**

**A** Work with Words **Use the clues below to complete the crossword puzzle.**

Across

1. Movement started by Martin Luther

5. A sincere change of mind, heart, and desire to turn away from sin and evil and turn toward God

6. The Apostles' ___ is said during Mass and at Baptism

8. Forgiveness of sins and the return to goodness for which humans were first created

Down

2. The Catholic Church is this because the popes and bishops trace their leadership back to the Apostles.

3. One of the two main branches of the Catholic Church

4. Season that helps us focus on what would make our lives more just and right

7. Lazarus' sister and a close friend of Jesus

**B** Check Understanding **Complete the sentences with the correct term.**

9. _____ was the first person Jesus appeared to after he rose to new life.

10. _____ was a businesswoman in Philippi, who offered her home to Paul and Silas.

11. Peter, James, and _____ were the only disciples who came with Jesus to pray the night he was arrested.

12. _____ means to have been declared "free of blame" or absolved.

13. _____ life is life forever with God for all who die in his friendship.

14. _____ is the process of turning away from sin and toward God that happens throughout our lives.

15. When we are _____, we live in accordance with God's will, in his friendship, free from guilt or sin.

16. As Catholics, we are united in our belief of one Lord, Jesus, and by the celebration of the _____.

17. The _____ Catholic Churches unite all three Sacraments of Initiation.

18. The event of the Risen Jesus being taken up into Heaven is called the _____.

19. A person who learns from and follows the example of a teacher is called a _____.

20. The movement toward building unity and community among all Christian people is called _____.

21. The _____ were chosen by Jesus to be his closest followers and to share in his work and mission in a special way.

**C** Make Connections  **Write a short answer to these questions.**

22. Jesus prayed for his Church to be "one." What steps could you take to make this happen?

_____

_____

_____

_____

_____

23. Imagine you are one of the disciples at Pentecost—the day the Holy Spirit first descended. What is happening around you? What are your thoughts and reactions?

_____

_____

_____

_____

_____

24. The fact that Peter was one of Jesus' closest friends, and that Jesus called him "the Rock," tells us that Jesus saw the best in his friends and knew what they could become. What do you think friendship with Jesus would be like?

_____

_____

_____

_____

_____

25. Jesus is the Light of the World, Bread of Life, and the Vine. Select one of these images. What does this image mean in terms of relationship with God?

_____

_____

_____

_____

_____

# THE CHURCH

*How is the Church an instrument of salvation through her teaching and missionary work?*

## CHURCH HISTORY TIMELINE

**33**     The Holy Spirit appears at Pentecost

**35**     Saint Paul's conversion

**1565**     St. Augustine, Florida becomes first Catholic presence in America

**1769**     Juniperro Serra establishes the first of the California missions

Go to page 348 for more

© Our Sunday Visitor

## Our Catholic Tradition

- The Church continues the mission Christ gave to his Apostles. She continues to teach the truth of Christ through the Magisterium—the Pope, and bishops in union with him, guided by the Holy Spirit. (CCC, 890)

- As members of the Church, we are called to proclaim the Good News of Christ to the world. We are called to share in the missionary work of the Church. (CCC, 942)

- All baptized Catholics are called to share in Jesus' ministry as Priest, Prophet, and King to serve the mission of the Church, but there are different roles in serving. These roles help the Church as she seeks to unite all people. (CCC, 783)

## Our Catholic Life

- The faith we profess in the Creeds is the faith we celebrate in the liturgy, live out by following God's will for us, and strengthen through prayer. (CCC, 26, 1064)

- The Church is universal, going out to the whole world, welcoming people of all cultures and ages. (CCC, 868)

- Members of religious orders consecrate their lives as a sign of God's love and holiness and serve an important part of the Church's mission. (CCC, 916)

# The Church Is Apostolic

## 💗 Let Us Pray

**Leader:** Father of us all, may your Spirit guide us as we reach out to others and serve in your name.

"I sing of mercy and justice; to you, LORD, I sing praise." **Psalm 101:1**

**All:** Lord, teach us.

### 📖 Scripture

"They devoted themselves to the teaching of the apostles and to the communal life, to the breaking of the bread and to the prayers. Awe came upon everyone, and many wonders and signs were done through the apostles." **Acts 2:42-43**

Religious sister Maria helps clean up after serving meals to the homeless in Kamagaski, Japan

### Have you ever thought...

- How are things we think and do today as a Church connected to people from the past?

- Why should we care about what people in the Church believed long ago?

# Getting Started

In this chapter, you will explore how the Catholic Church traces her authority, leadership, and teaching back to Christ and his Apostles. You will also learn about the role of ordained ministers in carrying on the work of the Apostles.

Catholic Faith Words

- Pope
- Apostolic Succession
- Magisterium
- infallible
- Nicene Creed

## Ordained Ministry in the Church

Fill in the chart with the ordained minister who leads and/or serves the Church in the manner described. ✱

The _____ leads the _____.

↓

A _____ leads a _____.

↓

A _____ leads a _____.

↓

A _____ serves in a _____.

© Our Sunday Visitor

## IDENTIFY AND DESCRIBE

**Traditions Passed On** The earliest Christian communities established new rituals and traditions following Jesus' command to baptize, teach, and celebrate the Eucharist.

List some traditions that have been passed on in your school, family, and parish.

_____

_____

_____

_____

_____

_____

_____

_____

_____

_____

_____

Then, in each category above, circle the ones that seem most important to you. Describe how you know about these traditions.

_____

_____

_____

_____

_____

What do you know about their origins?

_____

_____

_____

_____

_____

## Upon This Rock

**How has the Catholic Church kept the faith of Jesus after so many centuries?**

People like to follow traditions that have been passed down from generation to generation. Maybe it makes us feel connected to the people who came before us, or helps us see that we are part of something important.

Or, it might be that following the tradition identifies us as a group. Many things identify us as Catholics. Catholics make the Sign of the Cross. We do not eat meat on the Fridays of Lent and are asked to make a sacrifice every Friday of the year. While these are some of the traditions of the Catholic Church, we use the word Tradition to mean something even more vital. It refers to Sacred Tradition, the teaching handed on to us from Jesus and his Apostles. It is sacred because it is one source of the Word of God. Although some of our practices may have changed since Jesus

called his first disciples, the Catholic Church has always proclaimed the same Gospel handed on to us from Jesus and his Apostles.

## Peter the Apostle

As Jesus began his public life, he called many followers. From among those disciples, he chose twelve men to be his Apostles. He taught them everything he could. He sent them out to share in his mission to tell others the Good News he brought, and to build up God's Kingdom. Jesus gave his Apostles and their successors the authority to act in his name.

Jesus chose the Apostle Simon, who was a fisherman, to be the leader of the Apostles and his Church. Jesus gave him the name "Peter." This was a play on words—the word *Peter* means "rock."

> ### 📖 Scripture
>
> "And so I say to you, you are Peter, and upon this rock I will build my church, and the gates of the netherworld shall not prevail against it. I will give you the keys to the kingdom of heaven. Whatever you bind on earth shall be bound in heaven; and whatever you loose on earth shall be loosed in heaven." **Matthew 16:18–19**

Once Jesus ascended to Heaven to be with the Father, he was no longer visible to us. So he gave the Church a visible head, Saint Peter, who was his Vicar, or representative on Earth. Jesus formed the Apostles into a permanent gathering or assembly (also called a "college"), which together leads the Church. The authority given to that college of Apostles with Peter at its head has stayed with the Church ever since.

## Leaders of the Church

All of the Apostles, along with Mary, were present on the day of Pentecost. Their successors, the Pope and bishops, are present to lead the Church today.

The **Pope** is the successor to Saint Peter as bishop of Rome and as the leader of the entire Catholic Church. He is also called the "Vicar of Christ," the Church's visible head. Another title the Pope has received from Saint Peter is "Pastor of the universal Church." Jesus not only gave Peter authority over the Church, but he also told Peter to be a pastor, or shepherd, and to "feed my sheep" (John 21:17).

Jesus gave all his twelve Apostles authority to lead the Church under Saint Peter. This authority has been handed down directly from the Apostles to the Pope and bishops of the Church today. This is called **Apostolic Succession**.

We can trace the leadership of the Church all the way back to Jesus, Saint Peter, and the other Apostles. As the Apostles traveled to spread the Gospel, they appointed other leaders to continue the work Jesus had given them. From the Apostles to the Pope and bishops today, the Holy Spirit has helped us to know the truth that Jesus came to reveal through his life, Death, Resurrection, and Ascension. We call that truth the Sacred Tradition of the Church—the truth that guides the decisions of each member of the Catholic Church.

### Catholic Faith Words

**Pope** the successor of Peter, the bishop of Rome, and the head of the entire Catholic Church

**Apostolic Succession** the term used to describe that the authority to lead and teach the Church can be traced through the centuries from the Apostles to their successors, the Pope and bishops

© Our Sunday Visitor

### IDENTIFY

Read the parable in Matthew 7:24–27. Do you think Jesus might have had this parable in mind when he called Peter a "Rock"? What kinds of floods and storms has the Church had to endure?

_______________________________________________

_______________________________________________

_______________________________________________

_______________________________________________

_______________________________________________

_______________________________________________

_______________________________________________

What qualities do you think Church leaders need today?

# Teaching from the Apostles

**Where do the Church's teachings come from?**

Our Sacred Tradition starts with Jesus. After his Resurrection and Ascension, Jesus sent the Holy Spirit to continue teaching the Apostles. Everything Jesus entrusted to them, the Apostles handed down to the whole Church by their preaching and writing. Until Christ returns at the end of time, the Church faithfully hands down his teachings to all generations.

The teaching office of the Church is the Pope and all of the bishops in union with him. The **Magisterium** has the teaching authority to interpret the Word of God found in Sacred Scripture and Sacred Tradition. To this day, the college of bishops, in union with the Pope as bishop of Rome, makes up the authentic teachers who pass on the faith to the People of God and make pronouncements on moral questions.

The most important teachings from the Church are **infallible**, free from error. That is, when the Pope, as head of the

## Catholic Faith Words

**Magisterium** the teaching office of the Church, which is all of the bishops in union with the Pope. The Magisterium has the teaching authority to interpret the Word of God found in Sacred Scripture and Sacred Tradition.

**infallible** the quality of being free from error. A teaching is infallible when the Pope, as head of the Magisterium, speaks officially on a matter of faith or morals that is to be believed by everyone in the Church.

**Nicene Creed** a summary of foundational truths about the Holy Trinity, the Church, and eternal life. We usually say the Nicene Creed at Mass.

Magisterium, speaks officially on a matter of faith or morals that is to be believed by everyone in the Church, his teaching is infallible. This infallibility also extends to the full body of bishops when they teach, in union with the Pope, about faith and morals, most especially in ecumenical councils. We can trust that it comes from Christ because he has handed on his teaching authority and sent the guidance of the Holy Spirit to the Pope and bishops today through the ages from the Apostles. This is why one of the Marks of the Church is that she is **apostolic**.

## Creeds

From the beginning of the Church, believers have professed their faith using summaries called creeds. We have two main creeds, the Apostles' Creed you already studied, and the **Nicene Creed**. The Nicene Creed was written at the Council of Nicaea in A.D. 325. The Council of Constantinople added even more detail to the Creed later, in A.D. 381. We profess the Creed at Sunday Mass.

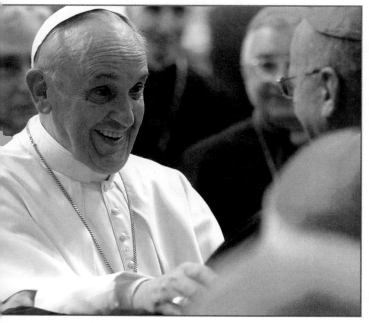

**Pope Francis meets with bishops of the Italian Episcopal conference.**

© Our Sunday Visitor

## WHERE IT HAPPENED

Why is the Nicene Creed so much longer than the Apostles' Creed? At the time the Nicene Creed was written (A.D. 325), there were heresies (false teachings) being spread that Jesus was not really a man, but was God who made himself look like a man, and did not already exist as the second Divine Person of the Holy Trinity before he was born on Earth.

The Pope and bishops met together in several councils at Nicaea and Constantinople expressly to answer these heresies. They declared that Jesus Christ is both true God and true man. The councils wrote the Nicene Creed with very clearly defined details, which stated this belief once and for all.

**Iznik, Turkey, formerly Nicaea**

## Unity Amid Diversity

The Christian churches of the world can be called a world Christian family. But not every Christian is a member of the Catholic Church. There are Christian faith communities that are not in union with the Pope, but they share some of the same important beliefs about Jesus. Only the Catholic Church contains all the teachings of Christ handed on directly to us from Peter and the Apostles to the Pope and the bishops. But we hope for and work toward unity among all Christians. We do this by praying together, discussing what we have in common, respecting one another, and learning more about what other Christians believe.

Of course, down through the ages, the Church has grown to be a worldwide community, and there is a lot of diversity in the ways people worship and express their faith. However, all Churches in communion with the Pope and the Catholic Church are united by fidelity to Apostolic Tradition: they are in union with the Pope and bishops. They carry on the faith and the Seven Sacraments that came from Christ through his Apostles.

## IDENTIFY

Name three truths of faith we profess in the Nicene Creed.

1. _____

2. _____

3. _____

# The Work of the Apostles

**How do ordained ministers continue the work of the Apostles?**

As the Church grew, the Apostles ordained more bishops who later ordained priests, deacons, and more new bishops. The line of succession from the Apostles has never been broken. People still come to faith in Christ through the Pope, bishops, priests, and deacons.

Saint Paul reminds us that God wills that everyone be saved, but it cannot happen unless someone is sent to preach the Good News:

## Scripture

"For 'everyone who calls on the name of the Lord will be saved.' But how can they call on him in whom they have not believed? And how can they believe in him of whom they have not heard? And how can they hear without someone to preach? And how can people preach unless they are sent?" Romans 10:13–15

The Sacrament of Holy Orders is "the sacrament of apostolic ministry" (CCC, 1536). The mission Christ gave to his Apostles continues in the Church until the end of time through this Sacrament. We speak of orders, instead of just one order, because Holy Orders are conferred in three degrees: bishops, presbyters (priests), and deacons.

**Bishops** receive the fullness of the Sacrament of Holy Orders. A bishop was first ordained a deacon and then a priest. Under the authority of the Pope, he is the visible head of the particular Church entrusted to him.

The bishop is the chief teacher, shepherd, and priest for his particular Church, called a diocese. Each diocese is divided into smaller faith communities called parishes. The bishop acts as Christ's representative.

Presbyters, or **priests**, belong to the second degree of Holy Orders. A priest can celebrate most of the Seven Sacraments; however, he cannot confer the Sacrament of Holy Orders. Under certain circumstances, a priest can confirm.

Priests share the dignity of priesthood with their bishops, but they also depend on the bishops to delegate them to act as priests in the diocese. Priests are called to be the bishops' co-workers. Each priest receives the charge of a parish or some other ministry.

**Deacons** belong to the third degree of Holy Orders. A deacon is ordained for tasks of service to the Church. They have a special role in the ministry of the Word (Scripture), the worship of the Church, works of charity and service, and outreach to the community. A deacon can preside at the Sacrament of Baptism and witness at Matrimony.

All three roles are necessary for the Catholic Church's mission to be carried out.

> **What would be missing if we didn't have each of these orders today?**

### INTERVIEW

Does your own parish have a full-time pastor or does your parish share a pastor with another parish? Do you have more than one priest in your parish? Make a list of the ways priests serve your parish. Write a question you would like to ask your priest about his role.

## IN SUMMARY   Catholics Believe

The Church is apostolic, continuing the mission Christ gave to his Apostles.

- Jesus named Peter to be head of his Church and gathered the rest of the Apostles as a united "college" to help lead it. The Pope is the direct successor of Peter as head of the Church, and the bishops are direct successors of the Apostles.

- The Church continues to teach the truth of Christ and his Church through the Magisterium—the Pope, and bishops in union with him, guided by the Holy Spirit.

- Particular Churches, or dioceses, are led by bishops, who appoint priests to be pastors and deacons to perform important works of service.

## Our Catholic Life

The **Nicene Creed** is a summary of the foundational truths of the Catholic faith. In it, we profess our belief in the Triune God—Father, Son, and Holy Spirit—and we proclaim that belief at Mass every Sunday throughout the world. The proclamation of the Nicene and Apostles' Creeds are two of the many elements of the Catholic Church. We end the Nicene Creed with "Amen," which, in Hebrew, has the same root word as "believe." By saying "Amen," we are saying God is faithful to us and we trust in him and his faithfulness. We will celebrate our "I believe" by participating in the liturgy, and live it out by following God's will for us, and strengthen it by praying.

> **What part of the Nicene Creed speaks to you the most? Why?**

## People of Faith

### Saint Peter Damian, 1007–1072

Peter Damian was a Benedictine monk in Ravenna, Italy, who saw ordinary people and Church officials engaged in practices that violated Church principles. He lashed out at corrupt practices, and defended celibacy at a time when many priests and bishops were married and had families. He preferred a monastic life, but Peter's intelligence made several Popes ask for his help. He resolved disputes among clergy and helped keep the Church intact during a time of schism. Peter was declared a Doctor of the Church in 1828. The Church celebrates his feast day on **February 21**.

For more, go to **aliveinchrist.osv.com**

## LIST

Obtain a copy of your parish bulletin or visit your parish or diocesan website. What does it tell you about the universal Church?

_____

_____

_____

_____

_____

What does it tell you about your bishop or diocese?

_____

_____

_____

_____

_____

## ♥ Prayer of Petition

**Leader:** Let us take this time to allow the Holy Spirit to enter our hearts.

**All:** Lord, lead us as children of light.

**Reader 1:** Father of us all,
through your Son, Jesus,
you called friends and disciples,
servants and teachers,
to spread your Word,
your Good News, and your mission.

We want to be called
to reach out to others
and serve in your name.

**All:** Lord, lead us as children of light.

**Reader 2:** Lord,
through those Saints and leaders
who have gone before us,
your story continues
to heal, to teach, to spread hope
through all the world.
We want to be called
to keep sharing the message of your love
and your care.

**All:** Lord, lead us as children of light.

**Reader 1:** Father,
you have chosen us to be your "Church,"
a living, breathing,
spirit-filled community,
that challenges all
to live with passion and joy,
care and compassion,
and to spread the Good News
and hope that you bring meaning to life.

Call us to be like your Son, Jesus,
and all those who have followed him,

We ask this through your Son, Jesus,
our Lord. Amen.

**All:** Amen.

▶ *Sing or play "Go Light Your World"*

Go to **aliveinchrist.osv.com** for an interactive review.

**A** **Work with Words** Circle the letter of the choice that best completes the sentence.

1. When the Pope speaks officially on a matter of faith or morals that is to be believed by everyone in the Church, the teaching is ____, free from error.
   a. apostolic      c. Papal law
   b. infallible     d. Tradition

2. The teaching office of the Church, which is all of the bishops in union with the Pope, is called the ____.
   a. Magisterium       c. Scriptures
   b. Tradition         d. Apostolic Succession

3. The particular Church that is led by a bishop is called a ____.
   a. vicar       c. parish
   b. presbyter   d. diocese

4. ____, or priests, belong to the second degree of Holy Orders.
   a. Presbyters   c. Bishops
   b. Deacons      d. Cardinals

5. Because of ____, we can trace the leadership of the Church all the way back to Jesus, Saint Peter, and the Apostles.
   a. Tradition   c. Papal Infallibility
   b. Scripture   d. Apostolic Succession

**B** **Check Understanding** Complete each sentence with the correct term from the Word Bank.

| | |
|---|---|
| cardinal | Pope |
| Nicene Creed | Tradition |
| presbyters | archbishop |
| Vicar of Christ | deacons |

6. The Pope, as the successor to Saint Peter and the leader of the entire universal Church, is called the _____.

7. To this day, the bishops in union with the _____ are the authentic teachers who pass on the faith to the People of God and make pronouncements on moral questions.

8. The _____ is a profession of faith in foundational truths about the Holy Trinity, the Church, and eternal life.

9. Apostolic _____ unites all Churches in communion with the Pope and the Catholic Church.

10. _____, who are ordained for tasks of service to the Church, belong to the third degree of Holy Orders.

**C** **Make Connections** On a separate sheet of paper, write a one-paragraph response to the question: What is the importance of Apostolic Succession to the Church?

# The Church Is Catholic

## ♥ Let Us Pray

**Leader:** O God of every good gift, help us to love your people by sharing our gifts with each other. May we help others believe in you.

"How good and how pleasant it is, when brothers dwell together as one!" **Psalm 133:1**

**All:** Lord, give us the right words to say.

## ✝ Scripture

"'For the promise is made to you and to your children and to all those far off, whomever the Lord our God will call.'

"All who believed were together and had all things in common; they would sell their property and possessions and divide them among all according to each one's need." **Acts 2:39, 44–45**

### Have you ever thought...

- How does the Good News reach every corner of the Earth?

- How can you explain your Catholic faith to a friend?

# Getting Started

In this chapter, you will explore the importance of sharing the Good News. You will better understand the Church's mission of establishing God's Kingdom and examine the ways that the Church carries out her mission.

In the circle, describe ways people and groups grow—in understanding and knowledge, or in size, or in influence. Why is it important to grow? Who or what can help us to grow?

**Ways Individuals Grow**

**Ways Families Grow**

**Ways a Group or Organization Grows**

**Ways a Community Grows**

**Top Ten Catholic** In the Acts of the Apostles, you read about how the Apostles shared their faith and the Christian community grew (see Acts 2:39, 43–46). A friend wants to learn more about what you believe and how you practice your faith. Create a Top Ten List of Catholic beliefs and practices that you could share with your friend.

top TEN list

1.

2.

3.

4.

5.

6.

7.

8.

9.

10.

## Believers Spread the Good News

**Am I willing to tell other people about Jesus and his Church?**

Sometimes talking about your faith is easy and natural. Sometimes it feels awkward. Sometimes it feels competitive—or preachy. When it comes to talking about your Catholic faith, speak simply and from your heart.

When you speak from the heart about what you believe, others tend to respect it—whether they get it or not. Talking about God comes with being a disciple.

## Evangelists

The four authors of the Gospels—Matthew, Mark, Luke, and John—are called the Four **Evangelists**. Inspired by God to record his Word, they were certainly bearers of the Good News.

Before any of the Gospels were written, a woman brought an entire town to meet Jesus, even though many of the townspeople did not like her very much. She became known as the Woman at the Well. (See John 4:4–42.) She was a woman with a bad reputation.

Jesus knew all about her, and he told her so. He also told her he was the Messiah who could give her life-giving water. She believed what Jesus told her and she told others about him. And they came to believe too.

> If Jesus came to stay with you, what would you want to ask him and learn from him?

### 📖 Scripture

"Many of the Samaritans of that town began to believe in him because of the word of the woman who testified, 'He told me everything I have done.' When the Samaritans came to him, they invited him to stay with them; and he stayed there two days. Many more began to believe in him because of his word, and they said to the woman, 'We no longer believe because of your word, for we have heard for ourselves, and we know that this is truly the savior of the world.'" John 4:39–42

📖 **Go to the Source**
What did Jesus say to the woman? Read *John 4:13–26* to find out.

© Our Sunday Visitor

## An Urgent Mandate

Jesus sends his disciples out with urgency. He says, "For God so loved the world that he gave his only Son, so that everyone who believes in him might not perish but might have eternal life" (John 3:16). After his Resurrection, Jesus told his Apostles to make disciples of all nations. The Church is the sign of salvation and new life sent by God to all nations in all times to bring the saving message of Jesus to everyone. Salvation can only come through faith in Christ and his Church, so the Church must spread the Gospel everywhere. This is her **missionary mandate**.

Christ did not send only the leaders to spread the Gospel. He sent the whole Church. This means he also sent and continues to send each of us. There is no other way for us to truly be disciples of Jesus. He expects us to spread his Good News.

We might doubt our ability to spread the Good News or be afraid of how people will receive us. Jesus reassures us: "And behold, I am with you always, to the end of the age" (Matthew 28:20). He has stayed with his Church down through the ages. He is with us now.

**A missionary priest in Cambodia**

### Catholic Faith Words

**Evangelists**  the four inspired human authors of the Gospels: Matthew, Mark, Luke, and John

**missionary mandate**  the responsibility given by Jesus to the Church to bring his saving message to everyone

## LIST AND APPLY

List some ways people can tell that you are a Catholic.

_____

_____

Think of other Catholics you know. Explain some of the ways their faith is visible.

_____

_____

What is one thing you can learn from the ways their faith is visible?

_____

Church of Mary Girgis, Cairo, Egypt

✝ Go to the Source

Read Acts 1:8–9 to discover how the Apostles would be able to carry out Jesus' command to be his witnesses.

# Meant for Everyone

**Why does the Church want to reach everyone in the world?**

The word *catholic* means "universal." When something is universal, it is for everyone. It is total and complete.

The word fits the Catholic Church in two ways:

- The Church proclaims all the truths of the faith. In the Church we have the total message and everything we need for salvation with nothing left out.
- The Church is for everyone. She is sent out to all people everywhere in every time. When Jesus was ascending to his Father, he told his Apostles, "You will be my witnesses in Jerusalem, throughout Judea and Samaria, and to the ends of the earth" (Acts 1:8).

This is why we say that one of the Marks of the Church is that she is **catholic**.

## Universal Doesn't Mean Identical

The Church has to reach out to everyone in the world in order to be herself. From the beginning, Jesus wanted the Church to be universal, welcoming, and open to everyone. In order for this to happen, we, like the first disciples, have to spread the message.

Although the Church strives to be universal and reach everyone in the world, she does not have to look and act the same in every place she is established.

The Church takes on different cultures, customs, and appearances in each part of the world where she puts down roots. The rich variety of liturgical traditions and cultural expressions of the faith are part of the Church's great glory.

> **Catholic Faith Words**
>
> **catholic** a Mark of the Church. The church is catholic because her mission is to the whole world.

## Everything Needed

The Catholic Church has everything needed to be reconciled with God and to be made one with him. The Fathers of Vatican Council II listed all that is necessary for salvation:

- correct and complete instruction in the faith
- the full sacramental life of all Seven Sacraments
- ordained ministry that follows in direct succession from the Apostles

These things can only be found completely in the Catholic Church. People who are not members of the Church can be saved, but only because of the grace of God present in the Church.

**Palm Sunday liturgy in Ethiopia**

## WRITE

Write down some ways the Church is for everyone, welcoming all people, and going out to people everywhere. Then, explain how your parish acts in the same way on a local level.

**The Universal Church:** _____

_____

_____

_____

_____

**My Parish:** _____

_____

_____

_____

_____

# A Missionary Church

**How does the Church carry out her missionary mandate?**

God, in his great love, wants everyone to know and love him. Everyone who searches for the truth is on the path to salvation, but the whole truth has been given to the Church. So, the Church goes out to those seeking the truth, offering them salvation through faith in Christ. The Church has been missionary from the very beginning and continues to be so today.

Missionary work requires patience; it doesn't succeed overnight! The Church acts like water on a seed—a whole tree doesn't grow instantaneously. It gradually leads people to Christ in these stages:

- proclamation of the Gospel to nonbelievers
- establishment of Christian communities
- foundation of local churches

**Missionaries** enter into "respectful dialogue" with those who do not yet accept the Gospel. They respect other traditions and

cultures and try to incorporate symbols and traditions of cultures into the way they teach about the Gospel.

Catholic missionaries have been among the greatest world explorers. Missionaries have found isolated tribes, explored unmapped lands, and gained new knowledge about cultures, languages, and even plant and animal life from distant places.

Missionaries help people needing food, shelter, medical care, education, and even protection from war and violence. Catholic missionaries are lay people, deacons, priests, bishops, or religious brothers and sisters. They work in every country in the world today, and are often in danger. There have been missionaries martyred in every land and time, including now.

> **Why is it important for missionaries to respect other religions and cultures?**

© Our Sunday Visitor

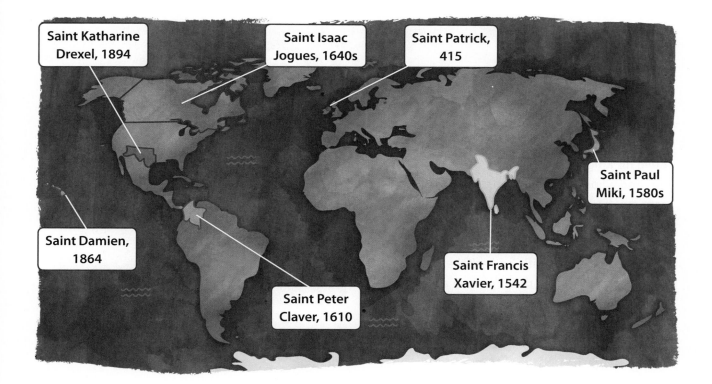

Saint Katharine Drexel, 1894

Saint Isaac Jogues, 1640s

Saint Patrick, 415

Saint Paul Miki, 1580s

Saint Damien, 1864

Saint Francis Xavier, 1542

Saint Peter Claver, 1610

## Everyone Is Called

You might be called to become a missionary someday. If not, you are still called to be part of the Church's missionary work—in fact, all Catholics are! One of the patron Saints of missionaries is Saint Thérèse of Lisieux, who never left her convent! Her prayers for the missions contributed so much that she has been recognized as a missionary herself. There are many opportunities to share in the missionary work of the Church with prayers and donations, and even projects in your local area. Your parish may even be a sister Church working with missionaries around the world.

> **If you could be a missionary in a distant land, what kind of work would you do?**

### SUMMARIZE

Find out about the life of one of the missionaries listed above and write a short summary of their work. Then spend some time in prayer for missionaries around the world.

## IN SUMMARY   Catholics Believe

As members of the Church, we are called to proclaim the Good News of Christ to the world.

- While Matthew, Mark, Luke, and John are the four Evangelists of the Gospels, all Church members are called to spread the Good News of the Gospel.

- The Church is universal, going out to the whole world, welcoming people of all cultures and ages.

- Missionaries continue Christ's mission of healing and bring the message of salvation to people who have not yet come to know and believe in Jesus. Each of us is called to share in the missionary work of the Church.

## Our Catholic Life

The Church's **missionary mandate** continues Jesus' mission of spreading the Good News by what we say and do, by loving one another, and by working for peace and justice as we work with God to help build his Kingdom: "Whoever receives you receives me, and whoever receives me receives the one who sent me" (Matthew 10:40). It is our responsibility to study, know, and live our faith so that we can share it with others. Talk to someone you know who is an example of Catholic faith, and ask them how they share their faith with others. You can also decide how to share in the missionary work of the Church right now. Choose a mission to pray for and think of ways you can help that mission financially.

> **What aspect of the Church's missionary mandate interests you most?**

## People of Faith

### Saint Agnes, c. 291–304

Agnes was born to a Christian family in Rome. A high-ranking official wanted her to marry his son, but Agnes didn't want to marry a non-Christian. This made the official angry, so he had her sentenced to death. She was dragged through the streets, then tied to a stake to be burned, but the wood wouldn't catch fire. One of the soldiers in charge of the execution then cut off her head. She was buried in the catacombs under Rome, but today her bones are in two churches named after her in Rome. Saint Agnes is the patron Saint of girls and engaged couples. The Church celebrates her feast day on **January 21.**

For more, go to
**aliveinchrist.osv.com**

## DISCUSS

Form groups of three and talk about being Catholic. Make notes here.

My favorite Catholic symbol is

_____

because

_____

My favorite Catholic season is

_____

because

_____

One thing I still don't understand about being Catholic is . . .

_____

_____

## ♥ Prayer of Acknowledgment

**Leader:** God calls all of us, his disciples, to be Saints.

Let us listen well to the words of Jesus.

**Reader 1:** Be attentive to the wisdom of the Gospel according to Matthew.

Jesus approached and said to them, "All power in heaven and on earth has been given to me. Go, therefore, and make disciples of all nations, baptizing them in the name of the Father, and of the Son, and of the holy Spirit, teaching them to observe all that I have commanded you. And behold, I am with you always, until the end of the age." (Matthew 28:18–20)

*At the conclusion, pause for silent reflection; then continue with the following:*

**Reader 2:** Let us pray.

O God, give us the strength we need, to take up the cause of those who so willingly gave their lives to serve others.

**All:** We will go out and tell the Good News.

**Reader 3:** God of light, help us to see as you would want us to see.

**All:** We will go out and tell the Good News.

**Reader 4:** God of all goodness and mercy, open our hearts to be compassionate,

open our minds to understand the needs of others.

**All:** We will go out and tell the Good News.

**Leader:** God, we know and believe that you have chosen us to be your servants, your missionaries, your Saints.

Help us to respond to your call; help us to receive this challenge with confidence and trust knowing you are with us.

We ask this through your Son, who is Jesus Christ, our friend and brother.

Amen.

▶ *Sing or play "Go Ye Out"*

Go to **aliveinchrist.osv.com** for an interactive review.

**A** Work with Words **Complete each sentence with the correct term.**

1. Matthew, Mark, Luke, and John are

   "the Four _____,"
   the four inspired human authors of the Gospels.

2. Jesus told the Apostles to make

   _____ of all nations.

3. Because salvation can only come through
   faith in Christ and his Church, the Church has

   a _____ to spread
   the Gospel.

4. The Church is _____
   or "universal" because she is sent on a mission
   to the whole world.

5. Jesus told his Apostles, "You will be my

   _____ in Jerusalem,
   throughout Judea and Samaria, and to the
   ends of the earth."

**B** Check Understanding **Indicate whether the following statements are true or false. Then rewrite false statements to make them true.**

6. In the Catholic Church we find everything
   necessary for salvation, with nothing left out.
   **True/False**

   _____

   _____

7. Full sacramental life of all Seven Sacraments is
   present in the Catholic Church. **True/False**

   _____

   _____

8. The Church looks and acts the same in
   everyplace she exists. **True/False**

   _____

   _____

9. To be a missionary, we have to travel.
   **True/False**

   _____

   _____

10. Many great world explorers have been
    Catholic missionaries. **True/False**

    _____

    _____

**C** Make Connections **Write a one-paragraph response to the question: Who do you know who needs to hear some Good News? Write about some specific ways you can share your faith with this person.**

_____

_____

_____

_____

_____

_____

_____

_____

_____

_____

© Our Sunday Visitor

# The Christian Faithful

## ♡ Let Us Pray

**Leader:** O Lord, you give us gifts to share. You call us to echo your Word and your love in the world. Help us to live the Gospel every day.

"Your word is a lamp for my feet,
a light for my path." **Psalm 119:105**

**All:** Holy God, be with all of those who serve the Church.

## 📖 Scripture

"You are the salt of the earth. But if salt loses its taste, with what can it be seasoned? It is no longer good for anything but to be thrown out and trampled underfoot. You are the light of the world. A city set on a mountain cannot be hidden. Nor do they light a lamp and then put it under a bushel basket; it is set on a lamp stand, where it gives light to all in the house. Just so, your light must shine before others, that they may see your good deeds and glorify your heavenly Father."

**Matthew 5:13–16**

### Have you ever thought...

- What does it mean to be salt for the Earth and light of the world?

- What is your place in the Catholic Church?

# Getting Started

In this chapter, you will learn about the importance of each person's membership in the Church and the role of the laity in the Church. You will also examine the call to serve as religious priests, brothers, and sisters.

In the chart below, record how each group serves the needs of the Church. As you complete the chapter, add new information to the chart.

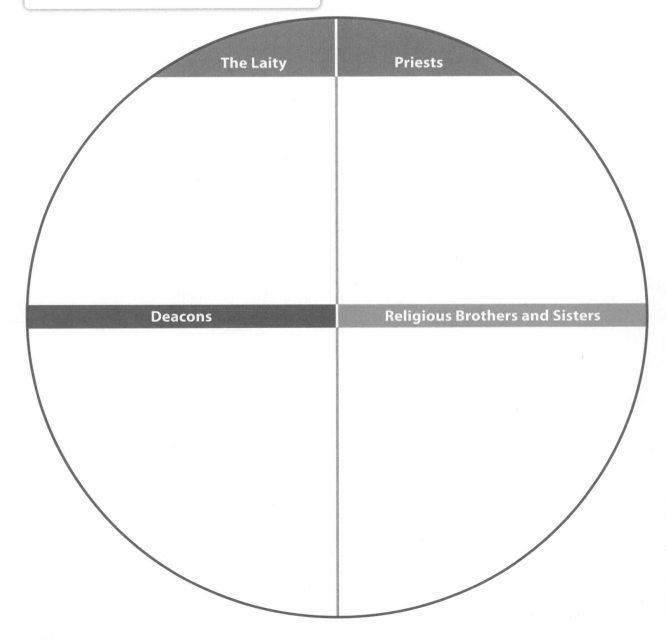

**The Laity**

**Priests**

**Deacons**

**Religious Brothers and Sisters**

© Our Sunday Visitor

**Welcome Home**  A Catholic family has moved to your town and is searching online for a new parish. The search lands them on your parish's homepage. What will they discover about the groups, activities, and ministries? How can you communicate how your parish is salt for the earth and light of the world (see Matthew 5:13-16)? Write some information the family might find on each of these navigation tabs:

**Parish Staff**

_____

_____

_____

**Ministries**

_____

_____

_____

**Faith Formation/Religious Education**

_____

_____

_____

**Daily and Sunday Mass Schedule**

_____

_____

_____

_____

**Stewardship**

_____

_____

_____

_____

## Priestly People

**How are all Church members important to the Church?**

The Apostles knew that it was important to divide responsibilities in the early Church. As more and more members joined, there was more work to be done. We learn from the sixth chapter of the Acts of the Apostles that some new Christians were concerned that poor widows were being neglected. The Apostles realized they needed help.

### Priest, Prophet, and King

Every member of the Church has an important role to play in carrying out her mission. Through our Baptism, we all share in the priestly, prophetic, and kingly offices of Christ. The **clergy** are ordained and given sacred authority to serve the Church by teaching, through divine worship, and through pastoral leadership. The **laity** serve in their personal, family, and community lives and in the parish.

Our participation differs depending on our state in life and our circumstances, but we are all called to bring the Good News to the world. As diverse as the Church is, we are united by our mission.

Jesus gives us this share in his mission. They are not honors we have earned. When Jesus showed us what a king should do, he showed us the job of a shepherd taking care of a flock of sheep. When he showed us how to exercise authority, he washed the feet of each Apostle and then told them to do the same (see John 13:3–15).

When you were baptized you became part of the common priesthood of the faithful, sharing in the priesthood of Christ. As you pray and discover what God wants you to do with your life, you will be called to be part of the clergy or the laity.

> **What roles have you noticed that people have in the Church? How are they all part of the same mission?**

## The Church's Hierarchy

From that earliest division of Church leadership started by the Apostles, we have come to a more complex division of leaders called the "hierarchy." Each member of the Church's hierarchy has clearly defined roles and responsibilities. They are ordained to serve the Church.

The Pope has "supreme, full, immediate, and universal power in the care of souls"

 **Go to the Source**

Read Acts 6:1–7. What are the different roles described in this passage? How is the work in your parish divided among the clergy (priests and deacons) and laity?

(CCC, 937). Bishops share with the Pope concern for all the Churches, but they are the visible successors of the Apostles in their own dioceses. The bishops must authentically teach the faith, celebrate divine worship, and guide their Churches as true pastors.

Priests—by their ordination into the ministerial priesthood—have sacred authority for the service of the faithful. They help their bishops by teaching, conducting worship, and governing in the name and the person of Christ in the community.

Deacons are ordained not to the ministerial priesthood but to ministry of works of service to the community. They assist the

## Catholic Faith Words

**clergy** men who are ordained and given sacred authority to serve the Church by teaching, divine worship, and pastoral leadership

**laity** all baptized members of the Church who share in Jesus' mission and witness to him and his message but are not priests or consecrated sisters or brothers; sometimes called lay people

bishops and priests in worship, especially in proclaiming the Gospel and preaching, in presiding at Baptisms, marriages, and funerals, and in dedicating themselves to different works of charity and outreach to the parish and beyond.

## NAME AND DESCRIBE

Look at the pictures below. On the lines under each picture, describe the ministry shown.

_____    _____    _____

_____    _____    _____

Name someone you have seen faithfully serving your parish. What role does this person play? What can you tell about this person based on what you have observed?

_____

_____

_____

# The Lay Faithful

**What is the role of the laity in the Catholic Church?**

Faithful Catholic lay men and women are essential to the work of the Church. Everyone who is baptized is called to be holy. In both Baptism and Confirmation, all Catholics receive grace to help them lead holy lives.

By cooperating with God's grace, all Christians can be faithful to Christ in all aspects of their lives—personal, family, social, and parish.

## Leaven in the Heart of the World Community

Lay people work in offices, factories, schools, farms, labs, stores, and any number of other busy places. Many do not spend their entire day focusing on religious matters, but they are called to bring their faith with them into all parts of their lives. The *Catechism of the Catholic Church* says lay people "are called to be witnesses to Christ in all circumstances and at the very heart of the community of mankind" (CCC, 942). Some lay people serve the Church in full- or part-time ministry. They are called "lay ecclesial ministers."

Jesus described those who serve the Kingdom of Heaven as leaven, which means to lighten or raise something, much like yeast makes bread rise. (See Matthew 13:33.) Lay people are called to be like "leaven in the world."

> Think about a finished loaf of bread. Can you take it apart and find the yeast in it? How can we know the yeast is there?

> What are some ways you have seen lay people bring Christ to a group of people or a certain place?

## The Laity at Worship

The clergy lead the worship of the Church, but there are liturgical roles for the laity, too. Perhaps you are already performing some of them. Lay people can be altar servers, readers at Mass (lectors) and the rest of the Seven Sacraments, cantors and/or choir members, organists, or extraordinary ministers of Holy Communion.

All of these roles help the assembly give praise and thanks to God during the Mass and the rest of the Seven Sacraments. Roles such as greeters and ushers, although not liturgical, help to bring people into the celebration.

## Other Parish Ministries

It is hard to imagine a parish today where the priests do all the work! It takes a whole community with many different gifts and talents to accomplish the mission of a parish. In addition to liturgical ministry roles, lay

**A priest prepares for morning Mass inside the sacristy**

men and women volunteer their time and talents to serve the Church. They may have busy secular (nonreligious) jobs, but they can be found on weekends and at other times in the week helping at the parish.

Keep your eyes open to see how things get done at your parish. Who decorates the sanctuary? Who washes the altar linens? Who teaches religious education classes?

Who ministers in Catholic schools? Who visits the sick and shut-ins? Who answers the phone, shovels snow, or counts money? Every time you see your parents or other lay people doing any of these things, you are seeing the laity helping accomplish the mission of the Church.

Every time you help out in any way, you are part of the mission, too. For more information on the work of the laity, see page 378 in the Our Catholic Tradition section of your book.

## EXPLAIN

Write a paragraph finishing this phrase:

By my Baptism, I was called to serve . . .

_____

_____

_____

_____

_____

_____

_____

_____

_____

Underline the ministries you and members of your family have been part of in your parish. Talk with a classmate about roles would you like to try in the future.

© Our Sunday Visitor

# Consecrated Religious Life

**Why do some people decide to become religious priests, brothers, or sisters?**

At Baptism, Jesus calls every disciple to follow him. Some Catholic men and women find Christ calling them to a different kind of dedication. They want to be more closely united with him, devoting their entire lives to God. These people choose some form of **consecrated religious life** so they can dedicate themselves to God's service and to the good of the whole Church.

Consecrated religious life is a special vocation in the Church that draws members from both the clergy and the laity. Priests, lay men, and lay women answer the call to become members of one of the many religious communities in the Church.

People who live a consecrated religious life make a public vow or promise to follow the **evangelical counsels** of poverty, chastity, and obedience. They join a religious order or congregation, that is, a vowed community of people carrying out the Church's mission.

These three special gifts—poverty, chastity, and obedience—are not commands. The

## Catholic Faith Words

**consecrated religious life** a state of life lived by religious sisters, brothers, and priests in community and characterized by the vows of poverty, chastity, and obedience

**evangelical counsels** poverty, chastity, and obedience. Those in consecrated religious life take public vows to live these counsels.

Commandments tell us what we must do. The evangelical counsels tell us what more we can do beyond what is required.

Consecrated religious men and women understand these gifts in a particular way and vow to live these three counsels. For consecrated religious, these vows have these meanings:

- Poverty: owning nothing in one's own name
- Chastity: giving oneself to God completely by living a celibate life for the Kingdom
- Obedience: promising to serve God and neighbor in one's religious community

In this way those who have chosen consecrated religious life as their vocation are free to serve God wholeheartedly.

© Our Sunday Visitor

## Many Forms of Religious Life

All through history, there have been men and women who felt a call to religious life in response to events and needs in the world. Some individuals felt led to gather other like-minded people around them to form religious communities.

The founders of religious orders established a way of life that others could follow. They selected the ministries to be done, and appealed to the bishop, or sometimes the Pope, to recognize their group as an official religious community in the Church. Lay women religious are often called "sisters." Lay men religious are called "brothers." Priests who join religious orders are called "fathers," as all priests are.

Some members of religious orders live a cloistered and contemplative life. They remain inside one convent or monastery, dedicating their lives to prayer for everyone in the world and to the study and preservation of Scripture and other religious texts. Often, cloistered women are called "nuns" and cloistered men are called "monks."

Other members live in active religious communities, where they go out to serve as missionaries, teachers, or hospital workers, and to do many other good works.

> **What memories do you have of a faith-filled sister, brother, or priest?**

### LIST AND PRAY

List three things that would be appealing to you about living the consecrated religious life. Then write a prayer for those who have accepted the call to consecrated life.

## IN SUMMARY  Catholics Believe

All baptized Catholics are called to share in Jesus' mission as priest, prophet, and king to serve the mission of the Church.

- The Pope and bishops belong to the Church's hierarchy, and lead the priests, deacons, religious communities, and the lay faithful. Priests serve in the ministerial priesthood and assist bishops in their role of teaching, governing, and sanctifying. Deacons assist the bishop and priests in sacramental ministries and the ministry of service.

- The laity in the Church act as leaven, bringing the raising and lightening power of God's Kingdom to the secular world where they live and work.

- Members of religious orders consecrate their lives as a sign of God's love and holiness and serve an important part of the Church's mission.

## Our Catholic Life

No matter what career you follow, you can live the life of a faithful Catholic. It's not the career that matters as much as how we bring the love of God to what we do. There are many **ways to be faithful:** some are called to priesthood, some are called to married life, some are called to be part of a religious congregation, others are called to the committed single life. Pay attention to God speaking to your heart to see what he is calling you to do. To live our vocation—our call from God—is to be who God made us to be. It's not always easy to know what work God wants us to do, but one way to start is by praying to the Holy Spirit to guide you to know what your vocation in life will be.

> Have you thought about vocations? What do you hear God telling you about your future?

## People of Faith

### Blessed Edmund Ignatius Rice, 1762–1844

Born into a large family in Ireland, Edmund Rice married at age 25, but his wife died two years later and Edmund spent much time caring for their infant daughter alone. He thought about becoming a monk, but instead arranged for the care of his daughter, and began his work of founding Catholic schools for troubled youth. He took the name "Ignatius," and founded the Institute of the Brothers of the Christian Schools, better known as "Irish Christian Brothers." He founded 23 schools in Ireland, England, and Australia. The Church celebrates his feast day on **May 5**.

For more, go to
**aliveinchrist.osv.com**

## CONSIDER

Think and pray about your own vocation in life. Begin by writing a paragraph that finishes this sentence:

I think I may be called to . . .

_____

_____

_____

_____

_____

_____

Together, pray this vocation prayer: Lord, show me how to be of service in your Church and in the world. Help me to see what you want me to do. Give me vision, courage, and friends who encourage me to do your work. Amen.

## ❤ A Prayer for Guidance

**Leader:** O Lord, open my lips.

**All:** That my mouth shall proclaim your praise.

**Leader:** Lord,

You have given each of us gifts and talents that can benefit others.

You call us to echo your Word and your love in the world.

Help us to understand your wisdom and your teachings.

Amen.

**Side 1:** How can young people keep their way pure?

By guarding it according to your Word.

With my whole heart I seek you; do not let me stray from your Commandments.

**Side 2:** The Lord is my portion;
I promise to keep your words.
I implore your favor with all my heart;
be gracious to me according to your promise.

**All:** Your word is a lamp to my feet and a light to my path.

**Side 1:** Your hands have made and fashioned me;

give me understanding that I may learn your Commandments.

Those who fear you shall see me and rejoice, because I have hoped in your Word.

**Side 2:** The Lord exists forever;
your Word is firmly fixed in Heaven.

Your faithfulness endures to all generations;

you have established the Earth, and it stands fast.

**All:** Your word is a lamp to my feet and a light to my path.
Based on Psalm 119:9, 10, 57, 58, 73, 74, 89, 90, 105

▶ *Sing or play "There Is a Light"*

Go to **aliveinchrist.osv.com** for an interactive review.

**A** Work with Words **Circle the letter of the choice that best completes the sentence.**

1. People who live a consecrated religious life make a public vow or promise to follow the evangelical ____ of poverty, chastity, and obedience.
   a. traditions
   b. orders
   c. laws
   d. counsels

2. The ____ are given sacred authority to serve the Church by teaching, leadership in divine worship, and pastoral ministry.
   a. laity
   b. ordained
   c. professors
   d. nuns

3. Cloistered men and women are typically called ____ and ____.
   a. laity, nuns
   b. monks, nuns
   c. clergy, brothers
   d. priests, nuns

4. ____ share with the Pope concern for all the Churches and are the visible successors of the Apostles in their own dioceses.
   a. Bishops
   b. Deacons
   c. Priests
   d. Cardinals

5. The ____ serve(s) through their Baptism and Confirmation in personal life, family life, social life, and parish life.
   a. laity
   b. priest
   c. clergy
   d. monk

**B** Check Understanding **Indicate whether the following statements are true or false. Then rewrite false statements to make them true.**

6. We all share in the offices of Christ, sharing in his work as priests, prophets, and kings. **True/False**

   _____

   _____

7. Consecrated religious life is a special vocation in the Church. **True/False**

   _____

   _____

8. Deacons are ordained to the ministerial priesthood and can preside at the Eucharist. **True/False**

   _____

   _____

9. Men and women who feel a call to religious life gather with other like-minded people to form religious communities. **True/False**

   _____

   _____

10. Only consecrated religious are called to live out the evangelical counsels. **True/False**

   _____

   _____

**C** Make Connections **On a separate sheet of paper, write a one-paragraph response to the questions below: Think of opportunities to serve in your parish. How have you served or how would you like to serve? What effects do you think this ministry would have on you and on others?**

© Our Sunday Visitor

**A** **Work with Words** Match the terms on the left with the correct definitions or descriptions on the right.

____ **1.** Apostolic Succession

____ **2.** Magisterium

____ **3.** infallible

____ **4.** diocese

____ **5.** presbyters

____ **6.** catholic

____ **7.** the clergy

____ **8.** the laity

____ **9.** evangelical counsels

____ **10.** bishops

____ **11.** missionaries

____ **12.** deacons

____ **13.** monks

____ **14.** Pope

____ **15.** Apostolic Tradition

**a.** belong to the second degree of Holy Orders

**b.** those ordained and given sacred authority to serve the Church

**c.** universal

**d.** the teaching office of the Church

**e.** poverty, chastity, and obedience

**f.** meaning free from error

**g.** the authority of the Pope and bishops traced back to Jesus, Saint Peter, and the other Apostles

**h.** the visible successors of the Apostles in their dioceses

**i.** Catholics who serve through Baptism and Confirmation in personal, family, social, and parish life

**j.** particular Church led by a bishop

**k.** ordained to tasks of service in the Church

**l.** successor to Saint Peter

**m.** cloistered men are typically called this

**n.** unites all Churches in communion with the Pope and the Catholic Church

**o.** many great world explorers have also been these

**B** Check Understanding Circle the letter of the best answer to complete the following statements.

16. The Pope, as the successor to Saint Peter and the leader of the entire universal Church, is called the ___.

    a. Presbyter

    b. Deacon of Christ

    c. Vicar of Christ

    d. Archbishop

17. The ___ lead our worship but there are liturgical roles for the ___, too.

    a. laity/clergy

    b. servers/lectors

    c. lectors/clergy

    d. clergy/laity

18. From the beginning of the Church, believers have professed their faith using summaries called ___.

    a. canons

    b. creeds

    c. doctrines

    d. encyclicals

19. Matthew, Mark, Luke, and John are called "the Four ___" because they were bearers of the Good News.

    a. Evangelists

    b. Messengers

    c. Heralds

    d. Horsemen

20. In the ___, we can find everything we need for salvation, with nothing left out.

    a. Word

    b. Catholic Church

    c. Eucharist

    d. Apostles

21. Because salvation can only come through faith in Christ and his Church, the Church has a ___ to spread the Gospel.

    a. missionary mandate

    c. covenant mandate

    b. missionary creed

    d. none of the above

22. We all share in the offices of Christ; he wants all of us to be priests, ___, and kings.

    a. disciples

    b. bishops

    c. monks

    d. prophets

**C** Make Connections **Write a short answer to these questions.**

**23.** Is the unity of the Catholic Church or the diversity within the Church more important to your personal faith? Explain your answer.

_____

_____

_____

_____

_____

_____

_____

**24.** What are some of the common elements of the major creeds of the Church?

_____

_____

_____

_____

_____

_____

_____

**25.** Using the Creeds as a model, write a summary of the ways you express and show the faith of the Church.

_____

_____

_____

_____

_____

_____

_____

_____

# MORALITY

*How does observing the First Commandment keep right order in our relationships?*

## CHURCH HISTORY TIMELINE

**34** Death of Stephen, the first Christian martyr

**451** Council of Chalcedon

**1950** Assumption of Mary is defined as dogma

**1979** Blessed Mother Teresa wins Nobel Peace Prize

Go to page 348 for more

## Our Catholic Tradition

- God calls us into relationship. We honor him when we love and respect him and his name, connecting what we believe with how we live. (CCC, 2084, 2142)

- Families are called to be schools of faith where we learn how to love, act, and treat others. The obedience, love, and respect found in the Holy Family is a model for our families. (CCC, 1657)

- God created us with equal human dignity, so we must work for the common good. The common good comes about in a society when the fundamental rights of the person are met, social well-being of all people is the goal, and there is security and peace. (CCC, 1924–1925)

## Our Catholic Life

- The First Commandment calls us to put God first in our lives, to give him the praise and honor he deserves as the Creator of everything. (CCC, 2093)

- Within the family, we develop personal character, grow in our understanding of right and wrong, and learn what's truly important. (CCC, 2223)

- Our individual actions to promote Catholic Social Teaching, peace, and love begin close to home. We can make a difference. (CCC, 2224)

# Honoring God

## ♥ Let Us Pray

**Leader:** God, you alone are God. We honor you. Help us make you a priority in our lives. Help us see your presence in each other.

> "The precepts of the LORD are right,
>     rejoicing the heart."  **Psalm 19:9**

**All:** Dear Lord, help us to live for you.

### 📖 Scripture

"One of the scribes, when he came forward and heard them disputing and saw how well he had answered them, asked him, 'Which is the first of all the commandments?' Jesus replied, 'The first is this: "Hear, O Israel! The Lord our God is Lord alone! You shall love the Lord your God with all your heart, with all your soul, with all your mind, and with all your strength."'" **Mark 12:28–30**

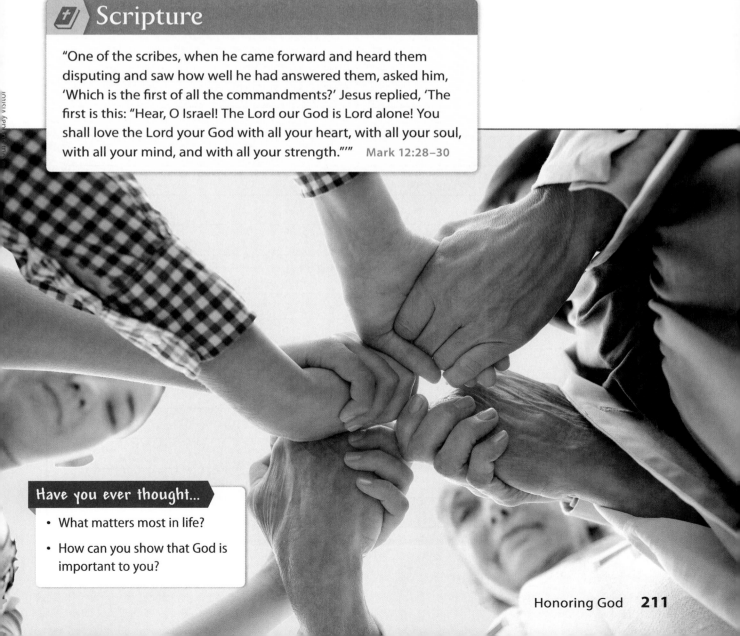

### Have you ever thought...

- What matters most in life?
- How can you show that God is important to you?

# Getting Started

In this chapter, you will explore how we respond to God and identify how we can keep God the primary focus of our lives. You will also learn about the importance of the Second Commandment.

1. Write each Commandment.

2. Name ways that you can observe each Commandment. You can add to the list as you complete the chapter.

| The First And Second Commandments | |
|---|---|
| **First Commandment** | **Ways to Follow It** |
| | |
| | |
| | |
| | |
| | |
| | |
| | |
| **Second Commandment** | **Ways to Follow It** |
| | |
| | |
| | |
| | |
| | |
| | |
| | |

**Priorities, Priorities!** Reflect on your past week. Fill in the week-at-a-glance to indicate the type of activities that filled your days and nights. Then complete the sentence.

**Monday**

_____
_____
_____
_____

**Tuesday**

_____
_____
_____
_____

**Thursday**

_____
_____
_____
_____

**Wednesday**

_____
_____
_____
_____

**Friday**

_____
_____
_____
_____

I can follow the Great Commandment (see Mark 12:28–30) by using my time

wisely to _____.

# I Am the Lord, Your God

**What do we owe God?**

If we say God is our number one priority in life, how do we live so that we aren't the only ones in our lives who know it? The best way to witness is to live like Jesus did, connecting what we say and do with what we believe. When we do that, we honor God, who is the source of all that is good.

## God's Covenant with Us

Long ago God chose a people for himself—the Israelites—and made a covenant, or sacred promise, with them. He declared, "I am the LORD your God, who brought you out of the land of Egypt, out of the house of slavery. You shall not have other gods beside me" (Exodus 20:2–3). God made a commitment to the Israelites and their descendants, who became known as the Jewish people.

God honored his covenant and then made a new covenant in Jesus Christ. He promises to take care of us, and to give us new life, and he calls us together as his People, the Body of Christ. Our part of the covenant relationship with God requires that we show that we are his People. Followers of Christ honor God for the life he gives us and follow the law and Jesus' teachings. One important way we do that is by living a life that shows gratitude to God; we owe him everything!

The Ten Commandments are the laws of the covenant God established with the Israelites, and they still hold true today. Jesus summed them up with the **Great Commandment**: to love God above all else and to love your neighbor as yourself. "The whole law and the prophets depend on these two commandments" (Matthew 22:40).

The first three of the Ten Commandments focus on our relationship with God, with loving God with all our heart, soul, and mind. This seems like a mighty task, but Jesus gives us many examples of how to do this.

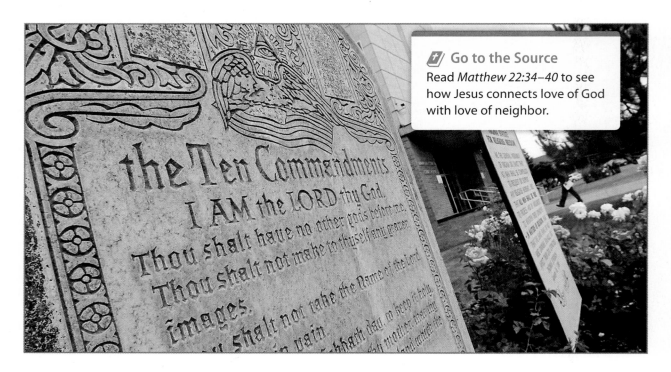

**Go to the Source**
Read *Matthew 22:34–40* to see how Jesus connects love of God with love of neighbor.

## Making Connections by Faith

The first of the Ten Commandments is "I am the Lord your God . . . you shall have no other gods before me." This Commandment calls us to live our faith and to have a relationship with God; to believe in God, hope in him, and love him above all else. Our lives are connected to God. This number one priority gives shape and meaning to everything else we do.

The word *religion* comes from the same Latin root word for "ligament." The purpose of religious practice is the same as the ligaments in our body: to hold us together.

There are several ways we can follow the First Commandment and give God the honor and importance he deserves. We show that God is our number one priority by

- adoring God, recognizing that he is God and Creator, the source of all things, praising him as we realize that we need him to have life,
- praying to him,
- worshipping him, and
- fulfilling the promises we make to him.

## Virtues and the First Commandment

The three Theological Virtues of faith, hope, and charity (love) give us the foundation for living by the First Commandment. They are called Theological Virtues because their source is God himself, and because those who live in faith, hope, and charity (love) are pointed back to God.

These virtues help us keep on track, believing all that God has revealed to us, putting all our trust in his care for us, and returning to him, albeit on a much smaller scale, the love that he gives us.

### Catholic Faith Words

**Great Commandment** the twofold command to love God above all and your neighbor as yourself. It sums up all of God's laws.

### EXPLAIN

How do you practice the First Commandment and "honor the Lord your God"? Explain your answer to a classmate.

"Empty idols make their worshippers empty..." (CCC, 2112)

# We Can't Replace God

What are some ways people fail to give God the honor he deserves?

Your parents may put limits on you in ways that you don't agree with. You may disagree on things or argue. But your relationship with your parents is more than a temporary disruption. A lifelong relationship is irreplaceable.

## Putting Others in God's Place

Our heavenly Father is irreplaceable, too. God is the only God there is. There is no other. No one and nothing can occupy his place in our lives, or his importance to us. When we try to put other people or things in God's place, it dishonors God, disorders our lives and his plan for us, and is unfair to those people or things.

### Catholic Faith Words

**idolatry** the sin of putting other people or things in God's place, or before God, in our lives

The name we give to putting other people or things in God's place is **idolatry**. Idols are empty, powerless false gods. When we confuse what's important in our lives, we can elevate these idols—such as power, prestige, money, pleasure—to the place of God, making them the number one priority in life. It's like we worship them because we give them all our time and attention. When we practice idolatry, our lives eventually fall apart. The idols that we are worshipping cannot satisfy us, and will keep us from experiencing true faith, hope, and love.

> What are two types of false gods or idols that we, as a society, try and put in God's place?

## Leading Away from God

When you get your driver's license, you will notice a lot more street signs warning drivers in advance that particular roads are "Dead Ends" or "Wrong Ways."

Likewise, there are a number of attitudes and practices that take you down a dead end or wrong way in your relationship with God. They challenge all Catholics to pay attention to where they are heading in their spiritual lives. Because these actions are all dead ends or take you the wrong way along the path of discipleship, they are sinful. They are contrary to the First Commandment.

### Sins Against the First Commandment

- **Tempting God:** testing God's goodness or power by word or deed, such as "If you give me an A on this test, I will go to church every weeknight."

- **Sacrilege:** treating holy people, places, and things in an unworthy way, such as not consuming the Eucharist, the Body of Christ; or defacing a crucifix or statue

- **Simony:** buying or selling spiritual things, such as paying for the Sacraments of Baptism or a wedding Mass (donations can and should be made, but a price is never set on the Seven Sacraments because their source is God and we receive them from the Lord as a grace, the free, loving gift of God's life and help)

- **Atheism:** rejecting or denying the existence of God, such as "We human beings are in total control of our lives. We are the makers of our world."

- **Superstition:** identifying certain objects or practices with a religious power, such as walking under ladders, voodoo dolls, Ouija boards, seances, and crystal balls.

> Place a check mark next to the issues you think most affect people your age.
>
> ✱

## WRITE

In the space below, write your own prayer to God by finishing the three sentences.

Dear Lord, you are God. I have faith in you because . . .

_____

I have hope in you because . . .

_____

I love you because . . .

_____

# What's in a Name?

**Why is it important to respect God's name?**

When we hold someone in tremendous respect, we speak of that person with an almost hushed voice. The Second Commandment—You shall not take the name of the Lord your God in vain—reminds us that the way we use the Lord's name must always show great respect for him. God is awesome. He is holy. So, his name is holy.

We can defame the name of God in a variety of ways. **Blasphemy** is showing contempt or lack of reverence for God and his name. It includes

- speaking words of hate or defiance against the Lord: for example, damning God
- speaking ill of God: for example, attributing evil to God
- misusing God's name: for example, using "God" itself as an expletive or curse word

The Commandment not to use God's name in an offensive way also extends to respecting the names of Jesus (the Son of God), the Virgin Mary, and the Saints.

Jesus tells us "Do not swear at all; not by heaven, for it is God's throne; nor by the earth, for it is his footstool; nor by Jerusalem, for it is the city of the great King" (Matthew 5:34–35).

> **When has your name—or the name of someone you care about—been "dragged through the mud"? What did it feel like?**

## The Truth in God

God is holy, awesome, and totally good. That would be reason enough to treat his name with respect.

However, God is also the measure by which all truth is calculated, for in the Lord there is no falsehood or lie. This means that the Second Commandment also forbids us from making false oaths (swearing to God that something is true when it isn't). We cannot call on God, in whom all truth resides, to be a witness to a lie on our part.

### Catholic Faith Words

**blasphemy** the sin of showing contempt or lack of reverence for God and his name

**perjury** making a promise under oath which the maker does not intend to keep

**Perjury** is when we make a promise to tell the truth under oath and do not intend to keep it. The Lord is always faithful to his promises. Every promise that we make under oath involves a reference to God, who is the Speaker of all truth. God's truthfulness and his own reliable promises must be respected in the oaths we ourselves take.

## Scripture

"O LORD, our Lord, how awesome is your name through all the earth!"  Psalm 8:2

 **Go to the Source**

Read *Matthew 5:33–35, 37* to find out what Jesus teaches us about swearing and oaths.

**Law and medical students participate in a mock trial**

## LIST

List three promises you could make to yourself, to others, and to God.

I promise myself . . .

_____

I promise others . . .

_____

I promise God . . .

_____

## IN SUMMARY   Catholics Believe

God calls us into relationship. We honor him when we love and respect him and his name, connecting what we believe with how we live.

- The First Commandment calls us to put God first in our lives, to give him the praise and honor he deserves as the Creator of everything.

- We need to avoid putting so much importance on things or other people that they take God's place in our lives.

- The Second Commandment states that God's name is holy, and we must always refer to his name with respect and reverence.

## Our Catholic Life

Do you focus too much on what you wear, or the things you own? Do you place too much value on your friendships and what people think about you? There are more important things in life, and your **faith** is among them. Find ways to include God in your thoughts and decisions, even about your ideas of friendship and who or what means most to you. Rely on God when you are unsure of something or need a friend. Be open to what the Spirit is telling you when a new person or idea comes into your world, and give that person or idea the thought he, she, or it deserves. Most of all, consider ways to be in friendship with God. It's the most important relationship in your life.

> What do you hear God telling you about your relationships? How will you respond?

## People of Faith

### Saint Blaise, d. c. 316

When the bishop of Sebasteia (now Sivas, Turkey) died, Saint Blaise was named to succeed him because people knew he was a pious and good man. He is said to have performed many miracles. When the emperor ordered that Christians had to renounce the faith or be killed, Blaise refused to deny Christ. On his way to execution, a mother allegedly placed her son, who had a fishbone in his throat, before Blaise. The Saint stopped to bless and cure the child before he was killed. The explorer Marco Polo mentions the place where Blaise was martyred. The Church celebrates his feast day on **February 3**.

For more, go to
**aliveinchrist.osv.com**

## LIST

List two things you can do to intentionally strengthen the amount of attention you are giving to your relationship with God.

1. _____
   _____
   _____
   _____
   _____

2. _____
   _____
   _____
   _____
   _____

## 💙 Prayer for Guidance

**Leader:** A reading from the book of Psalms.

**Reader 1:** I will bless the Lord at all times;
his praise shall be always in my mouth.

My soul will glory in the Lord;
let the poet hear and be glad.

Magnify the Lord with me;
and let us exalt his name together.
(Psalm 34:2–4)

**Leader:** This is a prayer by Saint Teresa of Ávila, a sixteenth-century Doctor of the Church, who was sometimes uncertain what path God wanted her to take.

We follow this path to symbolize the way we hope to follow Jesus.

**Reader 2:** Lord, grant that I may always allow myself to be guided by you,

always follow your plans, and perfectly accomplish your holy will.

**Reader 3:** Grant that in all things, great and small, today

and all the days of my life, I may do whatever you may require of me.

**Reader 4:** Help me to respond to your grace, so that I may be your trustworthy instrument of your honor.

**Reader 5:** May your will be done in time and eternity—by me, in me, and through me. Amen.

**Leader:** God, you led Saint Teresa to do great things for your Kingdom.

Today, we offer these prayers, asking you to guide us, too.

*Each person is invited to take turns and add his or her intentions.*

**All:** God, guide me to be fair and caring.

▶ *Sing or play "Take Me"*

Go to **aliveinchrist.osv.com** for an interactive review.

**A** Work with Words  **Complete each sentence with the correct term from the Word Bank.**

| | |
|---|---|
| superstition | blasphemy |
| Theological Virtues | simony |
| idolatry | perjury |
| sacrilege | atheism |

1. The name we give to putting other people or things in God's place is

   _____.

2. Identifying certain objects or practices with religious power is called

   _____.

3. Faith, hope, and charity (love) are

   _____ because they come from God and point us back to him.

4. _____ is showing contempt or lack of reverence for God and his name.

5. When we lie under oath we are committing

   _____.

**B** Check Understanding  **Circle the letter of the choice that best completes the sentence.**

6. Jesus taught that the ___ Commandment is to love God above all else and to love your neighbor as yourself.
   a. Tenth          c. Golden
   b. Great          d. First

7. The purpose of ___ can be compared to the ligaments in our body: to hold us together.
   a. religion       c. simony
   b. Commandments   d. virtue

8. ___ is buying or selling spiritual things, such as having to pay for the Sacrament of Baptism.
   a. Sacrilege      c. Superstition
   b. Simony         d. Atheism

9. The ___ Commandment calls us to put God first in our lives, to give him the praise and honor he deserves as the Creator of everything.
   a. First          c. Fifth
   b. Second         d. Third

10. ___ is rejecting or denying the existence of God.
    a. Blasphemy     c. Atheism
    b. Idolatry      d. Tempting God

**C** Make Connections  **On a separate sheet of paper, write a one-paragraph response to the question: What effect do "Dead End" attitudes and practices have on your relationship with God? Pick one specific attitude or practice, and consider how you can apply the Theological Virtues to head back toward God.**

# Honoring the Family

## ❤ Let Us Pray

**Leader:** Lord God, you give us the gift of family. Help us to be signs of God's love to one another.

"Come, children, listen to me;
   I will teach you the fear of the LORD." **Psalm 34:12**

**All:** God, help us love our families like you do.

### 📖 Scripture

"Children, listen to me, your father;
   act accordingly, that you may be safe.

For the Lord sets a father in honor over his children
   and confirms a mother's authority over her sons.

Those who honor their father atone for sins;
   they store up riches who respect their mother.

Those who honor their father will have joy in their own children,
   and when they pray they are heard.

Those who respect their father will live a long life;
   those who obey the Lord honor their mother."

The Wisdom of Ben Sira (Sirach) 3:1–6

### Have you ever thought...

- What are our responsibilities toward our parents?

- What do our families teach us about life?

# Getting Started

In this chapter, you will explore the responsibilities of family members, and identify the core ideals in our families that help us learn and grow. You will also see how the Holy Family is a model for respecting and caring among family members.

In the chart below, record the qualities of a good relationship. As you work through the chapter, you may want to add to the chart.

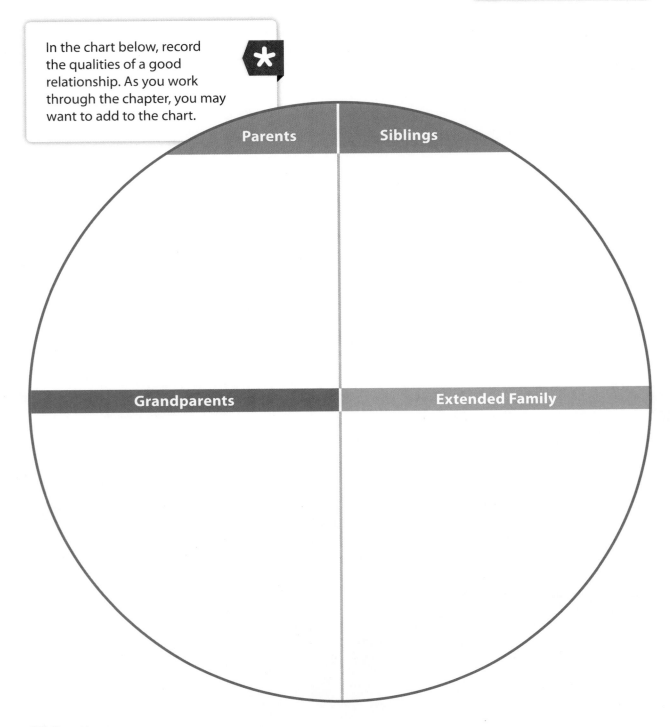

Parents

Siblings

Grandparents

Extended Family

© Our Sunday Visitor

**Your Family Tree** On the branches, write the names of some of your family members (parents or grandparents, siblings, cousins, aunts or uncles) who have served as positive role models for you.

Choose one and describe how he or she has influenced you.

_____

_____

_____

in a family is very important, especially during challenging or difficult times.

Because we are not born as adults, we need our families to teach us about life. As we grow physically and mentally and mature socially, we learn from our parents and teachers. We rely on our family members to take care of us, love us, laugh with us, and show us things by example.

The Fourth Commandment tells to honor our parents and guardians by giving them obedience, respect, gratitude, and assistance.

This fourfold response that children have toward their parents is called **filial respect**. Obeying, respecting, and helping our parents and guardians, and being genuinely grateful for all they do, helps children and families grow and interact in positive ways.

> **What is one way you have shown filial respect this week?**

## The Holy Family

We know that Jesus obeys his heavenly Father. At the same time, Jesus was born into a family, as we all are. His mother is Mary. His foster father is Joseph. Sometimes it's hard to think of Jesus as a six-year-old, learning how to play a game, or as a teenager having fun with friends. But Jesus truly was a child, growing up in a real family.

Mary and Joseph did not always understand Jesus, just as our own parents can be confused by the things we say or do. You may be familiar with the story of Jesus in the Temple. Mary and Joseph are on their way home from Jerusalem. They attach themselves to a busy caravan, where it is entirely possible for each to think the other is watching the Child Jesus. When they realize their mistake, they search for him until he is found in the Temple.

# Being A Family

**What responsibilities do family members have toward one another?**

We expect our family to be there for us. When they need us, they want us to be there for them, too. Every family is unique, and each family member has a different role. No family is perfect, and no human being is perfect.

Sometimes it's hard to respect what others in our family need or have to do when we're focused on what we need or want. But respect

## Catholic Faith Words

**filial respect** the response children are called to have toward their parents, which includes obedience, respect, gratitude, and assistance

**Feast of the Holy Family** the day celebrating the special family relationship among Mary, Joseph, and Jesus

##  Scripture

Jesus asks Mary and Joseph, "Why were you looking for me? Did you not know that I must be in my Father's house?" But they did not understand what he said to them. He went down with them … and was obedient to them, and his mother kept all these things in her heart. And Jesus advanced [in] wisdom and age and favor before God and man." **Luke 2:49–52**

###  Go to the Source

Read *Luke 2:41–52* to find out what Jesus was doing in the Temple and why it was so surprising to Mary and Joseph.

Jesus had, in effect, two homes: one in Nazareth and one in the Temple. His foster father, Joseph, headed the home in Nazareth. But his heavenly Father's home is symbolized by the Temple.

## CATHOLICS TODAY

The Holy Family is a role model for us, showing us how to live in a domestic Church where family members learn and live out their faith. Because all human beings are called to holiness, we can find it in the daily routines and minor details of family life. Mary, Joseph, and Jesus spent a majority of their time living out the demands of family: cooking, cleaning, earning a living, and doing household chores. Holiness can also be doing ordinary things with heartfelt compassion, kindness, humility, gentleness, and patience. We celebrate the **Feast of the Holy Family** on the first Sunday after Christmas. This day celebrates the special family relationship among Mary, Joseph, and Jesus, and reminds us that they are our models.

## DISCUSS

Look back at the four attitudes that make up filial respect. Which of the four is easiest for you to practice?

_____

_____

_____

_____

Which is hardest?

_____

_____

_____

_____

# Families and Relationships

**How do families help us have friendships and relationships with others?**

The Holy Family of Jesus, Mary, and Joseph is certainly unique. There is no other family quite like it. No other family has a child who is the Son of God. Nevertheless, the Holy Family provides a model for all families.

What is the purpose of a family? What lessons can we learn from the Holy Family?

- Parents and guardians should nurture and support their children so that they can grow up in a safe, loving environment.
- A family ought to be where we learn about our faith and where all family members learn about and relate to God.
- Families should pray together.
- Families should seek to promote living by the virtues.
- Parents are the prime movers in a family. As adults, they are responsible for the physical and spiritual needs of their children so that younger members can grow.
- Families draw out the best in all the members—adults and children—when they grow and work together.
- Parents should support their children as they reflect and pray about their God-given vocation.

> **What role models or sources do members of your family use for advice about living together the way God intends?**

## Our Families

Families come in all shapes and sizes, and each has its own way of communication, its own emphasis on what's important, and its own favorite activities. The most important ingredients in a family are the adults, who

provide a safe, loving environment for the children. When this happens, then the family itself can become a school of faith, with all its members learning from one another to live as God intends.

The purpose of a family will be helped or hurt by the quality of the relationships among all the members. To relate to another person means that we are connected in some way or that we are important to each other.

## Keys to a Healthy Relationship

____ **Time:** We need to make time for a person to be a significant part of our lives. Giving time does not just mean being in the same room or the same town.

____ **Loyalty:** Every good relationship demands that the people involved in it be true to each other, trust each other, be there for each other, and depend on each other's support.

____ **Truth:** A relationship built on lies will not go far. Only upfront, honest communication grows a healthy, strong relationship.

____ **Flexibility:** Not everything can be planned in a relationship. Sometimes spontaneous things are the most surprising and life-giving. Those in authority should ensure that each person's needs are met.

____ **Joy:** The bonds between people cannot be formed solely by grief or by mutually confronting a dangerous or difficult situation; every relationship requires some laughter, fun, and finding joy.

> ✱ Rank the importance of these components of a healthy family relationship from 1 to 5, with 1 being most important and 5 least important. Compare your answers with a classmate.

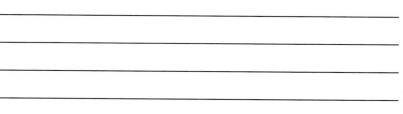

## IDENTIFY

Think about your relationship with a member of your family. Identify some steps you can take to increase one or two of the elements in the chart above in that relationship.

I can strengthen my relationship with _____

by _____

_____

_____

_____

_____

_____

# A Place to Grow

**What are some things we can learn in our families?**

We begin life within a family and from there we move into the larger world. We first form our core values within our family. Personal character is developed within a family first because it's there that we first form a sense of who we are and what we are capable of. We learn what's important, how to act and treat others, and what it means to be in a relationship.

It is within our families that we first learn to take responsibility for our own actions. We get a sense of what is acceptable and appropriate. Our **conscience**—the

God-given ability to judge actions as right or wrong, good or evil—begins to be formed and built up by the example of our parents, other adults, and siblings. A person has a moral obligation to follow his or her well-formed conscience when the person is sure about what it is judging to be right or wrong. We learn how to make decisions based upon the Word of God in Scripture and Tradition, the guidance of the Magisterium, what we judge to be right or wrong, discussions with people we trust, the example of Jesus, and prayer.

However, sometimes a conscience is not formed properly, perhaps because a person has not learned the example of Jesus, does not know Church teaching, does not get good advice, or hasn't been taught correctly. If that happens, the conscience can sometimes lead the person to make incorrect judgments, and this doesn't always free the person of guilt. That's why it's so important to have a an **informed conscience**. But if a person acts out of fear, or ignorance, or because of pressure put on them by someone, the person's moral responsibility for the action could be lessened or removed. To find out

## Catholic Faith Words

**conscience** the God-given ability that helps individuals judge whether actions are right or wrong

**informed conscience** a conscience that is educated and developed through constant use and examination and learning about the teachings of the Church

more about examining your conscience, go to page 371 in the Our Catholic Tradition section of your book.

> **What things have you learned from your family that are important to the way you act outside of the home?**

## It Takes Work

All families struggle to build strong relationships among their members. Why? Because relationships take work. They don't just happen. It takes a lot of time and energy to keep a relationship going. With all the demands placed on you by school and friends, sometimes you forget to take care of those with whom you should be the closest!

There is life inside and outside the family, and sometimes there is a mix and blending of the two. The key is working for a balance and giving all of your relationships the attention they deserve.

Family contributes immensely to who we are later in life. This does not mean that when a family does not function well or when its members have hurt each other, members cannot ever get beyond their painful experiences or harmful memories.

Sometimes a family is so hurt it can't help itself. That is why it is important for your family to be part of a bigger family—the

Church. Is there something deeply damaging occurring to you within your family, something you can barely acknowledge to yourself, much less to someone else? The first step is the hardest but also the most important. Talk to a trusted teacher, guidance counselor, or a parish priest or other minister for help.

### WRITE

What does your family need most in order to improve the relationships among your family members? Compose a prayer asking God to help you and your family grow.

## IN SUMMARY   Catholics Believe

Families are called to be schools of faith in which we learn how to love, act, and treat others.

- The obedience, love, and respect found in the Holy Family serves as a model for our own families.

- The relationships within a family demand as much care, concern, and energy on our part as with any of our other relationships.

- Within the family, we develop personal character, grow in our understanding of right and wrong, and learn what's truly important.

## Our Catholic Life

Make a commitment to spend time with your family and **examine your relationship** with each member. How does your family show care and concern for each person? Has it become hard to communicate with some members? Have you been patient enough with younger siblings or older people in your extended family? Have you shown filial respect to your parents? Sometimes, there are broken relationships within our families that we alone cannot fix. Trust in God and offer him your prayers for your family, and ask Mary and the Saints for their intercession as well. You may also pray the Lord's Prayer to help you in forgiving others as you seek forgiveness.

> What would you say to God in a prayer for your family's happiness or well-being?

## People of Faith

### Saint Helena, c. 248–330

Helena was the mother of Constantine the Great, who sent her to the Holy Land to try to find where Jesus lived and died, to build churches, and bring back relics. Tradition says that while Helena was at the site of Jesus' tomb, she found three crosses. She had a dying woman touch each one in turn. When the woman touched the third cross, she was healed. Helena took this to be the True Cross of Christ. Constantine had the Church of the Holy Sepulchre built on the site of the discovery. Helena is the patron of archaeologists because of her work in the Holy Land. The Church celebrates her feast day on **August 18**.

For more, go to
**aliveinchrist.osv.com**

## PLAN

Take time now to make a plan to improve yourself as a member of your family. You may have to repair damage done to a relationship within the family, or spend more time on one particular relationship that is weaker than others. Be specific as you make yourself a plan.

**Three things I can do this week . . .**

1. _____

_____

_____

2. _____

_____

3. _____

_____

## ♥ Celebration of the Word

**Leader:** Glory be to the Father
and to the Son
and to the Holy Spirit,

**All:** as it was in the beginning
is now, and ever shall be
world without end. Amen.

**Leader:** Let us quietly reflect on our families
and how we can better be signs of God's
love to one another.

*Reflect in silence.*

**Reader:** A reading from the letter of Paul to
the Colossians.

Put on then, as God's chosen ones,
holy and beloved, heartfelt compassion,
kindness, humility, gentleness, and patience,
bearing with one another and forgiving
one another. ... Let the peace of Christ
control your hearts; the peace into which
you were called into one body. ... And
whatever you do, in word or in deed, do
everything in the name of the Lord Jesus,
giving thanks to God the Father through
him. (**Colossians 3:12–13, 15, 17**)

The word of the Lord.

**All:** Thanks be to God.

**Leader:** We each belong to some type of
family, and all families are called to be loving,
respecting, caring, and responsible for one
another.

Let us thank God for those who love and
care for us, and ask him to bless our families
today and always.

*Silently offer your prayers for your family.*

Loving Father,
You know the love of a parent for a child.
We ask you to strengthen our families so
that we model that love.

We ask you to bless us with patience,
courage, and hope, so that we can become
the people you call us to be.

We ask this through your Son, Jesus.

**All:** Amen.

▶ *Sing or play "We Are One Body"*

Go to **aliveinchrist.osv.com** for an interactive review.

**A Work with Words** Circle the letter of the choice that best completes the sentence.

1. An informed ____ is educated and developed through constant use and examination and learning about the teachings of the Church.
   a. friendship
   c. family
   b. conscience
   d. judgment

2. The fourfold response children have toward their parents that is addressed in the Fourth Commandment is called ____.
   a. adoration
   c. filial respect
   b. conscience
   d. compassion

3. Every good relationship demands ____.
   a. trust
   c. loyalty
   b. respect
   d. all of the above

4. Our ____ enables us to judge whether something is right or wrong.
   a. free will
   c. obedience
   b. conscience
   d. none of the above

5. The obedience, love, and respect found in the ____ serves as a model for our own families.
   a. Holy Fathers
   c. Apostles
   b. Church
   d. Holy Family

**B Check Understanding** Indicate whether the following statements are true or false. Then rewrite false statements to make them true.

6. The Church is where we first learn about faith and how to relate to God. **True/False**

_____

_____

7. Family bonds must be formed based on a range of emotions and experiences, including grief, joy, and fun. **True/False**

_____

_____

8. Communication and faith are essential parts of healthy family relationships. **True/False**

_____

_____

9. If a person acts out of fear, or ignorance, or because of pressure put on him or her by someone, the person's moral responsibility for the action is always removed. **True/False**

_____

_____

10. The purpose of the religious life is to nurture and support children so that they can grow up in a safe, loving environment. **True/False**

_____

_____

**C Make Connections** Write a short response to the following: Write your prescription for a healthy family that models what we know about the Holy Family.

_____

_____

_____

_____

_____

_____

# The Dignity of All

## ♥ Let Us Pray

**Leader:** God of all that is loving and just, challenge us, humble us, and call us to reach out with open hands and hearts to our brothers and sisters.

"LORD, what is man that you take notice of him;
   the son of man, that you think of him?" **Psalm 144:3**

**All:** LORD, remind us that you are in every one of us.

### 📖 Scripture

"The community of believers was of one heart and mind, and no one claimed that any of his possessions was his own, but they had everything in common. With great power the apostles bore witness to the resurrection of the Lord Jesus, and great favor was accorded them all. There was no needy person among them, for those who owned property or houses would sell them, bring the proceeds of the sale, and put them at the feet of the apostles, and they were distributed to each according to need." **Acts 4:32–35**

### Have you ever thought...

- How are we supposed to take care of each other?
- What can you do to show others the dignity they are due?

# Getting Started

In this chapter, you will begin to comprehend what the Catholic Church means when we speak about "the common good," explore the role of the Church in today's society, and realize that Jesus is the core of how we live and show our faith.

© Our Sunday Visitor

## Catholic Faith Words

- common good
- New Commandment
- solidarity
- personal sin
- social sin

In the chart below, describe a situation when you thought someone was treated with dignity in each setting.

**At School**

_____

_____

_____

_____

_____

**With Friends**

_____

_____

_____

_____

_____

**Dignity and Respect**

**At Home**

_____

_____

_____

_____

_____

**In Your Community**

_____

_____

_____

_____

_____

## DESCRIBE AND EXPLAIN

**The Good of Everyone**  In the space provided, reflect on the following questions.

Describe a time when you saw someone make a sacrifice so someone else could have a need met.

_____

_____

_____

_____

_____

When have you experienced personal fulfillment?

_____

_____

_____

_____

Why does everyone deserve the opportunity to seek and reach fulfillment?

_____

_____

_____

_____

_____

_____

_____

_____

# The Common Good

**What is the common good, and how is it achieved?**

Preschool teaches children a basic lesson: the need to share. One child cannot hoard all the toys. Everyone shares. They have to "play nice," or chaos erupts.

Humans are social beings. Each individual must take others into account. We live with others. As Catholics, however, we know this is more than just a matter of cooperation. It is more than just the notion of "you work with me, and I'll work with you."

Society functions best when each person respects everyone else as "another self," as real people like himself or herself, with real needs, hopes, and dreams: In other words, not seeing others as a means to get something for one's self, but as people with the same basic rights that need to be respected and met.

## Catholic Faith Words

**common good** the good of everyone; the Christian principle that all people, either in groups or as individuals, have the opportunities to reach their fulfillment more fully and easily

## The Basis of a Just Society

The right kind of society is one that remains at service to people on every level. Societies that are organized in this way promote the **common good**, which means that all people, either in groups or as individuals, are given the opportunities to reach their fulfillment more fully and easily.

The common good is made possible by three essential elements:

- respect for the person and promotion of the fundamental rights that flow from human dignity
- social well-being and prosperity for everyone
- security and order as well as global peace

Not one single part of society is exempt from the common good. Society itself owes to every group, organization, and association the conditions that promote their own

## The Common Good

In his papal writing and in a 1979 speech to the General Assembly of the United Nations, Pope Saint John Paul II specified what is meant by the common good.

Write an example that expands on one item in each of these three categories.

| | |
|---|---|
| **What are the fundamental rights of persons?** | • the right to life (from conception to natural death)<br>• the right to live in a united family<br>• the right to develop oneself in a moral environment<br>• the right to develop one's intelligence<br>• the right to seek and know the truth<br>• the right to share in work that wisely uses Earth's resources<br>• the right to support one's family<br>• the right to establish a family<br>• the right to religious freedom<br>• _____ |
| **What does prosperity mean?** | • general development of spiritual goods so all may benefit<br>• general development of physical goods so all may benefit<br>• _____ |
| **How can peace and security be achieved?** | • the absence of war, along with:<br>• effective and fruitful justice between individuals and nations and<br>• the practice of love between individuals and nations<br>• _____ |

effectiveness and liveliness according to the common good. When society does this, it promotes social justice.

Every group, organization, and association must try to improve human life and the common good. Likewise, those in political authority cannot exercise leadership beyond the boundaries of these three essential elements that define the common good.

## IDENTIFY

In small groups, choose a basic right and discuss how it is being met. Identify some ways that people your age could promote that right.

_____

_____

_____

© Our Sunday Visitor

Cardinal Timothy Dolan, Archbishop of New York, greets people waiting for groceries at an interfaith Feeding Our Neighbors event.

# Living as a Catholic Today

**Why does the Church comment on political authority and structures?**

The Church is concerned with the way in which society is organized and the way in which it functions because everyone and everything in this world is oriented—or should be oriented—toward God.

The Church speaks out about social and economic matters, because sometimes groups or individuals undermine our human rights. The Church takes action to help society function properly.

In striving for the common good, the Church teaches about family and marriage as the basic "unit" of society, the value of human work and workers' rights, economic institutions in service to people, political authority, the international community, safeguarding the environment, and promoting peace.

Each of us has a responsibility to respect the rights of others and to make sure our actions do not make it hard for people to have their needs met. We are called to accept Gospel values and the Church that teaches them. We say "yes" to things that make the common good possible. We work within society to promote virtue in all aspects of life.

This means that sometimes we will have to say "no" to practices in society that do not correspond to the common good, that go against the Gospel and Church teaching. The standard by which we judge our "yes" or "no" is the good of every human person. What truly helps people in their physical needs by giving them access to food, shelter, and basic human rights? What helps people become closer to one another and God? What deprives people of their human rights and dignity? What brings them down and prevents them from becoming closer to God?

> What are some things that you can say "yes" to in society?

> What are some things that you should say "no" to in society because they do not promote the dignity of the person?

## Society

The structure and character of society should be geared toward love. Jesus says: "This is my commandment: love one another as I love you" (**John 15:12**). His **New Commandment** is not meant just for individuals, but is also to be followed by groups and organizations, and even by nations in how they deal with their citizens and with other nations.

Political authority and governments are not higher than God. Their authority is legitimate when they are committed to the common good and use morally good actions to lead and govern. It is the responsibility of citizens to work with the authorities to build up a society based on truth, justice, freedom, and solidarity. Members of society have the right to information (such as news) based on the values of truth, justice, and freedom. We all have to be careful in the ways we use the media to communicate.

**Solidarity** means that we stand with and are related to people who are deprived of their human rights. We don't just help from afar those who are poor or oppressed; we get to know them and their situations.

Sometimes, citizens must disobey the immoral directives of civil authorities and follow their consciences to uphold truth, justice, solidarity, and freedom.

Global peace and security is one of the three elements of the common good. So the Church teaches that everything possible must be done to avoid war. The impact and result of war is devastating for the entire human race, and especially harms the poor, because it diverts precious resources that could be used to make their lives better.

Entering into war as a last resort does not relieve a country or its armed forces from following national laws and the moral law. For example, targeting innocent civilians or harming an enemy soldier who has surrendered goes against the moral law.

The highest compliment we could pay to society is the same that we would pay to an individual: love. Each of us can take action to build society according to Jesus' command.

## Catholic Faith Words

**New Commandment** Jesus' command for his disciples to love one another as he has loved us

**solidarity** a Christian principle that motivates believers to share their spiritual gifts as well as their material ones

## RESEARCH

What are some ways that a government does or does not promote the common good through laws, programs and organizations, and policies? Record three ways here, and then explain to a classmate how each does or does not reflect Jesus' command to love one another as he has loved us.

1. _____

_____

2. _____

_____

3. _____

_____

# The Significance of One

**How do the actions of some affect the whole group?**

We can't underestimate the power of one. Building a just, loving world—contributing to the common good—starts with a single person, Jesus Christ. Like a stone that creates ever outward ripples in a pond, Jesus, through the continuing action of the Church, creates ripples in our world and society.

Justice, love, and peace are furthered by the specific, concrete actions of each individual. One small step within our own homes and in our neighborhoods, towns, and counties can have a real effect on the world. If every person waited for someone else to contribute to the common good, nothing good would happen. The good from each person's action to promote justice, peace, and love is combined to have a greater and greater influence on the world.

The same is true when we turn from God. Our sins do not damage just ourselves and our relationship with God. **Personal sin** wounds our human nature—who we are, and how we relate beyond ourselves—and therefore it injures human solidarity.

A personal act of discrimination against someone who is of a different skin color ends up wounding the common good. An individual act of bullying by one classmate against another will end up wounding the common good of the whole school.

Why? All sins are social, even thoughts or actions that seem to go no further than one's self, because we are social in nature. The same is true of our virtues, because what strengthens or makes each of us personally, individually better does not remain isolated. By our human nature, we are social. Therefore, **social sin**, the sum of personal sins that then become part of society—like discrimination and prejudice—can only be combated by an accumulation of virtue, that is, many just, peaceful, and loving actions by many individuals.

## Catholic Faith Words

**personal sin** a deliberate thought, word, deed, or omission that violates the law of God

**social sin** a term that refers to the sinful social structures that result from personal sin and that lead to social conditions that do not reflect or promote the New Commandment

Pope Francis has said, "The Son of God became incarnate in the souls of men to instill the feeling of brotherhood. All are brothers and all children of God." The Church condemns all forms of social and cultural discrimination as incompatible with God's design. Each person is created in the image of God and is gifted with dignity equal to all other humans. That equality—guaranteed by the Creator—requires our heartfelt efforts to reduce sinful social and economic inequalities.

## NAME

How often do you hear or make the statement, "It's not my problem!"? Name two social sins that might change if we stopped saying "It's not my problem."

_____

_____

Then explain how you would go about making this change if you could. Tell how your plan would benefit the common good and promote the human dignity of people in your community or around the world.

_____

_____

_____

_____

_____

## IN SUMMARY  Catholics Believe

Because God created us with equal human dignity, we are required to work for the common good so that all people have what they need and can reach their fulfillment more fully and easily.

- The common good comes about in a society when the fundamental rights of the person are met, social well-being of all people is the goal, and there is security and peace.

- The Church works to make sure that public and political authority acts within the truth, justice, freedom, and solidarity. Each and every member of the Church can do this by making wise decisions based upon the human dignity of the person.

- Our individual actions to promote Catholic Social Teaching, peace, and love begin close to home. We can make a difference.

## Our Catholic Life

The Catholic Church is active all over the world in charitable outreach missions that promote the **human dignity** of all. Go online to research outreach efforts that help people in poorer countries with better living conditions or more healthful diets. After investigating their activities, you may want to persuade your family members, friends, or classmates to contribute to these outreach efforts or become involved in some other way. Research the following Catholic organizations:

• Catholic Relief Services

• Catholic Fund for Overseas Development

• Catholic Near East Welfare Association

> Which organization's work interests you most? How could you help?

## People of Faith

### Saint John Chrysostom, 347–407

Saint John Chrysostom is one of the most important early Church fathers. He is best known for his writing and homilies on the Bible. He spoke in words that all could understand, but his teachings were so profound, he was given the title "chrysostomos," which means "golden mouthed" in English. John was particularly concerned with taking care of the poor. He wrote: "What good is it if the Eucharistic table is overloaded with golden chalices when your brother is dying of hunger? Start by satisfying his hunger and then with what is left you may adorn the altar as well." The Church celebrates his feast day on **September 13**.

 For more, go to
**aliveinchrist.osv.com**

## IDENTIFY

Make a point this week to find out about local and global political issues and needs, and what might be needed from you. For example, you might set aside part of your money from your allowance or jobs and donate to people in need in your neighborhood, school, or town, or clean out your closet and give away unnecessary clothes. List some of your ideas on the lines below:

_____

_____

_____

_____

_____

_____

_____

## ♥ A Prayer for Peace

**Leader:** God, you made Pope Paul VI a bold champion of peace and justice for our world. He understood so well that every single human being has a God-given dignity. Each person should be treated with loving respect and justice. We still remember his wise words, "If you want peace, work for justice." Let's pray his prayer for peace.

**Reader 1:** Lord, God of peace, who has created man, the object of your kindness, to be close to you in glory, we bless you and we thank you because you have sent us your beloved Son, Jesus, the source of all peace, the bond of true friendship.

**Reader 2:** We thank you for the desire, the efforts, which your spirit of peace has roused in our day: to replace hatred with love, shyness with understanding, unconcern with care. Open yet more our hearts to the needs of all our brothers and sisters, so that we may be better able to build a true peace.

**Reader 3:** Remember, Father of mercy, all who are in pain, who suffer and die in the cause of a more friendly world.

For people of every race, of every tongue— may your Kingdom come: your Kingdom of justice, of peace, of love; and may the Earth be filled with your glory.

**All:** Amen.

Adapted from a prayer by Pope Paul VI

**Leader:** Let's now conclude our prayer by praying the prayer Jesus gave us for the Kingdom—the Our Father.

**All:** Our Father, who art in heaven,
hallowed be thy name;
thy kingdom come,
thy will be done
on earth as it is in heaven.
Give us this day our daily bread,
and forgive us our trespasses,
as we forgive those who trespass against us;
and lead us not into temptation,
but deliver us from evil.

▶ *Sing or play "Justice Shall Flourish"*

Go to **aliveinchrist.osv.com** for an interactive review.

**A** Work with Words  **Circle the letter of the choice that best completes the sentence.**

1. Societies organized to promote the ____ give opportunities to all people to reach their fulfillment more fully and easily.
   a. common good      c. global peace
   b. justice system   d. Theological Virtues

2. The ____ of people include(s) the right to life, to a moral environment, to a united family, and to religious freedom.
   a. Theological Virtues
   b. fundamental rights
   c. common good
   d. fundamental values

3. The standard by which the Church judges "yes" or "no" to social practices is the good of every ____.
   a. liturgy          c. human person
   b. Tradition        d. social sin

4. ____ mean(s) that we stand with and are related to people who are deprived of their human rights.
   a. Common good      c. Solidarity
   b. Justice          d. Fortitude

5. ____ is the effect of personal sins over a period of time that affect society.
   a. Social sin       c. Discrimination
   b. Common sin       d. Prejudice

**B** Check Understanding  **Indicate whether the following statements are true or false. Then rewrite false statements to make them true.**

6. Human dignity and global peace are essential to the common good.  **True/False**

   _____

   _____

7. Pope Saint John Paul II founded many of his writings in the area of human rights.  **True/False**

   _____

   _____

8. Three essential elements to promote the common good are respect for fundamental rights, prosperity, and security for some.  **True/False**

   _____

   _____

9. Citizens must obey the directives of civil authorities unless the directives are immoral.  **True/False**

   _____

   _____

10. Personal sin does not wound our human nature and therefore cannot contribute to social sin.  **True/False**

   _____

   _____

**C** Make Connections  **On a separate sheet of paper, write a response to the question: "Justice, love, and peace are furthered by the specific, concrete actions of each individual." What specific, concrete actions can you take to promote the common good?**

**A** Work with Words  Use the clues below to complete the crossword puzzle.

Across

**2.** Putting other people or things in God's place

**6.** These Virtues include faith, hope, and charity (love)

**7.** Lying under oath

**8.** Identifying certain objects or practices with religious power

Down

**1.** Showing contempt or lack of reverence for God and his name

**3.** Standing with and relating to people who are deprived of their human rights

**4.** Buying or selling spiritual things

**5.** The purpose of this can be compared to the ligaments of the body: to hold us together

**B** Check Understanding  **Indicate whether the following statements are true or false. Then rewrite false statements to make them true.**

9. Jesus taught that the First Commandment is to love God above all else and to love your neighbor as yourself.  **True/False**

   _____

10. Perjury is when we make a promise to tell the truth under oath and do not intend to keep it.  **True/False**

    _____

11. The fourfold response children have toward their parents that is addressed in the Fourth Commandment is called filial honor.  **True/False**

    _____

12. Our free will enables us to judge whether actions are right or wrong.  **True/False**

    _____

13. Children need to give parents and guardians obedience, respect, loyalty, gratitude, and assistance.  **True/False**

    _____

14. Societies organized to promote the common good give opportunities to some people to reach their fulfillment more fully and easily.  **True/False**

    _____

15. The fundamental rights of people consist of the right to life, liberty, freedom of religion, and the pursuit of happiness.  **True/False**

    _____

16. The standard by which the Church judges "yes" or "no" to social practices is the human person.  **True/False**

    _____

17. Common sin is the effect of sins over a period of time that affect society.  **True/False**

    _____

18. Every good relationship demands loyalty—that the people are true to each other, trust one another, and depend on each other's support.  **True/False**

    _____

**19.** Faith, hope, and modesty are the Theological Virtues. **True/False**

_____

**20.** Pope Saint John Paul II founded many of his writings in the area of human rights. **True/False**

_____

**C** Make Connections **Write a short answer to these questions.**

**21.** Why do you think the First Commandment is first? How do you follow this Commandment in your life?

_____

_____

_____

**22.** Name one thing you see in society today that does not promote the dignity of the person. How does this practice devalue people? What effect does this practice have on society?

_____

_____

_____

**23.** Explain the Great Commandment in your own words.

_____

_____

_____

**24.** What are the elements that promote the common good?

_____

_____

_____

**25.** Name two essential parts of healthy family relationships, and explain which is most important to you.

_____

_____

_____

# SACRAMENTS

*Why and how is the Paschal Mystery the basis for our worship, the Sacraments, and the liturgical year?*

## CHURCH HISTORY TIMELINE

| | |
|---|---|
| **590** | Pope Saint Gregory the Great elected |
| **910** | Monastery of Cluny founded |
| **1992** | New *Catechism of the Catholic Church* is published |
| **2000** | Divine Mercy Sunday added to Church calendar |

Go to page 348 for more

## Our Catholic Tradition

- The liturgy is the official public worship of the Church. The symbols and rituals of the liturgy form us in prayer and communicate God's gift of life. Our spiritual life strengthens our moral life. (CCC, 1190, 2047)

- The Sacraments at the Service of Communion celebrate a commitment to serve God and the community and help build up the People of God. (CCC, 1534)

- The seasons and feasts of the Liturgical Year emphasize different aspects of the Paschal Mystery of Christ. The Eucharist is at the heart of what it means to be Catholic. Participation in Sunday Mass and our own regular personal prayer help us live the life of Christ. (CCC, 1194)

## Our Catholic Life

- As the Lord's Day, Sunday observance includes required attendance at Mass, the omission of unnecessary work that would distract from the day's purpose, and attention to living a good life. (CCC, 2192–2195)

- Practicing and living by the virtues of modesty and chastity can help all people, no matter whether they are married, ordained, or single. The grace of the Eucharist and Reconciliation can strengthen all of us to be pure and self-respecting. (CCC, 2348, 2533)

- Because we are different each year, we enter into the Church's seasons and feasts with different needs, hopes, and relationships with God and others. (CCC, 1168)

# Worship and Grace

## ♡ Let Us Pray

**Leader:** God our Father, you bless us with your grace. You invite us to participate in your life. Send your Spirit to be with us every day.

"Enter, let us bow down in worship;
  let us kneel before the LORD who made us.
For he is our God,
  we are the people he shepherds,
  the sheep in his hands." **Psalm 95:6–7**

**All:** God, we rely on you.

### 📖 Scripture

"Every day they devoted themselves to meeting together in the temple area and to breaking bread in their homes. They ate their meals with exultation and sincerity of heart, praising God and enjoying favor with all the people. And every day the Lord added to their number those who were being saved." **Acts 2:46–47**

### Have you ever thought...

- How does the Church worship?
- What is the relationship between worshipping God and living a holy life?

# Getting Started

In this chapter, you will explore how God acts through the symbols and rituals of the Church, investigate the relationship between worship and moral living, and learn the importance of a day of worship and rest.

In the chart below, record the Third Commandment and three different ways that we keep this Commandment.

| Keeping the Third Commandment |
|---|
| **The Third Commandment tells us …** |
| _____ |
| _____ |
| _____ |
| **I keep this Commandment when I …** |
| 1. _____ |
| 2. _____ |
| 3. _____ |

**Routines** The first Christians followed Jesus' commands and his example. In doing so, they established routines that helped them grow spiritually and live holy lives (see Acts 2:42–43, 46, 47).

What routines do you practice every day?

_____

_____

_____

_____

Which ones keep your mind healthy? Which ones keep your body healthy?

_____

_____

What routines do you and your family follow that keep your spiritual life healthy?

_____

_____

_____

_____

_____

_____

_____

_____

_____

_____

_____

_____

# The Church Worships

### What are liturgy and the Seven Sacraments?

The Church uses patterned actions called rituals in her **liturgy**, the official public worship of the Church. The word *liturgy* originally meant a "public work," or an action in the name of or for the people. To Catholics, the term describes the participation of all the faithful in the work of God. When we worship, we give praise and thanks to God.

Rituals use actions and symbols. Symbols have layers of meaning. Symbolism means you always see the same material object (ring, candle, bread, water) but can find additional meanings besides the obvious outer layer. A symbol is a sign of something that is abstract or spiritual, like the concepts of justice or country. Symbols use real elements to get across a deeper meaning.

Because rituals generally remain the same and use symbols and repeated gestures, they free us to go beyond the actions that make them up to enter more deeply into the spiritual meaning "layer by layer."

## Effective Signs

We all participate in the liturgy. The priest leads the assembly, the deacon assists, and others serve in the celebration, but we all take part through prayers, singing, silences, and gestures. In the celebration of each Sacrament, there are visible signs—our words and actions—and Divine actions—things we can't see—that give grace and allow us to share in God's work. Jesus is present with us, in the assembly gathered, acting in and through the priest, Scripture readings, and most especially in the Eucharist. The latter is known as Christ's *Real Presence*. This term is used to describe the Catholic teaching that Jesus is really and truly with us in the Eucharist—Body, Blood, Soul, and Divinity.

The liturgy is truly a work of the whole Body of Christ, Jesus the Head, and all of her members. The liturgy includes the celebration of the **Seven Sacraments** and the forms of daily prayer. The Sacraments are effective signs of God's grace, instituted by Christ and given to his Church. The visible symbols and rituals of the Sacraments illustrate the graces and effects that are received.

The Church celebrates Seven Sacraments: Baptism, Confirmation, Eucharist, Penance and Reconciliation, Anointing of the Sick, Holy Orders and Matrimony.

The Real Presence of Christ in the Eucharist begins at the moment of consecration during Mass and lasts as long as the **Blessed Sacrament** exists. Christ is completely present in every part of the Eucharist (see *CCC*, 1377). The Church has always offered the Eucharist for adoration during Mass, but also outside of it. The Eucharist not consumed at Mass is reserved

### Catholic Faith Words

**liturgy**  the official public worship of the Church. It includes the Seven Sacraments and forms of daily prayer.

**Seven Sacraments**  effective signs of God's grace, instituted by Christ and given to his Church. In the celebration of each Sacrament, there are visible signs and Divine actions that give grace and allow us to share in God's work.

**Blessed Sacrament**  a name for the Holy Eucharist, especially the Body of Christ reserved in the Tabernacle

**Tabernacle**  the special place in the church where the Blessed Sacrament is reserved after Mass for those who are ill or for Eucharistic Adoration in the **Tabernacle**. For adoration outside of Mass, the Eucharist is exposed with great care for the veneration of the faithful and often for carrying it in procession (see *CCC*, 1378).

Eucharistic Adoration is an expression of faith that takes place in the presence of Christ in the Blessed Sacrament. Worship of the Eucharist outside of Mass begins with Exposition. Eucharistic Exposition provides us with the opportunity to worship the Lord in the Blessed Sacrament exposed in either a ciborium or monstrance, which are vessels that hold the Eucharist.

Eucharistic Adoration consists of people spending time kneeling or sitting in silent prayer before the Blessed Sacrament, much like the Magi must have done when they first saw Jesus.

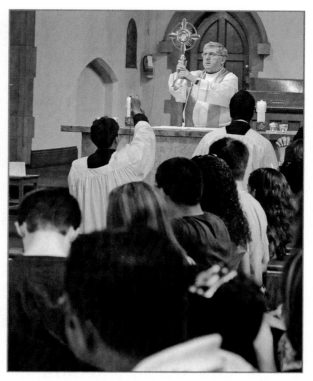

**Eucharistic Adoration can include prayers, readings, and songs.**

## REFLECT

In the chart, write what the average person might know about these objects or symbols used in the Church's worship. Then write the meanings you associate with that symbol when worshipping.

| Symbols in Worship | | |
|---|---|---|
| **Object** | **What People Know About Them** | **Their Meaning in Worship** |
| Ashes | | |
| Bells | | |
| Candles | | |

# Visible and Invisible Realities

**What is the connection between worship and moral living?**

Perhaps the most famous line in *The Little Prince*, by Antoine de Saint-Exupéry, is this: "It is only with the heart that one can see rightly; what is essential is invisible to the eye." God's gift of grace is the free and undeserved gift he gives us so we can become his adopted children. Grace is an invisible but essential part of our lives.

God takes the first step with us, loving us, and offering us his life. Because we are made in his image and have free will, we are free to respond to his grace.

His grace makes it possible for us to respond, but we still make the choice of whether to do so or not. Grace connects to what makes us truly human, to our desire to be with God and to be like him, to be free and to be in union with him.

## Our Response

How do we respond to God's grace? And what does our response look like? One important way to respond is to live a holy (God-like) life by participating in the Seven Sacraments and following Jesus' example. Our spiritual life includes our prayers, celebration of the liturgy, and participation in the Seven Sacraments. It strengthens our moral life—how we live by Jesus' example and Church teachings. The reverse is also true.

We need God's help to face the challenges and temptations of everyday life. We can find his help through prayer and the Seven Sacraments. We need the spiritual life to

---

### Catholic Faith Words

**Precepts of the Church** some of the minimum requirements given by Church leaders for deepening our relationship with God and the Church

**sanctifying grace** God's Divine life within us that makes us his friends and adopted children

**actual grace** the help God gives us in our particular need or to do a particular good act or to avoid evil

---

have a moral life. It is vital that we pray, and prayer is always possible. As Saint Paul reminds us, "Pray at every opportunity in the Spirit" (Ephesians 6:18). Prayer and the Christian life are inseparable.

We can give praise and thanks to God by leading moral lives. Although worship in a church building is visible, we can worship in an invisible or spiritual way every minute of the day by leading moral lives. We obey the Ten Commandments, live out the Beatitudes, pray, and follow the **Precepts of the Church**, Church laws that name specific actions that all Catholics must carry out to help them grow in love of God and neighbor. God makes it possible to follow his commands and do all these things by his grace. Grace strengthens our moral life, which will only be complete and perfect when we are together with God in Heaven.

- **Sanctifying grace** is God's Divine life within us that makes us his friends and adopted children. The Holy Spirit fills our souls to heal us of sin and make us holy.
- **Actual grace** is the help God gives us in our particular need or to do a particular good act or to avoid evil.
- **Sacramental grace** is a grace specific to each of the Seven Sacraments. It is the Gift of the Holy Spirit that helps us fulfill our particular calling.

- **Special graces** (called charisms in Saint Paul's letter to the Corinthians) are special Gifts of the Holy Spirit connected to one's state in life or ministry in the Church, such as teaching or giving aid. Special graces might include the extraordinary, like the gift of miracles. They are intended for the good of all members of the Church. The Church also teaches that we have the responsibility to help provide for the material needs of the Church, based upon our ability.

Place check marks next to the two Precepts that can most help you grow right now in your relationship with God.

| Precepts of the Church | |
|---|---|
| ○ | Attend Mass on Sundays and avoid unnecessary work. |
| ○ | Celebrate the Sacrament of Reconciliation at least once a year if there is serious sin. |
| ○ | Receive Holy Communion at least once in the Easter season. |
| ○ | Fast and abstain on days of penance. |
| ○ | Give your time, gifts, and money to support the Church. |

## IDENTIFY AND LIST

Discuss with a classmate which of the Precepts of the Church are easiest for you to follow, and which are the most difficult. Then create three additional "Personal Precepts" as a way to challenge yourself and for continued spiritual exercise and growth.

1. _____

2. _____

3. _____

# Sunday

**How can we make Sunday a day for worship and rest?**

From the earliest times of Christianity, Sunday has been celebrated as the Lord's Day: the first day, the eighth day, the day beyond time, the day of Jesus' Resurrection and the day of post-Resurrection appearances, the day of Eucharist. Sunday is a symbolic day for all that Christianity is!

Sunday is the major celebration of the Eucharist because it is the day of the Resurrection. It is the day we gather together as God's family to give God thanks and praise for all he is and all he does for us. It is a day of joy and rest, when we can set aside the things that take up most of our attention during the rest of the week.

## The Third Commandment

The Third Commandment required the people of the Old Law to observe the Sabbath. We observe Sunday. The Sabbath represented God's rest at the end of the first creation, as told in the Book of Genesis.

At one time, "keeping the Sabbath" meant people could not work or play on Sunday. It's come to mean the spiritual practices you engage in that help you care for your soul. Christians celebrate it on Sunday because that was the day of the new creation begun by the Resurrection of Christ.

Because Sunday is the most important Holy Day of Obligation, we are required to participate in the Mass on Sunday or Saturday evening. It is the center of our worship and helps us keep our spiritual rhythm. In our celebration of the Eucharist, Christ is present in the community gathered together, in the Word of God proclaimed, in the person of the priest, and most especially his Body and Blood. Sunday Mass brings us all together to celebrate Jesus Christ and everything he has given the Church and her members to be and do for the world.

## Keeping Holy the Lord's Day

- Participate in Mass.

- Avoid work that would prevent us from attending Mass.

- _____

On the lines below, write one way you have followed this advice.

- Avoid unnecessary work that would take away from the needed relaxation of mind and body.

- Perform "good works" that strengthen family bonds and friendships. Contact the lonely or sick or attend parish gatherings.

- _____

- Set aside some leisure time—broaden your interests at museums (even virtual tours), walk outdoors, read, play music, and do restful activities.

- Don't place demanding athletic practices or long hours of work on others that could prevent them from observing the Lord's Day.

- _____

It is highly recommended that we receive Holy Communion every time we attend Mass, provided we are free from mortal sin.

Christ longs to give himself to us and be close to us; partaking of his Body and Blood is our response in saying, "Yes, I want to become like you. I wanted to be nourished by your life and love so I can live as you live and love as you love."

**PLAN**

In addition to taking part in Mass, what are other ways for you to take time on Sundays to remember who you are and whose you are?

_____

_____

# IN SUMMARY  Catholics Believe

The way we worship and pray has an impact on the choices we make and the ways we live our daily lives.

- The liturgy is the official public worship of the Church. The symbols and rituals of the liturgy form us in prayer and communicate God's gift of life.

- Our spiritual life—our prayer and worship— strengthens our moral life—how we live by Jesus' teachings and follow the Precepts of the Church.

- Observing Sunday as the Lord's Day includes required attendance at Mass, the omission of unnecessary work that would distract from the day's purpose, and attention to living a good life.

## Our Catholic Life

You can make your personal relationship with Jesus Christ and his Church stronger by following the Precepts of the Church, including **honoring the Lord's Day** every Sunday, both by participating in the Mass with your family and by avoiding unnecessary work. Use this time to get close to God in a special way through your full participation in the liturgy. Your voice is needed to respond to the prayers at Mass, your mind is needed to listen to the readings, and your presence is needed to show the world that you are part of the People of God. Participation on the Lord's Day and other Catholic holy days helps you treasure and reflect on your favorite Catholic symbols and seasons. Allow them to join the Word of God to lead you to a deeper understanding of spiritual truths.

> **What is one way you feel part of the Church as you celebrate Mass on Sundays?**

© Our Sunday Visitor

## People of Faith

### Saint Thomas Becket, 1118–1170

Thomas Becket was Lord Chancellor and Archbishop of Canterbury under King Henry II. The appointment changed Thomas' life. He began to wear a monastic habit instead of fine clothes and opposed the king on certain matters. Henry became angry at this rebellion, especially after Thomas excommunicated clergymen who supported Henry. Four of Henry's knights traveled to Canterbury Cathedral and murdered Thomas. As he lay dying, he said, "For the name of Jesus and the protection of the Church, I am ready to embrace death." The Church celebrates his feast day on **December 29**.

For more, go to
**aliveinchrist.osv.com**

## IDENTIFY

Reflect on which times give you the best opportunity to pray.

When are you most likely to feel God's presence?

_____

_____

_____

What can you do to remind yourself to pray and listen at these times? What form does your prayer normally take?

_____

_____

_____

_____

## ❤ A Gospel Reflection

**Leader:** In faith and in hope we gather here this day, to hear the Word of God.

**Reader:** Let us listen to the Gospel according to Luke.

*Read Luke 18:1–8.*

The Gospel of the Lord.

**All:** Praise to you, Lord Jesus Christ.

*Share your Gospel reflections.*

**Leader:** O God,
we are your newest generation,
who long to know the stories of our faith;
to grow in our understanding of the message
your Word has for us,
and to share the Good News
with all your people.

**All:** Teach us, Lord, we pray.

**Leader:** O God,
We are your people, who long to grow
in the practices of our faith;
to share fully in the celebrations, rituals,
songs and prayers;
to be active participants in the Body of
Christ.

**All:** Teach us, Lord, we pray.

**Leader:** O God,
We are your people, your newest generation;
we long to serve all your poor ones
with the gifts you freely gave us,
and with the love and compassion
of your Son, Jesus.

**All:** Teach us, Lord, we pray.

**Leader:** O God,
Like the widow who persisted,
we dare ask for more . . .
We long to be people of prayer,
who turn to you in times of trouble and
fear, who talk with you in our loneliness
and doubt, who cry out to you in our pain
and sorrow, who reach toward you with our
questions and searching,
and who share with you
our joys and our praise.
We ask this through your Son, Jesus. Amen.

Go to **aliveinchrist.osv.com** for an interactive review.

**A** **Work with Words** Complete each sentence with the correct term from the Word Bank.

| | |
|---|---|
| ritual | liturgy |
| Mass | actual grace |
| Church canon | Seven Sacraments |
| sanctifying grace | Precepts of the Church |

1. Catholics must follow the _____, minimum requirements given by Church leaders for deepening our relationship with God and the Church.

2. _____ is the official public worship of the Church.

3. God gives us _____ to help in our particular needs, or to do a particular good act or to avoid evil.

4. God's Divine life within us that makes us his friends and adopted children is called _____.

5. The _____ are effective signs of God's grace instituted by Christ and given to his Church.

**B** **Check Understanding** Circle the letter of the choice that best completes the sentence.

6. ___ is/are present through the rituals and symbols of all of the Seven Sacraments.
   a. Virtue   c. Jesus
   b. Signs    d. Mystery

7. The liturgy includes the celebration of the Seven Sacraments and the ___ of daily prayer.
   a. hymns    c. liturgy
   b. forms    d. Precepts

8. ___ refers to Jesus really and truly with us in the Eucharist.
   a. Sabbath        c. Communion
   b. Reconciliation d. Real Presence

9. The Third Commandment requires us to keep holy the ___.
   a. Lord's Day  c. Law of God
   b. Precepts    d. a and c

10. ___ (called charisms) are intended for the good of all the Church.
    a. Special graces     c. Actual grace
    b. Sanctifying grace  d. Sacramental grace

**C** **Make Connections** On a separate sheet of paper, write a one-paragraph response to the question: What can you do to keep the Lord's Day holy? What difference do you think this might make in your life?

© Our Sunday Visitor

**262** Chapter 16

# Faithful Living

## ♥ Let Us Pray

**Leader:** Faithful God, you are always with us. Teach us to be faithful to one another and to you. May we be witnesses to your love and faithfulness.

"I keep the LORD always before me;
    with him at my right hand, I shall never be shaken.
You will show me the path to life,
    abounding joy in your presence,
      the delights at your right hand forever." Psalm 16:8, 11

**All:** Lord, help us keep our promises.

### ✝ Scripture

"Let no one have contempt for your youth, but set an example for those who believe . . . Be diligent in these matters . . . so that your progress may be evident to everyone." 1 Timothy 4:12, 15

**Have you ever thought...**

- How are you an example of a faithful person?
- What does it mean to be faithful to God, to yourself, and to others?

# Getting Started

In this chapter, you will examine the Sacraments at the Service of Communion. You will learn about the promises of the Sacrament of Matrimony and study Holy Orders. You will also study the Sixth and Ninth Commandments.

© Our Sunday Visitor

## Catholic Faith Words

- Matrimony
- fidelity
- vows
- Holy Orders
- *in persona Christi*

In the spaces provided, write information about each Sacrament at the Service of Communion.

| The Sacraments at the Service of Communion | |
| --- | --- |
| **Matrimony** | **Holy Orders** |
| Who Receives It: | Who Receives It: |
| Symbols: | Symbols: |
| The Commitment: | The Commitment: |

**Promises Made. Promises Kept** Write about four promises you have made: to yourself, to family, friends, and to God. Then, tell how you have kept these promises.

Promise I Made to Myself: _____

_____

_____

How I Kept It: _____

_____

_____

Promise I Made to My Family: _____

_____

How I Kept It: _____

_____

_____

Promise I Made to My Friends: _____

_____

How I Kept It: _____

_____

_____

Promise I Made to God: _____

_____

How I Kept It: _____

_____

_____

© Our Sunday Visitor

God's image and likeness, God did not create humans to be alone. From the beginning, men and women have been partners. We find our true selves in relationship with others. In other words, we know ourselves better when our ties with family, friends, and others are strong.

We become our best selves when we strengthen those ties by keeping our promises to others, whether the promise is small like helping around the house or large like committing our lives permanently to another person in marriage.

The Seven Sacraments give us grace to be faithful to our commitments and relationships. By his presence at the Wedding at Cana, and by performing his first miracle there (see John 2:1–11), Jesus showed the goodness and importance of marriage. Christian marriage is a Sacrament, an effective sign of Christ's presence.

## The Promises of Marriage

In Catholic marriages, a baptized man and baptized woman freely vow to be faithful and true to each other forever. **Matrimony** is a visible sign of the union of Christ and his Church. In this Sacrament, God gives spouses special graces to make their love more perfect and holy, and strengthen their unity.

# Marriage as a Sign of Christ's Love

**What does a couple promise in marriage?**

When you make a promise to do something with or for someone, that person plans on you keeping your promise. Keeping your promises strengthens your relationships by showing that you can be trusted. Making a promise enriches your life, but it sometimes makes life a little more complicated.

The same thing applies to your relationship with God. Making and keeping promises with God deepens your friendship with God. It also brings challenges.

God is a Trinity. His very being is communion. Because we are made in

### Catholic Faith Words

**Matrimony** the Sacrament at the Service of Communion in which a baptized man and a baptized woman make a permanent covenant of love with each other and with God

**fidelity** faithful presence; it is the most important rule of loving and lasting relationships

**vows** solemn promises that are made to or before God

As a sign of Christ's love for his people, married couples have a tremendous responsibility. They freely choose to make a permanent covenant of faithful love with each other. This covenant was founded by God the Creator and given special laws. The couple must be to each other and to all they meet what Christ is to the Church— totally loving and sacrificing, maintaining total **fidelity**, giving themselves in service, faithfully working to keep their marriage unbreakable. They also commit to be open to any children God may give them, and to be faithful stewards of this gift of life.

In a public celebration within the liturgy, before a priest or deacon, witnesses, and family, the couple **vows** to love each other as God loves us. Sometimes it's hard to believe that God is always with us, forgives us, cares about us, and loves us beyond our understanding. When in doubt, we can look to happily married couples and say,

## CATHOLICS TODAY

Some of the Eastern Catholic Churches use crowns at their marriage rite. In fact, the Sacrament is referred to as "holy crowning." The priest prays prayers of blessing and places the crowns on the heads of the bride and groom. The crowns symbolize that the couple are the king and queen of their home, that they should give themselves to each other, and that they are part of the Kingdom of God.

"That gives me a glimpse of God's love. If Dave and Maddie are that forgiving, that compassionate, that caring, how much greater must God's love be!"

> **What does a loving and faithful marriage teach us about God's love?**

> **How can your commitment to someone or something show God's love?**

## REFLECT AND WRITE

Wedding vows are the solemn promises you make to the person you marry. What kinds of values and ways of behaving do you think are important in a successful marriage? List some of those values and behaviors here.

**Values**

_____

_____

_____

**Behaviors**

_____

_____

_____

**Eastern Catholic Holy Crowning**

Seminarians participate in World Youth Day celebrations.

# The Ordained Life

### How is Holy Orders a Sacrament of Service?

Matrimony is not the only Sacrament that involves making a vow or being at the Service of Communion. The other is the Sacrament of **Holy Orders**, in which a baptized man is ordained to teach the faithful, lead divine worship, and govern the Church; ordained ministers serve as bishops, priests, or deacons.

Like Matrimony, Holy Orders involves making promises that deepen relationships to God and others through service and giving witness to faith in daily life. Although all followers of Christ must serve, bishops, priests, and deacons are ordained into the service of authority for the Kingdom through teaching, worship, and pastoral governance.

All the people in the Church are part of the priesthood of Christ. This is sometimes referred to as the "common priesthood of the faithful." However, some men are called to participate in the mission of Christ in another way, through the Sacrament of Holy Orders, where bishops and priests act in the name and in the person of Christ the Head in the midst of the community. Deacons are ordained to serve the People of God in liturgy, Word, and charity. In the ministerial priesthood the priest receives a sacred authority for the service of the faithful.

How does a man know he is called to serve as a deacon or a priest? Here are some ways:

- The man discerns through prayer, careful thought, and many conversations with others in the community, God's call to live out his baptismal promises in Holy Orders. He is invited by and receives this calling from a bishop (deacon and priest) or the Pope (bishop).

- The man has a solid spiritual life and the personal gifts needed by the Church. He must have certain talents and abilities that would help the Church family. The Sacrament of Holy Orders grants a special role of leadership on the priest. He has a distinctive relationship with Christ and the Church.

**Holy Orders** the Sacrament at the Service of Communion in which a baptized man is ordained to teach the faithful, lead divine worship, and govern the Church; ordained ministers serve as bishops, priests, or deacons

***in persona Christi*** term referring to the mission and ability of priests and bishops, granted through Holy Orders, to act in the person of Christ

## The Celebration of the Sacrament

After years of discernment, studying theology, working in a parish, and performing different ministries, the candidate for the priesthood is ordained. The Sacrament of Holy Orders usually takes place in the diocesan cathedral, and the bishop is the minister. After the Litany of the Saints, the bishop lays his hands on the candidates' heads, prays in silence, and then sings or recites a prayer of consecration, asking the Holy Spirit to bless the man with the graces needed to fulfill his ministry.

Like Baptism and Confirmation, ordination prints an indelible character, or permanent mark, upon the one ordained. He enters into a permanent relationship with the Church, as he acts in the person of Christ as a leader in the Church community.

> **Why do you think all three of these Sacraments mark the recipients?**

## Acting in Christ's Name

Priests act ***in persona Christi*** (in the person of Christ) and *in persona ecclesiae* (in the person of the Church). Through their membership in the Body of Christ and the special graces of the Sacrament of Holy Orders, priests are special signs of Christ, the Head of the Body. A priest's leadership should inspire the faith of the community. This happens when a priest's ministry flows from a heart transformed by the Spirit and open to God and his People. In choosing to live a celibate life in imitation of Jesus, the priest grows in deeper intimacy with God. In choosing obedience, in imitation of Jesus who was perfectly obedient to his Father, the priest obeys the bishop and Pope, knowing that Jesus works through them.

Everyone is called by God to serve. But God calls some to serve a deeper commitment as an ordained priest or as a religious brother or sister. Speaking to your priest or pastor or to a religious brother or sister is one way to begin identifying whether God might be calling you to the consecrated life. While speaking to others is an important part of the discernment process, continually turn to the Holy Spirit for guidance. To learn more about vocations and charisms, turn to page 378 in the Our Catholic Tradition section of your book.

## NAME

Name three ways a parish priest can make a difference in the lives of his parishioners.

1. _____

_____

_____

2. _____

_____

_____

3. _____

_____

_____

# Living Faithfully

**How can you live out the Sixth and Ninth Commandments?**

Faithful living in marriage means that you will be able to count on the goodness of your partner every day until old age. Being faithful in marriage involves many things.

Living out the marriage covenant requires the couple to follow the Sixth Commandment, "You shall not commit adultery," and the Ninth Commandment, "You shall not covet your neighbor's wife."

The Sacrament of Matrimony gives the couple the grace to be faithful and true to their marital vocation. Most importantly the husband and wife

- commit to each other and only each other. This results in a unique unity between the couple. Polygamy—the practice of having more than one spouse at a time—opposes this unity.

- make a permanent and unbreakable commitment that is blessed by God. Divorce would separate what God has joined together. It goes against God's plan and his laws. In order for a divorced person to remarry in the Catholic Church, the marriage must be annulled (a formal declaration by the Church that the marriage vows were not valid).

- are open to having children if they are blessed with them. The unwillingness to have children turns marriage away from its greatest gift—a child.

For a variety of reasons, sometimes couples separate and even divorce. This is often very painful for everyone involved. Making vows makes life richer, and sometimes more complicated. Our faith tells us that making a spouse, parent, or stepparent "the enemy" only makes the pain worse. The Church recognizes that those in pain need our prayers and support.

## Commandments for All of Us

The virtue of chastity helps you maintain the right balance of body and spirit in human sexuality. Your sexuality is part of who you are. It's more than whether you are biologically a male or female. Chastity helps you express your sexuality in the right way. It helps you remain pure in the ways you act and think. It helps you show love in the appropriate ways.

Some thoughts and actions harm a person's dignity and go against the virtue of chastity to such a degree that they are sins: masturbation, sexual intercourse outside of marriage, pornography, and homosexual actions. We all have the responsibility to develop the self-discipline necessary to live chastely. God's grace will help us if we are open to it.

The Ninth Commandment reminds us that the proper attitudes toward sexuality involve the ways people think, too. Desiring to act in improper ways can lead people to do the thing they desire, causing disrespect to their own bodies or those of others. Focusing your heart on what is good and practicing temperance are important.

The virtue of modesty is all about decency. It's about being discreet in the way you dress, and the things you say (or choose not to say).

The more you practice the virtues, like modesty and chastity, the more you'll be able to rely on them. Participating in weekly Eucharist and the frequent celebration of the Sacrament of Reconciliation can give you the strength to practice self-control and make good judgments.

## IN SUMMARY   Catholics Believe

The Seven Sacraments strengthen us to be faithful to our commitments and our relationships. The Sacraments at the Service of Communion celebrate people's commitment to serve God and the community and help build up the People of God.

- The Sacrament of Matrimony strengthens the couple to live out their promises to be true and faithful, to be open to the gift of children, and to be models of the love Christ has for his people.

- Holy Orders is the Sacrament in which a baptized man is ordained to teach the faithful, lead divine worship, and govern the Church; ordained ministers serve as bishops, priests, or deacons.

- Practicing and living by the virtues of modesty and chastity can help all people, no matter whether they are married, ordained, or single. The grace of the Eucharist and Reconciliation can strengthen all of us to be pure and self-respecting.

## Our Catholic Life

The Sacraments of Holy Orders and Matrimony honor the commitments of Catholics to be faithful to God and to each other. Even before you are old enough to enter into these kinds of commitments, you can make others. **Faithfulness** means being true and loyal, and your faithfulness to God should be one of the most important aspects of your life. Honor your commitments by being faithful to yourself (remembering who you are and what you believe), being faithful to God (following his Commandments and showing your belief to the world), and by being faithful to others (honoring their friendship, love, and lives). Think before you make promises, and honor your commitments.

> What commitments can you make to God, to yourself, and to others this week?

## People of Faith

### Saint Benedict the Black, 1526–1589

Benedict was a slave until age eighteen, but he still worked for his former master. Eventually he joined an order of hermits, then a friary, and was given the role of cook. At the friary Benedict was chosen to oversee reforms. He could not read or write and was not a priest, but he obeyed. Benedict led wisely, and spent the rest of his days cooking for his brothers and sharing the love of Christ. Upon his death, King Philip III of Spain paid for a special tomb for the simple friar. Benedict is the patron of African Americans in the United States. The Church celebrates his feast day on **April 4**.

For more, go to
**aliveinchrist.osv.com**

## IDENTIFY

Think about the promises you are living with now. Fill in the lines below to explore how you make and keep your promises. Answer the following questions:

What promises have you made?

_____

_____

What responsibilities come with them?

_____

_____

How are you doing in keeping them?

_____

_____

## ♥ Prayer of Petition

**Reader 1:** A reading from the holy Gospel according to Mark.

*Read Mark 12:28–33.*

The Gospel of the Lord.

**All:** Praise to you, Lord Jesus Christ.

**Leader:** Loving God,

Be with us now as we call out to your greatest gift, Jesus, and ask for strength and guidance.

Our response is . . . Jesus, give us strength.

**Reader 2:** To keep the promise of faithfulness:
in times of question and doubt.
For this we pray . . .

**All:** Jesus, give us strength.

**Reader 3:** To keep the promise of love:
of our God, of self, and others.
For this we pray . . .

**All:** Jesus, give us strength.

**Reader 4:** To keep the promise of friendship:
with those we walk with each day,
with those we find hard to love.
For this we pray . . .

**All:** Jesus, give us strength.

**Reader 5:** To keep the promise of service,
in times of indifference,
when we are busy, self-involved, or distracted.
For this we pray . . .

**All:** Jesus, give us strength.

**Leader:** Lord, Jesus,
Give us strength today and always,
to serve you in all we do,
and to faithfully follow wherever you lead.

**All:** Amen.

▶ *Sing or pray "I Love You, Lord"*

Go to **aliveinchrist.osv.com** for an interactive review.

**A** **Work with Words** **Circle the letter of the choice that best completes the sentence.**

1. Christian ___ is an effective sign of Christ's presence joining a man and a woman in a holy union.
   a. marriage
   b. priesthood
   c. Confirmation
   d. fellowship

2. The Sacrament of ___ is a symbol of the union of Christ and his Church.
   a. Confirmation
   b. Eucharist
   c. Matrimony
   d. Baptism

3. Married couples freely choose to make a permanent ___ of faithful love with each other.
   a. covenant
   b. character
   c. confirmation
   d. none of the above

4. The virtue of ___ helps you maintain the right balance of body and spirit in human sexuality.
   a. hope
   b. modesty
   c. chastity
   d. faith

**B** **Check Understanding** **Complete each sentence with the correct terms from the Word Bank.**

| | |
|---|---|
| modesty | miracle |
| Deacons | Holy Orders |
| Ministers | character |
| partners | chastity |

5. From the beginning, men and women have been _____.

6. Jesus performed his first _____ at the Wedding of Cana.

7. _____ are ordained to serve the People of God in liturgy, Word, and charity.

8. Through the Sacrament of _____, bishops and priests serve in the name of and in the person of Christ in the community.

9. Like Baptism and Confirmation, ordination prints an indelible _____ upon the one ordained.

10. The virtue of _____ helps you be discreet in the ways you dress, act, and talk.

**C** **Make Connections** **Write a short response to the question: Compare and contrast the way marriage is presented in two current movies or books. How are the principles of Christian marriage being lived out in both?**

_____
_____
_____
_____
_____
_____
_____
_____
_____
_____

# The Liturgical Year

## ♡ Let Us Pray

**Leader:**  Holy Lord, you are with us always. In every day of every
season of every year you draw us closer to yourself.
You call us to love you, each other, and ourselves
more deeply.

"Glory in his holy name;
let hearts that seek the LORD rejoice!
Seek out the LORD and his might;
constantly seek his face."  **Psalm 105:3–4**

**All:**  God, help us know how to live.

### 📖 Scripture

The works of God are all of them good; he
supplies for every need in its own time.

No cause then to say: "What is the purpose of this?"
Everything is chosen to satisfy a need.

The works of God are all of them good;
he supplies for every need in its own time.

There is no cause then to say: "This is not as good
as that";
for each shows its worth at the proper time.

So now with full heart and voice proclaim
and bless his name!
**The Wisdom of Ben Sira (Sirach) 39:16, 21, 33–35**

### Have you ever thought...

- What is life's purpose?
- What does the Church celebrate
through the year, year after year?

# Getting Started

In this chapter, you will explore what the Church celebrates through the year and look at how the liturgical year changes, yet remains the same. You will also come to understand the importance of regular prayer and regular reception of the Eucharist.

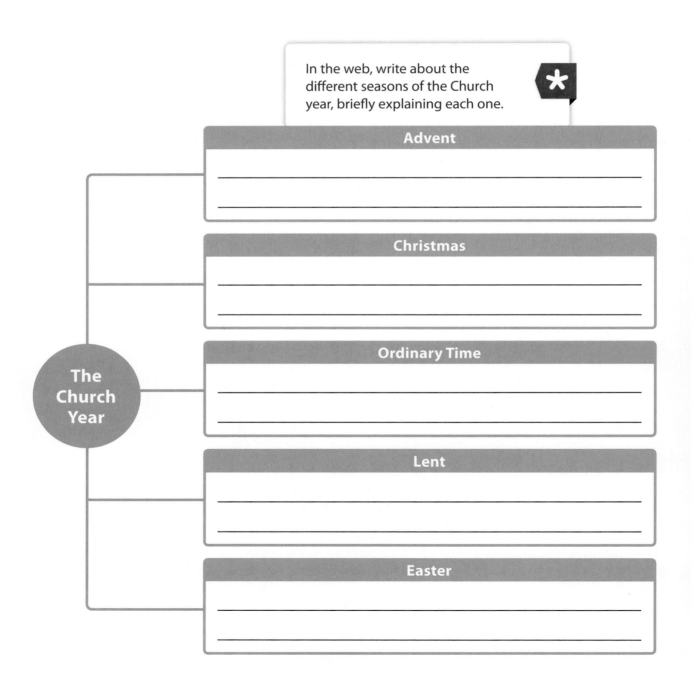

In the web, write about the different seasons of the Church year, briefly explaining each one.

**The Church Year**

**Advent**

**Christmas**

**Ordinary Time**

**Lent**

**Easter**

## IDENTIFY

**Through the Years**  Think of some of the changes that have happened over the course of your life thus far—the predictable things, and the unpredictable. Use the questions below to help you reflect on the past and look forward to the future.

What new beginnings have you experienced?

_____

_____

_____

_____

_____

What "works of God" (The Wisdom of Ben Sira 39:16) have you seen or experienced?

_____

_____

_____

_____

_____

_____

What changes are you looking forward to in the future?

_____

_____

_____

_____

_____

_____

_____

_____

_____

_____

_____

_____

**An Easter Vigil procession with the Paschal Candle**

# The Church Year

**What does the Church celebrate through the year?**

So many things in our lives change with each new year. Did you ever look back at last year and realize how different you are today from how you were a year ago? Things you worried about then may look easy now that you've been through them. It's like winning the big basketball game or passing final exams. You get ready for them by practicing or studying, and when the time comes, you take what you've learned and use it to win a victory.

When you've finished what you started, you celebrate—you might hang your final exam on the fridge or save a team photo in your album. You want to hold on to something that helps you remember how it all happened.

## Remembering and Celebrating

The Church does the same thing. We want to remember special events in the story of Jesus' life and our own story. We celebrate the Paschal Mystery through a cycle of seasons and feasts called the **liturgical year.**

One reason we call it the liturgical year is because the Scripture readings, prayers, and songs of the liturgy reflect what season or feast we are in. In the cycle of 365 days, the Church remembers the whole life of Jesus from his Incarnation and Nativity to his Death, Resurrection, and Ascension. We remember his continued presence with us through the sending of the Holy Spirit at Pentecost and the expectation of his coming again at the end of time.

As Catholics, you might say that we have our own calendar. Instead of celebrating President's Day, Valentine's Day, or the first day of spring, we celebrate different events from the life of Christ: his birth, miracles, prayer, preaching, suffering, Death, and Resurrection. On Passion (Palm) Sunday we emphasize his Death; on Easter we celebrate in a special way his Resurrection; and on other Sundays we may listen to the stories of Jesus' miracles and teaching.

## The Whole

Every day we celebrate everything that Jesus accomplished for us through his Passion, Death, Resurrection, and Ascension. Whether it's a holiday or the feast of a Saint, we celebrate the same thing in our liturgy: the Paschal Mystery. Every Sunday we celebrate the Risen Lord and what he has done for us.

The liturgical year begins in Advent, usually in late November or early December, moves to the Christmas season, then to the first, shorter part of Ordinary Time, on to Lent, the Triduum, and the Easter Season, then to the longer part of Ordinary Time that lasts many weeks. We end the year with the Feast of Christ the King.

Even though each season emphasizes one part of Jesus' life, ministry, or saving work, each also celebrates the whole of it.

### Catholic Faith Words

**liturgical year** the feasts and seasons of the Church calendar that celebrate the Paschal Mystery of Christ

In every season and feast, the Scripture we proclaim, prayers we pray, and songs we sing all come back to the great mystery we celebrate each and every Sunday of the year.

> **What is the religious significance of your favorite Church season or feast day?**

## DESCRIBE

Work with a classmate to describe what you already know about the Church's seasons in the two categories.

| Season | Symbols/Colors | Parish and Family |
|---|---|---|
| Advent | | |
| Christmas | | |
| Ordinary Time | | |
| Lent | | |
| Triduum | | |
| Easter | | |

# A Time for Everything

**How is the celebration of the liturgical year the same but different?**

The liturgical year helps you pattern your life on Jesus' life. It helps you live the life of Christ a little more deeply year after year.

Every year your experiences, needs, and dreams change. So do your relationships with your family and friends. Your relationship with God changes, too. Some years you find yourself really relating to Christmas; another year, you find yourself really paying attention to Lent, or All Saints Day, or simply "going to Communion."

## Past, Present, Future

So what you hear, feel, and think about during liturgical worship and family rituals may change, but you will continue to celebrate the same important seasons and feasts. We need that continuity in our lives. It's comforting to know that "There is an appointed time for everything, and a time for every affair under the heavens" (Ecclesiastes 3:1).

The Church celebrates these special times no matter what else is going on in our lives or in the world. While we are busy experiencing different things in our lives, she helps us join those experiences with the experience of Christ and the Church. The community of the Church and her customs keep us connected—to ourselves and to each other.

## The Trinity in the Liturgy

The Holy Trinity is present and active in our worship, making our liturgy possible, bringing about the mysteries of faith we celebrate throughout the liturgical year.

### Father

In creating the world, God the Father gave us all the gifts the Church uses in the Seven Sacraments: wheat, wine, oil, water, and

**Go to the Source**

Read Ecclesiastes 3:1–8. How many contrasting "seasons" are there in these verses? Can you think of any others? What does "under the heavens" mean to you?

© Our Sunday Visitor

more. More importantly, he gave us the gift of his Son, whose saving work is the source of all the grace flowing from the Seven Sacraments. In every liturgy, we bless and praise God the Father for these gifts. We acknowledge that he gave us the blessing of creation and the gift of salvation through his Son, Jesus. The Father has shared the Holy Spirit with us so that we might share in the new life his Son has made possible.

## Son

Jesus is the origin of the Sacraments. He is also the principal priest in every Sacrament. Bishops, priests, and deacons serve as his ministers. When the Church baptizes, Christ baptizes. When the Church confers Holy Orders, Christ ordains the priests. In every liturgy, Christ and his mystery of salvation are present through the work of the Holy Spirit and his own Body, the Church, that is a sign of hope, a means of grace, and a way to meet God.

When we participate in the Sacraments, we participate in Jesus' offering of himself to his Father. He established the Eucharist at the Last Supper and offers it through the work of the priest who leads the celebration. Only ordained priests can preside at Mass and consecrate the bread and wine, changing

them into Christ's Body and Blood. The **consecration** takes place during the part of the Eucharistic Prayer in which the priest prays the words of Jesus over the bread and wine, and these elements become the Body and Blood of Christ.

## Holy Spirit

The Holy Spirit prepares the assembly to meet Christ at Mass. His mission in the liturgy is to show us Christ, making him and his mystery of salvation present, and to work in the Church so that the gifts of Holy Communion can bear fruit.

## RECALL

Do you know by heart the words of consecration? Write here one phrase from the prayer and explain what it means to you.

_____

_____

_____

# To Live the Life of Christ

Why is participation in the Eucharist and regular prayer important?

We are always becoming what the Church already tells us we are: children of God, witnesses of our faith, forgiven people. The Mass makes this possible. We know it's a memorial of all God has done for us: Christ's Passover, his work of salvation finished through his Death on the Cross and Resurrection, and made present in the liturgy.

The Eucharist is at the very center of the liturgical year and all of the Church's life. Everything we do leads to and flows from the celebration of the Mass. In it Christ connects all of us to the sacrifice he made on the Cross and gives us new life.

The liturgical year commemorates the saving work of Christ. This is more than remembering Jesus' deeds recorded in the Gospels. It means we feel, act, think, and love in such a way that others can see what

© Our Sunday Visitor

## Catholic Faith Words

**Saints** those whom the Church declares led holy lives and are enjoying eternal life with God in Heaven

**Holy Days of Obligation** all Sundays, as well as designated holy days that Catholics are required to participate in the Mass

**Liturgy of the Hours** the Church's public prayer offered at set times during the day and night to mark each day as holy

Christ's actions and character are like when they observe our actions. That is the whole point of our memorial: to be transformed by remembering what Christ is like, to become like him.

Throughout the Church year we celebrate the lives of the **Saints**, who help us model Christ: Mary the Mother of God, the Apostles, the martyrs. Their feast days show that the Church on Earth is joined to the liturgy of Heaven. Our deceased relatives and friends can also help us see the connection between Heaven and Earth.

## An Invitation to Regular Prayer

Exercise programs and healthful diets have something in common: They are regular patterns or routines that are good for your physical health. The Church, too, has her regimen of regular prayer that helps keep Catholics in good spiritual health. Participation in the Sunday Eucharist, the Sacrament of Reconciliation, and the feasts of the Church year can help us grow spiritually and be strengthened to live as Christ did.

Catholics are required to participate in the Mass on all Sundays and on **Holy Days of Obligation** such as Christmas and All Saints Day. For a list of all six days, see page 372

in the Our Catholic Tradition section of your book.

Daily prayer and the Liturgy of the Hours are two more ways we can enter into a conversation with God and open our minds and hearts to him.

The **Liturgy of the Hours** is the Church's public prayer to mark each day as holy. This prayer is offered at set times during the day and night. In some monasteries and convents, monks and nuns gather throughout the day to praise God in the Liturgy of the Hours for his gifts and to mark the holiness of the day. Although women and men religious pray these

prayers, the Liturgy of the Hours is also the prayer of the whole People of God. All are encouraged to pray the principal hours, Morning Prayer, and Evening Prayer. Some parishes gather together to do so. Some use a special book called the Office containing the prayers of the Liturgy of the Hours.

However, any prayers of praise, thanks, and petition are great daily or weekly prayer routines. Your own personal daily prayers keep you in touch with God. You may have some favorite prayers like the Our Father and Hail Mary. Perhaps you simply sit in quiet or talk to God in your own words. What matters is the time spent with God.

## IN SUMMARY    Catholics Believe

We grow in our understanding of Jesus and in our relationship with him as we celebrate the different seasons of the liturgical year, which helps us pattern our lives on the life of Christ.

- The seasons and feasts of the liturgical year emphasize different aspects of the Paschal Mystery, connecting us more closely to Jesus' Passion, Death, Resurrection, and Ascension.

- Because we are different each year, we enter into the Church's seasons and feasts with different needs, hopes, and relationships with God and others.

- The Eucharist is at the heart of what it means to be Catholic. Participation in Sunday Mass and our own regular personal prayer help us live the life of Christ.

## Our Catholic Life

In this chapter you learned about the **Liturgy of the Hours**, the Church's public prayer that marks each day as holy with prayers, readings, hymns, and psalms. The Liturgy of the Hours also reflects the seasons and times of year, connects them to the Church as a whole, and reminds Catholics of their connection to the Paschal Mystery. Along with the readings from Psalms, other parts of Scripture are proclaimed, with commentaries on the readings by Fathers of the Church such as Saint Augustine. There are Catholics praying as part of the Liturgy of the Hours every day all around the world, constantly praising God and giving him thanks for all his gifts.

> How can you make prayer an essential part of your life every day?

# People of Faith

### Saint Maria del Transito de Jesus Sacramentado, 1821–1885

Maria's family was wealthy, but her father had a deep Christian faith. One of her brothers became a priest, and three sisters became nuns. When her mother died, Maria entered a Franciscan Order, then a Carmelite monastery. Illness forced her to leave that convent and another soon afterward. During this time of sickness and loss, Maria turned to God. With encouragement and help from friends, Maria started the Congregation of the Franciscan Tertiary Missionaries of Argentina to help the poor and orphans. The Church celebrates her feast day on **August 25**.

For more, go to
**aliveinchrist.osv.com**

## REFLECT

Reflect on and answer the following questions.

What joys have you had in life so far?

_____

_____

What losses or failures have you gone through?

_____

_____

What part of your faith do you need to develop in order to keep making your way through the Paschal Mystery of your life?

_____

_____

_____

_____

## ♡ Prayer of Blessing

**Leader:** God, your Church is the Body of Christ. The Church, established by Jesus, lives on with his life and his mission here on Earth. We pray now for our Church, which is our family of faith.

**Side 1:** God please bless . . . our journey as young Catholics.

**Side 2:** God please bless . . . the faith journey of everyone in our families.

**Side 1:** God please bless . . . all the parishioners of our parish.

**Side 2:** God please bless . . . the pastor and parish staff of our parish.

**Side 1:** God please bless . . . all who serve in parish ministries.

**Side 2:** God please bless . . . the bishops and clergy of our diocese.

**Side 1:** God please bless . . . all bishops and cardinals of our country.

**Side 2:** God please bless . . . all schools and programs that help us learn about our Catholic faith.

**Side 1:** God please bless . . . all Catholic ministries and missions serving those in need.

**Side 2:** God please bless . . . all religious sisters and brothers.

**Side 1:** God please bless . . . our Catholic brothers and sisters around the world.

**Side 2:** God please bless . . . the Pope and all who serve the worldwide Church.

**Reader 1:** Now let's pray together this Prayer for the Church written by Saint John Chrysostom, an early Church Father and Doctor of the Church from the fourth Christian century.

**Reader 2:** Remember, Lord, the city in which we dwell, and every city and region, and the faithful that inhabit it.

Remember, Lord, those that voyage, and travel, that are sick, that are laboring, that are in prison, and their safety.

Remember, Lord, those that bear fruit, and do good deeds in your holy churches, and that remember the poor.

And send forth on us all the riches of your compassion, and grant us with one mouth and one heart to glorify and celebrate your glorious and majestic name, Father, Son, and Holy Spirit, now and ever, and to ages of ages.

And the mercies of the great God and our Savior Jesus Christ shall be with all of us.

**All:** Amen.

▶ *Sing or play "Christ, Be Our Light"*

Go to **aliveinchrist.osv.com** for an interactive review.

**A** **Work with Words** **Complete each sentence with the correct term from the Word Bank.**

| | |
|---|---|
| Son | Hail Mary |
| liturgical year | Trinity |
| Liturgy of the Hours | Father |
| | Christmas |
| Advent | |

1. We celebrate the Paschal Mystery through a cycle of seasons and feasts called the

   _____.

2. The liturgical year begins with the season

   of _____.

3. The _____ is present and active in the liturgy of the Church, bringing about the mysteries of faith we celebrate.

4. In each and every liturgy, we bless and praise God the _____ for the blessing of creation and most importantly the gift of salvation.

5. The _____ is the Church's public prayer throughout the day to mark each day as holy.

**B** **Check Understanding** **Indicate whether the following statements are true or false. Then rewrite false statements to make them true.**

6. In the cycle of 365 days, the Church remembers the earthly life of Jesus from his Incarnation and birth to his Death. **True/False**

   _____

   _____

7. Jesus is the origin of the Seven Sacraments and the principal priest who celebrates them. **True/False**

   _____

   _____

8. The Holy Spirit's mission in the liturgy is to show Christ to us, making him and his mystery of salvation present by his power. **True/False**

   _____

   _____

9. In the Liturgy of the Hours, the sacrifice that Christ made on the Cross is renewed and gives all of his Church new life. **True/False**

   _____

   _____

10. Sundays are our Holy Days of Obligation. **True/False**

    _____

    _____

**C** **Make Connections** **On a separate sheet of paper, write a one-paragraph response to the question: What part of the liturgical year is most meaningful to you now and why? How has your experience of that season or celebration changed over time?**

**A** Work with Words  **Use the clues below to complete the crossword puzzle.**

**Across**

1. A Sacrament of Initiation

6. Effective signs of God's grace instituted by Christ and given to his Church

7. This virtue helps you be discreet in the ways you dress and the things you say

8. ____ grace is God's Divine life within us, which makes us his friends and adopted children.

**Down**

2. Beginning of the liturgical year

3. The Liturgy of the ____ is the Church's public prayer to mark each day as holy.

4. Some of the minimum requirements given by Church leaders for deepening our relationship with God and the Church

5. The official public worship of the Church

**B** Check Understanding  Complete each sentence with the correct
term from the Word Bank at right.

9. _____ is present through the rituals and
symbols of all of the Seven Sacraments.

10. The Third Commandment requires us to keep holy the
_____.

11. _____, called charisms, are intended for the
good of all the Church.

12. Christian _____ is an effective sign of Christ's
presence for the Church and the couple.

13. Married couples choose to make a permanent
_____ of faithful love.

14. The virtue of _____ helps you maintain the
right balance of body and spirit in human sexuality.

15. The feasts and seasons of the _____ celebrate
the Paschal Mystery of Christ.

16. The Holy Spirit's mission in the _____,
is to show Christ to us, making him present by his power.

17. In the _____, the sacrifice Christ made on
the Cross is renewed and his Church is given new life.

18. The Assumption and All Saints Day are Holy Days of _____.

19. The Liturgy of the _____ honors every part of the day with
prayers, readings, hymns, and psalms.

20. Jesus performed his first _____ at the wedding at Cana.

Word Bank:
Eucharist
special graces
Obligation
covenant
liturgical year
marriage
Jesus
Lord's Day
actual grace
miracle
rituals
oath
chastity
liturgy
Hours

**C** Make Connections **Write a short answer to the questions below.**

**21.** How do you experience God differently through the symbols or rituals of the Church? Give a specific example.

_____

_____

_____

_____

**22.** Think about a marriage that you think is strong. In what ways does that marriage reflect the relationship of Christ and the Church?

_____

_____

_____

_____

**23.** What authority does the Sacrament of Holy Orders confer on bishops, priests, and deacons?

_____

_____

_____

_____

**24.** What do the Precepts of the Church require Catholics to do?

_____

_____

_____

_____

**25.** Describe one of the Sacraments of Initiation and its effects.

_____

_____

_____

_____

# KINGDOM OF GOD

*How is Mary's faith-filled response the model for each member of the Communion of Saints throughout history?*

## CHURCH HISTORY TIMELINE

| | |
|---|---|
| **70** | Temple in Jerusalem destroyed |
| **787** | Second Ecumenical Council of Nicaea addresses iconoclasm |
| **1854** | Dogma of the Immaculate Conception is pronounced |
| **1962** | Second Vatican Council convenes |

Go to page 348 for more

## Our Catholic Tradition

- Catholics are connected with each other across time through prayer, practices, and the celebration of the liturgy. (CCC, 960–961)

- Mary has a special role in God's plan, and by saying "Yes" to God, she became the Mother of his Son and of all those who believe in him. She is the greatest of Saints. (CCC, 967–970)

- As the Church faced many internal and external challenges to unity and accurate expressions of faith, faith-filled men and women have made an impact on how the Church responded to the needs of the time. (CCC, 853)

## Our Catholic Life

- The Communion of Saints is everyone who believes in and follows Jesus: those Church members on Earth, the souls being purified in Purgatory, and the Saints in Heaven. (CCC, 962)

- All of us are called to be Saints, holy men and women who accept God's friendship and live lives of service to others. The Pope declares some people canonized Saints for their lives of heroic virtue and holiness. (CCC, 825–828)

- The documents and decisions from the Second Vatican Council invite all the members of the Church to give a Catholic response to the challenges and opportunities the modern world presents. (CCC, 748)

# The Communion of Saints

## ♡ Let Us Pray

**Leader:** O God, you are wonderful and loving to have called forth heroes in the faith. They show us by their lives the struggles and rewards of following the Lord every day.

"I believe I shall see the LORD's goodness
    in the land of the living.
Wait for the LORD, take courage;
    be stouthearted, wait for the LORD!" **Psalm 27:13–14**

**All:** Lord, bring us together.

## 📖 Scripture

"…are you unaware that we who were baptized into Christ Jesus were baptized into his death? We were indeed buried with him through baptism into death, so that, just as Christ was raised from the dead by the glory of the Father, we too might live in newness of life. For if we have grown into union with him through a death like his, we shall also be united with him in the resurrection. …. If, then, we have died with Christ, we believe that we shall also live with him. We know that Christ, raised from the dead, dies no more; death no longer has power over him. Consequently, you too must think of yourselves as [being] dead to sin and living for God in Christ Jesus." **Romans 6:3–9, 11**

### Have you ever thought...

• What does it mean to die in Christ so to live with him?

• How are you a part of the Communion of Saints?

# Getting Started

In this chapter, you will understand what the Catholic Church means by the term *Communion of Saints*, identify familiar sacramentals and learn how they add to our worship experience, and explore how art can enrich the prayer life of the Church.

Catholic Faith Words

- Communion of Saints
- sacramentals
- Stations of the Cross
- Paschal Candle
- icons

In the web, write the names of Saints, loved ones who have died, and prayer practices and devotions that remind you that the whole Church is united in Jesus Christ.

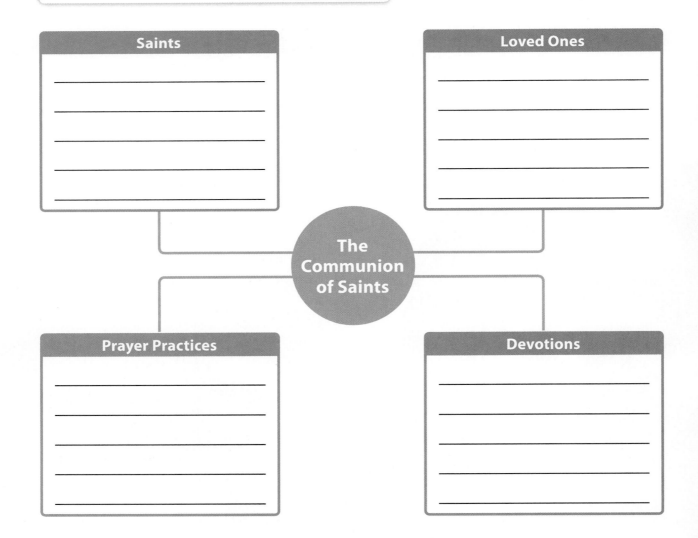

**Saints**

_____

_____

_____

_____

**Loved Ones**

_____

_____

_____

_____

_____

**The Communion of Saints**

**Prayer Practices**

_____

_____

_____

_____

_____

**Devotions**

_____

_____

_____

_____

_____

© Our Sunday Visitor

## WRITE

**Gone, but Not Forgotten**  Who is someone that you wish you could talk to but he or she has died?

_____

Tell that person what is going on in your life right now.

_____

_____

_____

_____

_____

_____

Write a short reflection telling God why that person is special to you.

_____

_____

_____

_____

_____

_____

_____

_____

_____

_____

Ask your loved one to pray for you.

# You Are Not Alone

**What is the Communion of Saints?**

You may have experienced a loss of a loved one, a friend, or relative. It can take a long time to see how the person who has died is still with you in your memories, the things you do now, or things you learned from and shared with the person. In the Catholic Church, we recognize this connection with those who have died in a special way.

## Celebrating Life

Living in New Orleans, Louisiana, is a unique experience. Funerals are often festive. Mourners march to the cemetery twirling colorful umbrellas, while a brass band plays "When the Saints Go Marching In."

This celebration draws a bridge between life and death, and shows how Catholics think differently when it comes to concepts like time and family. Spiritually, we live in the

past, present, and future. We are connected to Jesus, to all the Church members who lived in the past, and those who live now.

We call this unity of Church members on Earth, in Purgatory, and in Heaven the **Communion of Saints**. We all want to be included among the Saints—God's holy people, living and dead. That begins now, through holy things and events such as the Eucharist, which brings us together with many believers to form one Body in Christ.

This vision of the community of Saints goes back to the earliest days of our Church. When we remember those days, we have a "communion" with those early Christians who are alive with God today!

© Our Sunday Visitor

**A funeral procession in New Orleans**

## CATHOLICS TODAY

In Mexico on November 1 and 2, Catholics celebrate, honor, and pray for the dead in a gathering known as *Dia de los Muertos,* or Day of the Dead. Cemeteries and streets are lined with flowers, paper skeletons and skulls, and candy. People build altars to their departed, filled with offerings of candles, incense, marigolds, photos of their relatives, and *calaveras,* small skulls made out of sugar. People celebrate with food, music, and dancing, mocking the decorative skeletons with sayings such as, "Death is so skinny and weak she cannot carry me." The festivities reflect a tradition of living with joy in the face of death.

## Being in Communion

We call the Eucharist "Holy Communion" because it unites us with Christ and the Communion of Saints in a special way. We offer our prayers for those who have died not only at their funeral Masses, but every time we celebrate the Eucharist, when we pray for those "who have gone before us marked with the sign of faith."

We're also in communion with all the Church members—those with us and those who have died—when we share our talents to support each other and the Church. When we hug a friend who's hurting, sing in the choir, or share our lunch with someone who's hungry, we serve Jesus and live in solidarity with all people.

We connect with them in many ways, such as the names of Saints that we take at Baptism and Confirmation. But we especially remember them in our prayers. The Saints in Heaven are intercessors who pray with and for us to God. When we talk about praying to the Saints, what we really mean is that we are asking them to pray to God with and for us. We believe their holy friendship draws us closer to God. We also pray for the souls in Purgatory, that they will have eternal rest in Heaven.

On November 1, All Saints Day, we remember in a special way all the Saints who are with God in Heaven. On November 2, All Souls Day, we pray for the souls being purified in Purgatory.

## LIST AND DISCUSS

Choose three of the following Saints to discover what organizations or groups of people call them their patron Saints. Discuss why you think each Saint is the patron of that particular cause or group.

- Saint Thomas Aquinas
- Saint Cecilia
- Saint Clare of Assisi
- Saint Josephine Bakhita
- Saint Vincent de Paul
- Saint Augustine

## Holiness Is All Around You

How do sacramentals help us?

The moment you step inside your church, you're surrounded by sacred things. You dip your hand in holy water and make the Sign of the Cross. Your eyes are drawn to the cross near the altar. Candles, bells, and incense awaken your senses. There's no doubt you're on holy ground.

© Our Sunday Visitor

**Sacramentals** are sacred blessings, objects, and actions that help us respond to the grace received in the Seven Sacraments. Although they aren't actual Sacraments that bring us grace, these things do bring us closer to God and strengthen the spiritual side of our everyday lives.

On many Sundays, you'll see special blessings. Catechists or lectors might be blessed for their ministries in the Church. Mothers often are blessed on Mother's Day, and teenagers might be blessed when they get their driver's licenses. Even certain things that help us in our lives—everything from medals to motorcycles—can be blessed. In some parts of the world, Catholic fishermen even have their boats blessed. These blessings always include a prayer and some special sign, like the Sign of the Cross or the sprinkling of holy water, which reminds us of Baptism.

> **What sights, smells, or sounds make your parish church feel sacred to you?**

### Catholic Faith Words

**sacramentals** sacred blessings, objects, and actions that remind us of God, are made sacred through the prayers of the Church, and that help us respond to the grace received in the Sacraments

**Stations of the Cross** images of fourteen scenes that help us think and pray about Jesus' suffering, Death, and burial

**Paschal Candle** a large, white candle that is lit from the Easter fire, and is used during the Easter season and at Baptisms and funerals as a symbol of the Resurrection

## Special Sacramentals

One of the most uniquely Catholic sacramentals is the crucifix—a cross with the body of Christ on it. This connects us with Jesus, the sacrifice he made for us, and the joy of his Resurrection.

**Stations of the Cross** are often found on the walls of the church building. These show fourteen scenes that help us think and pray about Jesus' suffering, Death, and burial. At each station we pray, "We adore you, O Christ, and we bless you, because by your holy Cross you redeemed the world."

Incense is burned at special times, creating a fragrant scent and smoke. It has been used for ages as a way to honor God. One of the Magi brought frankincense to Jesus. Today we use it to bless the altar, the Book of Gospels, and people.

The Rosary is both a sacramental and a prayer devotion to Mary. The blessed Rosary beads—which are made up of five sets of ten smaller beads, some larger beads, and a small crucifix—help us mark the Hail Marys prayed as the various mysteries of the life of Jesus, Mary, and the Church are reflected upon. The Mysteries of the Rosary include the Joyous, Sorrowful, Glorious, and Luminous Mysteries.

Candles also have a lot of meaning. The **Paschal Candle** is lit from the Easter fire, and celebrates Jesus' rising at Easter. It symbolizes Resurrection at Baptisms and funerals. The sanctuary candle shines near the Tabernacle to show that Jesus is always present in the Blessed Sacrament. Smaller candles, or vigil lights, often glow near statues. They represent people's prayers and hopes.

Of all sacramentals, blessings have a special place. Blessings include praising God for his great works and gifts and praying that someone will use God's gifts wisely, be protected, grow in holiness, and more.

Underline the sacramentals that are in your home or classroom.

## IDENTIFY AND DESCRIBE

Think about the sacramentals you've seen or practices or prayers you've been involved in. Then, choosing one of the sacramentals described on this page (or another that is not shown), tell how you can use it to grow closer to God this week.

_____

_____

# Images and Imagination

How can art help you to pray?

For the past two thousand years, artists have been creating artistic paintings and other images of Jesus. Early on, **icons**, or religious pictures in a certain style, showed Jesus, Mary, and other holy people. It's said that Saint Luke drew some of the first icons of Jesus and Mary.

## Not Idolatry

Many beautiful paintings, mosaics, and statues were created in the early centuries of the Church. Unfortunately, during the early Middle Ages, some Eastern Tradition Christians in southern Europe and Asia treated these images as idols. Other people believed that such idol worship violated the First Commandment, which says we shouldn't worship false gods. In the year A.D. 730, Emperor Leo III ordered that all crucifixes, statues, and paintings be destroyed. Iconoclasts, or image breakers, were sent out to destroy Church artwork. This continued until A.D. 787, when a Church council ruled that icons, if used properly, can help

Christians worship God. Today, beautiful icons cover the walls of many Eastern Catholic churches.

When we venerate or honor an image, we honor the person that image portrays. It's like cherishing a portrait or possession of a beloved relative. It's a sign of respect for that person, but it doesn't replace the unique love and adoration we give to God. It doesn't violate the First Commandment. (See Exodus 20:2–5.)

Most churches, for example, have a statue of Mary, the Mother of Jesus. You often will see people pray in front of this statue. They are honoring Mary for the great love she showed by bringing God's Son into our world. Likewise, God greatly loves Mary, so we ask her to pray for us. We honor Mary, but we worship God. We pray *with* Mary and pray *to* God.

## Two Images, One Artist

There are many awesome pieces of religious art, but Michelangelo created two of the greatest around 1500. His marble sculpture *Pietà* shows Mary lovingly holding the body of Jesus after the Crucifixion. This statue is found in a chapel at St. Peter's Basilica in the Vatican. Michelangelo's best-known work is a mural on the ceiling of the Sistine Chapel, also in the Vatican. It shows many scenes from the Bible, including God creating the world. These two works are true labors of love.

## Artistic License

Back in the Middle Ages, artists often showed Jesus in fancy settings. Marble pillars and velvet curtains might surround him and he might be wearing clothes fit for royalty, perhaps holding a gold chalice. But the Holy Family was a working-class family, likely living in a very simple house, in solidarity with the poor.

Many images show a light-skinned, well-groomed Jesus. Chances are, as a roaming preacher in long-ago Palestine, he had darker skin and a scruffier style, like many of the people he taught. Artists often draw Jesus to look like those who will see their art, so their audience can relate to Jesus.

Other forms of art have developed to help us understand our faith. Catholic churches are known for their stained-glass windows. Although these are beautiful, they can also be practical. In the Middle Ages, when very few people besides the clergy could read, great churches were designed to include stained-glass windows that showed stories from the Bible. These helped common people learn the stories of their faith even though they could not read words—they "read" the stories in the windows.

**Michelangelo's *Pietá* (below) still inspires artists today to create sculpture and art depicting Mary and Jesus.**

### 📖 Go to the Source

Read Exodus 20:2–5 (the First Commandment). Discuss how statues and other religious images can help us in worshipping God.

## IN SUMMARY ▸ Catholics Believe

Catholics are connected with each other across time through prayer, practices, and the celebration of the liturgy.

- The Communion of Saints is everyone who believes in and follows Jesus: Church members here on Earth, souls being purified in Purgatory, and the Saints in Heaven.

- Sacramentals are holy objects, prayers, and practices that help us respond to God's grace and bring us closer to him.

- Religious art, especially icons, helps us to honor the Saints and glorify God.

## Our Catholic Life

Symbols and memories keep us in touch with loved ones who have died. Old letters and pictures—or even a holy card from their funeral service—help us remember them and hold them in our prayers. Rediscover a song, a scent, or a taste that brings you and your thoughts back to someone in your life who is no longer with you. And remember to pray for them even though they aren't with you on Earth. They are part of the **Communion of Saints,** and it is part of our faith to pray for the dead as well as those still alive. Pray as well to the Saints for their intercession on behalf of those who have died, and pray to God that our Church will be unified, in this world and across all time.

> This week do one thing to honor someone you knew who has died.

# People of Faith

### Saint André Bessette, 1845–1937

Alfred Bessette's parents died when he was young. He lived with relatives, but because he was often ill, he didn't receive much education. Because he'd been prayerful and devout from childhood, his pastor suggested that he join the Congregation of Holy Cross, where he took the name Brother André. André had a special devotion to Saint Joseph. Over the years, many miraculous cures were attributed to his prayers, although he insisted that the credit be given to Saint Joseph. When André died at the age of 91, a million people filed by his coffin. The Church celebrates his feast day on **January 6.**

For more, go to
**aliveinchrist.osv.com**

## WRITE

Think of someone special in your life who has died. Write a prayer or poem thanking God for the gift he or she was in your life, and asking your friend or relative to remember you while he or she is with God.

_____

_____

_____

_____

_____

_____

_____

_____

_____

_____

## ♥ Reflection on the Saints

**Leader:** Let us recognize that Jesus is present and listening to us now.

Close your eyes. Take a deep, relaxing breath, and enter into the reflection:

*Read the following, slowly and with reflection.*

Our God is a wonderful and loving God, who has called forth heroes in the faith who have shown us by their lives the struggles and rewards of commitment and of following the Lord every day.

*(pause)*

We look to the Saints
and ask them to pray for us,
to be with us as we walk the road of faith.

*(pause)*

We take into our hearts
these holy men and women,
as people who can teach us
what it means to follow Jesus.

*Read slowly and reverently. After each, all respond "pray for us."*

Holy Mary, Mother of God,
Saint John the Baptist,
Saint Joseph,
Saint Peter and Saint Paul,
Saint Andrew and Saint Stephen,
Saint Francis and Saint Dominic,
Saint Mary Magdalene,

*Other Saints can be added; then conclude with the following:*

All holy men and women,
those Saints in your own families.

Loving Father,
we thank you for those who have gone before us,
for those whose lives have taught us,
and who chose to embrace the life
of Jesus, your Son. Amen.

 *Sing or play "Litany"*

Go to **aliveinchrist.osv.com** for an interactive review.

**A** Work with Words **Complete each sentence with the correct term.**

1. Sacramentals are sacred

   _____ and

   _____ that help us
   respond to the grace received in the Seven
   Sacraments.

2. The _____ show(s)
   fourteen scenes that help us think and pray
   about Jesus' suffering, Death, and burial.

3. _____ are religious
   pictures of Jesus, Mary, and other holy people
   illustrated in a certain style and traditional
   among Eastern Christians.

4. The unity of Church members on Earth,
   in Purgatory, and in Heaven, is the

   _____.

5. The Emperor Leo III ordered that

   _____ destroy
   all crucifixes, statues, and paintings.

**B** Check Understanding **Indicate whether the following statements are true or false. Then rewrite false statements to make them true.**

6. When someone has died, Catholics offer
   prayers for them at their funeral Mass and in
   private prayer. **True/False**

   _____

   _____

7. Saints are our intercessors who pray with and
   for us to God. **True/False**

   _____

   _____

8. On All Saints Day, the Church prays for the
   souls being purified in Purgatory. **True/False**

   _____

   _____

9. Blessings are special sacramentals that include
   praising God for his great works and gifts.
   **True/False**

   _____

   _____

10. Catholics believe that when we venerate or
    honor an image, we worship the person that
    image portrays. **True/False**

   _____

   _____

**C** Make Connections **On a separate sheet of paper, write a one-paragraph response to the question: When have you been affected by a symbol or image that relates to Jesus? Write about the picture or symbol and its effect on you.**

# Examples for Living

## ❤ Let Us Pray

**Leader:** Lord, give us the courage we need to become saintly.

He will receive blessings from the LORD,
    and justice from his saving God.
Such is the generation that seeks him,
    that seeks the face of the God of Jacob." **Psalm 24:3, 4, 5-6**

**All:** Lord, help us follow your example.

## 📖 Scripture

"Blessed are the poor in spirit,
    for theirs is the kingdom of heaven.
Blessed are they who mourn,
    for they will be comforted.
Blessed are the meek,
    for they will inherit the land.
Blessed are they who hunger
    and thirst for righteousness,
    for they will be satisfied.
Blessed are the merciful,
    for they will be shown mercy.

Blessed are the clean of heart,
    for they will see God.
Blessed are the peacemakers,
    for they will be called children of God.
Blessed are they who are persecuted
    for the sake of righteousness,
    for theirs is the kingdom of heaven.

Blessed are you when they insult you and persecute you and utter every kind of evil against you [falsely] because of me. Rejoice and be glad, for your reward will be great in heaven." **Matthew 5:2–12**

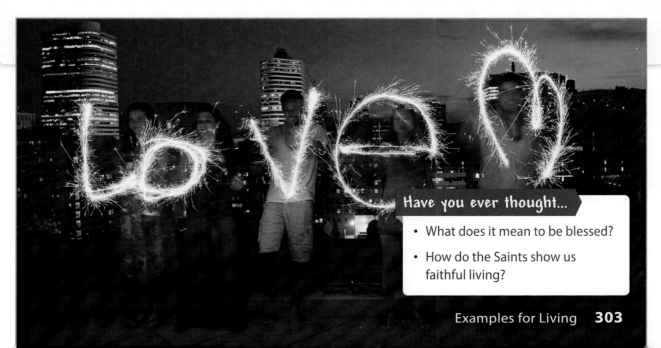

### Have you ever thought...

- What does it mean to be blessed?
- How do the Saints show us faithful living?

# Getting Started

In this chapter, you will learn to identify how particular Saints are examples of faithful living, look at Mary's special role in the Communion of Saints and how the Church honors her as the greatest of all the Saints, and study the process of how people are named as Saints by the Church.

Catholic Faith Words

- Assumption
- devotions
- Immaculate Conception
- canonization
- beatification

In the web below, name some feasts that honor Mary and her contribution to the Church. Write why each feast is important.

**Feasts that Honor Mary**

## WRITE

**Questions for Our Saints**  Read the Scripture passage Matthew 5:2–12 and think about the ways the Saints have lived out the Beatitudes. The Saints span the history of the Church, from her beginning to the 20th century. What questions would you ask one or more of the Saints? For each of the categories listed below, write some of your questions.

Family_____

_____

_____

_____

_____

Friends_____

_____

_____

_____

_____

Jesus _____

_____

_____

_____

_____

Work _____

_____

_____

_____

_____

**Go to the Source**
Read *Luke 1:39–45.*
How does Elizabeth
recognize that Mary will
be the Mother of God?

# Mary's Special Place in God's Plan

**How would life be different if Mary had not said "Yes" to God?**

Who are the everyday heroes in your life who inspire you? Who demonstrates a virtue that you want to also develop? As Catholics, we have always seen Mary as such a person, a person of authentic faith.

## Scripture

The Angel Gabriel came to Mary, saying "Hail, favored one! The Lord is with you."

But Mary was greatly troubled at what the angel said and pondered what sort of greeting this might be. Then the angel said to her, "Do not be afraid, Mary, for you have found favor with God. Behold, you will conceive in your womb and bear a son, and you shall name him Jesus. He will be great, and will be called the Son of the Most High . . . of his kingdom there will be no end."

Gabriel continued, "The holy Spirit will come upon you, and the power of the Most High will overshadow you. Therefore the child to be born will be holy, the Son of God."

Mary said, "Behold, I am the handmaid of the Lord. May it be done to me according to your word." *Luke 1:26–38*

## Humble, Yet Honored

Who could blame Mary for being confused and worried? This announcement must have puzzled her. But then Gabriel explained that it was by God's power that she was going to have a child. This incredible honor could cause great scandal. Did she wonder how Joseph would react? Mary took a leap of faith and said she would do God's will.

The Angel Gabriel's visit to Mary to announce that she would be the Mother of God is known as the Annunciation. After the angel's visit, Mary went to her cousin Elizabeth, who was also expecting a child.

Elizabeth's reaction when she saw Mary is quite famous: "Blessed are you among women, and blessed is the fruit of your womb" (Luke 1:42). Mary was a virgin at Jesus' conception, and she remained a virgin throughout her life.

Mary's "yes" was the first of many sacrifices she made for God. She gave birth to Jesus in a stable instead of in her home. She and Joseph spent the early days of Jesus' life protecting him from the wrath of an angry king.

Jesus' sacrifice on the Cross hurt Mary greatly as well. Her son was dying in a brutal way. But even at such a difficult and sad time, Mary believed in her Son and acted with courage. As she stood near the Cross with the Apostle John, she heard Jesus tell her, "Woman, behold, your son." And to John, he said, "Behold, your mother" (John 19:26–27). Mary would not only become mother to John, but to all who love and follow Christ. She is our Mother and a model of faith.

Mary lived her life in total obedience to God. She was without sin. At the end of her life, Mary's body and soul were "taken up" (assumed) into Heaven. We call this the **Assumption**. It's different from Jesus' Ascension because Mary's journey to Heaven happened through God's power. She could not do this herself. She shares in the glory of Jesus' Resurrection, and this gives us hope that someday we, too, will rise to share life in Heaven with Jesus and Mary.

### Catholic Faith Words

**Assumption** the Church teaching that, at the end of her life, Mary, body and soul, was "taken up" (assumed) into Heaven. The Church celebrates the Feast of the Assumption on August 15.

## LIST

When you say "Yes" to a big commitment, it really means that you have to say yes to a lot of things as you live through that commitment. Saying yes to owning a pet means yes to training, to feeding, to exercising, to grooming, etc. Think of a commitment that you have made. On the lines below write three times you had to say yes.

1. _____
2. _____
3. _____

# The Greatest of Saints

**How does the Church honor Mary?**

All four daughters of one Catholic family have some form of Mary in their name. One Catholic diocese has forty-five parishes named St. Mary's. In the Church's liturgical year, there are sixteen feast days marked to honor Mary. And, people in different parts of the world consider May and October special months to honor Mary with popular **devotions** and practices.

No one who knew this humble Jewish girl from Palestine would have imagined so much honor would one day be given to her. She is the greatest Saint, a person who led a holy life giving God glory and who enjoys eternal life with God in Heaven.

## Mark Your Calendar

People around the world celebrate on New Year's Day. It's an important day for the Church, too, as we celebrate the Solemnity of Mary, Mother of God. We honor Mary for bringing the Son of God to us.

This day is one of three Holy Days of Obligation devoted to Mary. Being so close to Christmas, it also reminds us that what we believe about Mary is based on what we believe about Jesus. Her life is a continuing inspiration to our faith. The more we learn about and get closer to Mary, the stronger our faith in Jesus becomes.

The second of these most special days is August 15, when we celebrate the Feast of the Assumption and our belief that God took Mary—body and soul—into Heaven. The third special day is December 8, the Feast of the **Immaculate Conception**, when we celebrate the special care God took by creating Mary free from Original Sin.

## Devotions

Devotions are prayers and practices that honor Jesus, Mary, and the Saints. One of the most popular devotions to Mary is the Rosary, which Catholics have prayed for eight hundred years. If you look at the Rosary as just a string of beads to hold as you pray lots of Hail Marys, you're missing

> ### Catholic Faith Words
>
> **devotions** popular prayers or practices that honor Jesus, Mary, and the Saints
>
> **Immaculate Conception** the truth that Mary was preserved free from Original Sin from the moment of her conception. The Church celebrates the Feast of the Immaculate Conception on December 8.

## WHERE IT HAPPENED

In 1917, three children experienced apparitions (special visions or appearances of Jesus, Mary, or other Saints) in the town of Fátima, Portugal. Mary told them that God wanted people to seek forgiveness and live faithful lives. She told people to pray the Rosary to help bring peace to our world. At least thirty thousand people from all over Europe—believers and nonbelievers alike—witnessed the final apparition of Mary, during which, they said, the sun danced in the sky.

In 1981, on the anniversary of the first apparition, Pope Saint John Paul II was wounded in an assassination attempt. He credited Mary with saving his life. Two years later, on that same anniversary date, he went to Fátima to consecrate the world to the Immaculate Heart of Mary. In doing so, he fulfilled one of Our Lady's promises made there in 1917 to three little children.

**Pilgrims honor Mary in Fátima, Portugal**

the point. The Mysteries of the Rosary help us focus on events in the lives of Jesus and Mary and apply them to the challenges and good times in our lives. For example, you might pray the Joyful Mysteries of the Rosary, thinking first about the Annunciation. As you pray the Hail Marys, you might also ask God to come into your life in a special way.

May is a month many people dedicate to Mary. Many parishes have a devotion called "May Crowning." Children set fresh flowers around a statue of Mary, and a crown is placed on the statue. This honors Mary, whom God chose as Mother of Jesus and Queen of Heaven.

> **How does our honoring Mary strengthen our relationship with Jesus?**

## DESCRIBE

How does your family, parish, and school honor Mary? Describe one of those ways here, then work with a small group to plan a special way for your class to honor Mary.

_____

_____

_____

_____

_____

© Our Sunday Visitor

# The Church of Saints

**Why are the Saints important to the Church?**

Raymond Kolbe had a vision of Mary when he was twelve years old. She offered him two crowns and asked if he'd accept either. One crown was white, symbolizing that he should live a pure and holy life. The other was red, meaning that he should die for his faith. Raymond said that he'd take both.

Five years later, when he began studying for the priesthood, he took the name "Maximilian." He became a great priest who founded monasteries and magazines, first in his native Poland, and then in Japan and India. He was very devoted to Mary and worked to bring sinners back to Christ.

Impressive as his life was, Maximilian is best known for how he died. After the Nazis invaded Poland in World War II, Maximilian protected refugees and published materials that criticized the Nazis. He was thrown into Auschwitz, the Nazi prison camp.

One day in 1941, a prisoner escaped. Camp rules required that ten men be killed to make up for the escape. When a married man who had young children was chosen to die, Maximilian volunteered to die in his place. He lived as Jesus commanded, so great was his love for his fellow man. "No one has greater love than this, to lay down one's life for one's friends" (John 15:13). After a holy life, he died a martyr's death. He had both crowns.

> **How do you think Maximilian found the courage to give up his life?**

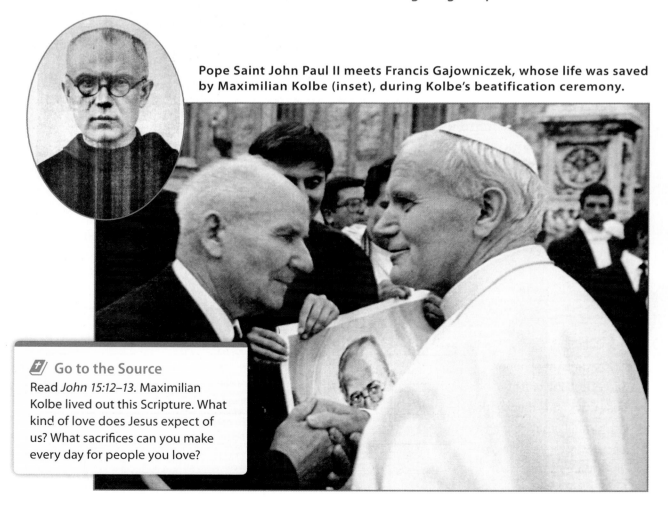

**Pope Saint John Paul II meets Francis Gajowniczek, whose life was saved by Maximilian Kolbe (inset), during Kolbe's beatification ceremony.**

### Go to the Source

Read *John 15:12–13*. Maximilian Kolbe lived out this Scripture. What kind of love does Jesus expect of us? What sacrifices can you make every day for people you love?

## Catholic Faith Words

**canonization** a declaration by the Pope naming a person a Saint. Canonized Saints have special feast days or memorials in the Church's calendar.

**beatification** the second step in the process of becoming a Saint, in which a venerable person is recognized by the Church as having brought about a miracle through his or her prayers of intercession

## Role Models

**Canonization** is the process by which the the Pope declares someone a Saint, after a process involving beatification. In 1971, Maximilian Kolbe was beatified, a step on the way to becoming a Saint. In the crowd at his **beatification** ceremony was Francis Gajowniczek, the man for whom Maximilian gave his life.

When the Church names Saints, it lifts up holy people as heroes of our faith. When Maximilian Kolbe was canonized, named a Saint, by Pope Saint John Paul II in 1982, he became a hero not just to the Gajowniczek family, but to all of us.

We celebrate the Feast of Saint Maximilian Kolbe on August 14. He is with Mary not only in Heaven, but also on the Church's calendar, as the Feast of Mary's Assumption is the next day, August 15. These feasts of Mary

and other holy women and men spiritually unite the Church on Earth with the Church in Heaven. When we remember Saints, we give glory to Jesus for using them to show us the way to his Father.

The Saints not only intercede for us in prayer, but they also serve as role models. Their stories inspire us to live holy lives. They made great sacrifices for their faith, often dying to protect their virtues.

## The Road to Sainthood

All faithful members of the Church are called Saints because Jesus has called us to be the holy People of God. In another sense, the term Saints refers only to some deceased members of the Church who have led lives of heroic virtue, have been canonized by the Church, and are in Heaven.

### DISCUSS

Because you have been united to Jesus in Baptism, by the power of the Holy Spirit you have been united to the Communion of Saints. Being part of the Church is like having a team that supports you, coaches you, and challenges you. Discuss one way the Church living and in Heaven supports you, challenges you, and coaches you.

## IN SUMMARY  Catholics Believe

The Church honors Mary and all the Saints with special feasts and devotions.

- Mary has a special role in God's plan, and by saying "Yes" to God, she became the Mother of his Son and of all those who believe in him. We believe she was born free of sin, remained free of sin, and was taken into Heaven body and soul.

- The Church honors Mary as the greatest of Saints and honors her with many feast days and devotions. Mary continues to care for us, praying and interceding for us.

- All of us are called to be Saints, holy men and women who accept God's friendship and serve others. Some people are canonized Saints for their heroic virtue and holiness.

## Our Catholic Life

We sometimes think of sainthood as something unreachable—something that's more about being perfect than about being one of God's people—or something achieved only through suffering or even martyrdom. But **sainthood** is something to which we can all work. Think about the everyday Saints in your own life, people who serve as good role models and show the love of Jesus Christ and his message through their work or just the way they interact with those they meet. From following the examples of Christ and these people, you can learn the qualities of a Saint. Pray to God for the strength to live your faith amid life's challenges, and ask the Saints for their intercession on your behalf as well.

> What is your biggest challenge as you follow the path toward sainthood?

## People of Faith

### Blessed Mariam Thresia Chiramel Mankidiyan, 1876–1926

Mariam Thresia grew up with a strong devotion to God. In her village of Kerala, India, she gave medical and spiritual care to the suffering. With the blessings of the Vicar Apostolic of her province, she had a prayer house built and moved in with three companions, where they ministered to the poor and sick. Under Mariam's guidance, the Congregation of the Holy Family came into existence. Over time, she opened three convents, two schools, two hostels, a study house, and an orphanage. The Church celebrates her feast day on **June 6**.

For more, go to
**aliveinchrist.osv.com**

## IDENTIFY

Pick two or three People of Faith from this text and write what you see in their lives as heroic virtue. Discuss those people's virtues and the good things they've done for others.

1. _____
_____
_____

2. _____
_____
_____

3. _____
_____
_____

## ♥ Litany of Mary

**Leader:** Mary, God chose you as the Mother of his Son and called all nations and generations to bless the gift of grace he gave you. In the company of those who have gone before us, we call upon you in prayer.

To each title, respond: *pray for us.*

Holy Mary
Mother of God
Mother of our redemption
Mother of a lost child
Mother of comfort and understanding
Mother who shares our joys
Mother who endures our sorrows
Mother whose heart was pierced by a sword
Mother most merciful
Woman responsive to God's Word
Woman willing to believe the impossible
Woman who rejoices in her lowliness
Woman with an undivided heart
Woman wrapped in mystery
Woman moved by the Spirit
Woman champion of the poor and lowly

Woman graced by a husband's love
Woman widowed by a husband's death
Woman at the Cross
Woman patient and waiting
Woman clothed with the sun
Queen of the fullness of times
Queen of beauty unalloyed
Queen of integrity
Queen of painful meetings
Queen of all our heart's treasure
Queen of our destiny
Queen of peace. ... pray for us.

Almighty Father, in your wisdom and goodness you chose Mary to be the Mother of your Son, Jesus. Through her intercession, remember us and our needs. Protect us from all that keeps us from you and bring us the happiness that comes from trusting in you alone.

**All:** Amen.

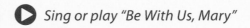 *Sing or play "Be With Us, Mary"*

Go to **aliveinchrist.osv.com** for an interactive review.

**A** **Work with Words** **Circle the letter of the choice that best completes the sentence.**

1. The title ____ Conception refers to the truth that Mary was preserved free from Original Sin from the moment of her conception.
   - **a.** Annunciation
   - **b.** Assumption
   - **c.** Immaculate
   - **d.** Ascension

2. The Angel Gabriel's visit to Mary to tell her she would be the Mother of God is called the ____.
   - **a.** Annunciation
   - **b.** Assumption
   - **c.** Aspiration
   - **d.** Ascension

3. A(n) ____ is a person who led a holy life on Earth giving God glory and enjoys eternal life with God in Heaven.
   - **a.** disciple
   - **b.** priest
   - **c.** angel
   - **d.** Saint

4. The ____ is the Church teaching that, at the end of her life, Mary—body and soul—was "taken up" into Heaven.
   - **a.** Annunciation
   - **b.** Assumption
   - **c.** Second Coming
   - **d.** Ascension

5. ____ are prayers and practices that honor Jesus, Mary, and the Saints.
   - **a.** Devotions
   - **b.** Obligations
   - **c.** Rosaries
   - **d.** Sacramentals

**B** **Check Understanding** **Complete each sentence with the correct term.**

6. The Solemnity of Mary, Mother of God, is one of three Holy Days of _____ devoted to Mary.

7. The Mysteries of the _____ help us focus on events in the lives of Jesus and Mary and apply them to our lives.

8. Special visions or appearances of Jesus, Mary, or the Saints are known as _____.

9. _____ is the process by which the Pope declares someone a Saint.

10. All faithful members of the Church are called _____ because Jesus has called us to be the holy People of God.

**C** **Make Connections** **Write a one-paragraph response to the question: Think of someone you know who could be on the way to sainthood. What do you see in his or her life that inspires you? Write an encouraging note to that person telling him or her about how his or her life has helped you.**

_____

_____

_____

_____

_____

_____

# From Age to Age

## 💙 Let Us Pray

**Leader:** God our Father, you have always loved us throughout all of history. In these times that can be filled with fear and doubt, you call us to be your Church. You call us to be your voice.

"Let everything that has breath
    give praise to the LORD!
Hallelujah!" **Psalm 150:6**

**All:** Lord, make us instruments of peace in the world.

## 📖 Scripture

"Beloved, do not be surprised that a trial by fire is occurring among you, as if something strange were happening to you. But rejoice to the extent that you share in the sufferings of Christ, so that when his glory is revealed you may also rejoice exultantly. If you are insulted for the name of Christ, blessed are you, for the Spirit of glory and of God rests upon you … The God of all grace who called you to his eternal glory through Christ [Jesus] will himself restore, confirm, strengthen, and establish you after you have suffered a little. To him be dominion forever. Amen."

1 Peter 4:12-14; 5:10-11

### Have you ever thought...

- How does God give you the strength you need to face challenges in life?
- How can you accept the call of serving God?

# Getting Started

In this chapter, you will come to understand what it means to grow in wisdom, explore the growth of the early Church and her progress during the Middle Ages and the Reformation, and consider how the Church responds to the needs of the world today.

## Catholic Faith Words

- martyr
- monastery

1. In the chart below, write some challenges that our world faces today.

2. Then write some possible ways the Church can, or does, help address the situation.

| Challenges and the Church | |
|---|---|
| **The Challenges the World Faces** | **What the Church Can Do** |
| | |
| | |
| | |
| | |
| | |
| | |
| | |
| | |
| | |
| | |

**Life's Struggles, Life's Lessons** Identify a problem you experienced that you'd rather not repeat. Perhaps it involved a friendship, or a challenge at school. What lessons have you learned from older people that could help you address the struggle? Is there a person whom you could ask for advice? How do the words of Peter (1 Peter 4:12-14; 5:10-11) give you hope?

**The Problem**

_____

_____

_____

_____

_____

_____

_____

**Lessons Others Have Taught Me**

_____

_____

_____

_____

_____

_____

_____

_____

_____

**Who I Can Turn to For Help**

_____

_____

_____

_____

# The Early Church

**How did the Church spread and grow?**

From age to age, brave Christians have struggled to witness to their faith, but it was especially hard being Christian in the early years. Although Christian communities were small and scattered, the Roman Empire saw them as a threat. Christians ignored Roman gods, who were seen as the source of the emperors' power. For over two hundred years, emperors persecuted people who didn't worship their gods, torturing and killing thousands of Christians whom we honor as **martyrs**, people who gave up their lives for witnessing to Christ. Still, many people were inspired to become Christians because of the martyrs' courage and the Church's vision and charity. Most Christians feared being arrested because of their faith. So they worshipped in hiding, often in one another's homes.

## Free to Worship

Things changed when the emperor Constantine dreamed that he would conquer his enemies through a special sign of Christ. His soldiers marked their helmets with a cross. They won, and Constantine issued the Edict of Milan in A.D. 313, giving Christians the freedom to worship. Constantine supported the Church and eventually tried to run it. In 381, Christianity became the religion of the Roman Empire. This connection between Church and state would have an influence on the Church's history for many centuries to follow.

## Power Struggles

Everybody wanted a piece of the Roman Empire. Europe was in chaos, and the Church was one of the few institutions people could depend on. One leader who shined in the early Middle Ages (A.D. 500 to A.D. 1000) was Pope Gregory the Great, elected in A.D. 590. Gregory fed the poor, rebuilt churches, and opened schools for children. He also worked to prepare better priests. Gregory converted the marauding tribes and helped make peace in Spain, England, and other lands.

## The Pope or the Emperor

In A.D. 799, King Charlemagne (Charles the Great) was a warrior who supported Pope Leo III against kings trying to take over Rome. To thank him, the Pope crowned him Emperor of the Holy Roman Empire.

Charlemagne tried to bring power and unity back to the empire. When he won a battle,

**Crowning of Charlemagne as Holy Roman Emperor in A.D. 800 by Pope Leo III**

he insisted that the people he conquered become Christians. He made Latin the language used at Mass in Western Churches, a practice that continued until the 1960s.

This close connection between the Church and state caused confusion. Sometimes the emperor would obey the Pope, and other times he ignored the Church. The emperor's power often allowed him to force the Church to support his actions. The relationship between faith and political power that started with Constantine continued through Charlemagne. The identity of the Church was tied to that of the empire, and lost in the middle were believers.

The future Saint Benedict was about twenty years old when he fled Rome. At first, he lived alone in a cave. Then people came to

**Saint Stephen preaching in Jerusalem**

### Catholic Faith Words

**martyr** a person who gives up his or her life to witness to the truth of Christ and the faith. The word *martyr* means "witness."

**monastery** a building where a community of religious men (or sometimes women) join together in spirituality and service

him, inspired by how he balanced prayer and work. In A.D. 530, he built a **monastery**, a community of men who have taken vows of poverty, chastity, and obedience and have joined in spirituality and service. Benedict wrote rules about prayer, work, fasting, and community life that are still followed today. During the early Middle Ages, monasteries protected people, art, and writings from invaders. They also sent missionaries to convert invaders and restore Christianity.

## INTERVIEW

If you could ask a question of someone from the Church's history, who would it be and what would you ask?

_____

_____

_____

_____

_____

# The Church in Transition

**What changes took place in the Church during the Middle Ages and the Reformation?**

Most people in the Middle Ages (A.D. 500 to A.D. 1450) lived faithful lives. Many were peasants, unable to read or write, but who worked hard, had little, and found hope and happiness in the Church. It was the center of their lives. Sunday was the highlight of their week. The Mass brought beauty and mystery to their lives.

## A Challenging Time

Pope Gregory VII made a bold move to free the Church of politics. He ruled in A.D. 1077 that the Holy Roman Emperor couldn't appoint bishops.

Still, the Church depended on the emperor's protection. Pope Urban II convinced Christian kings to join forces for the Crusades, military efforts on behalf of the Church. The First Crusade, started in A.D. 1095, sought to regain the Holy Land from the Muslims and keep Christians safe on pilgrimages to Jerusalem. The Crusades continued for 150 years, and most failed.

As towns grew, cathedral schools and universities were founded. New religious orders emerged. In A.D. 1209, Saint Francis founded the Franciscans, who helped reform the Church through simple living and trust in God. At about the same time, Saint Dominic founded the Dominicans, who were great teachers.

During this same time, some Church members created a court to fight heresy known as the Inquisition. Many Dominican and Franciscan priests were inquisitors. They were seen as educated and pious, good judges of heresy or faithfulness. If heretics refused to confess, they could be burned at the stake, but most were ordered to do penance or make a pilgrimage to prove their repentance.

## A Painful Change

In the early 1500s, some people thought they could buy their way into Heaven. This led to abuse, often in the form of indulgences.

Indulgences are specific works or prayers, offered by the Church, for the remission of temporal punishment due to sins already forgiven. You still had to be sorry for your sins, but through indulgences, you could avoid temporal punishment and you would not suffer punishment in Purgatory. In some places, indulgences were sold and profits were made, which was against Church teaching.

In A.D. 1517, a priest named Martin Luther nailed a poster to the door of the church in Wittenberg, Germany, with his Ninety-five Theses. Luther protested the indulgences. Eventually, Luther's protest began the Protestant Reformation. He was excommunicated from the Catholic Church. He had originally wanted reform, not separation. However, thousands of Germans followed him away from the Church. From this group, numerous other Protestant religions came into being.

Then, in England, King Henry VIII, eager for a son to succeed him and fearing his wife could not have one, sought to divorce her. When the Pope refused, Henry founded the Anglican Church and made himself its head.

Catholic leaders gathered in Trent, Germany, between A.D. 1545 and 1567. The Council of Trent worked to make Church teachings clearer and discipline stronger. Colleges for training priests were formed and the Church became rededicated to the Seven Sacraments. These efforts were part of the Counter-Reformation.

## New Lands

As Europeans came into contact with Asia and the Americas, explorers and missionaries brought Catholicism to parts of Asia, and to South, Central, and North America. At times they met resistance, especially when they tried to impose their culture on people they were evangelizing. But their efforts helped make Catholicism the truly universal faith it is today.

King Henry VIII and Saint Thomas More in a scene from the film *A Man for All Seasons*

### DISCUSS AND NAME

Discuss in small groups the challenges missionaries might face today in foreign lands and locally. Name some ways your parish and school help to spread the Good News.

_____

_____

_____

📖 **Go to the Source**
Read *Matthew 28:16–20*. What do you think of the challenge to "make disciples of all nations"?

# The Church in the Modern World

**How is the Church responding to the needs of our time?**

Catholicism in America rode the waves of immigration, first from Europe and then from Latin America, Asia, and other lands. In some large cities, earlier Catholic immigrants from Germany, Poland, Italy, and Ireland might have established four separate ethnic parishes in the same neighborhood. Today, these churches may be places where Anglos, Europeans, Asians, Hispanics, or other ethnic groups worship, often together in the same place.

More than a billion people—about one-sixth of the world's population—call themselves Catholic. About 24 percent of Americans are Catholic. These numbers may seem impressive, but they tell a small part of the story.

## Mission: Still Possible

The Church is still a force for justice in the world. For over a century, she has protected the rights of workers. Like Jesus, she speaks out for the poor and outcasts in our world. She supports basic human rights such as education, health care, and voting. The Church encourages all people to be good stewards of the environment. And she protects the most vulnerable members of society—especially the unborn.

Pope Saint John Paul II was a modern disciple who spread the Gospel around the globe. He lived out the call of the Second Vatican Council to collaborate with other churches and apply our beliefs to the world's needs. In his travels, he promoted peace and solidarity, and encouraged young people to take an active role in the Church. His funeral in 2005 showed the love and respect he earned, as people from every walk of life gathered to honor him.

## Are We Up to the Challenge?

Our Church also faces challenges from within. Pope Benedict XVI said that the sexual abuse crisis reminds everyone of the need to protect the dignity of all God's children. And forces such as greed continue to distract us from our calling. Pope Francis has called for a "poor Church for the Poor."

Still, with the strength and guidance of the Holy Spirit, our Church will continue to grow and be a sign of God's Kingdom. Jesus reminds us that he is always with us in our challenges "until the end of the age" (Matthew 28:20).

## CONSIDER

What is an issue that you, as a Catholic, would like to get involved with? What issue(s) do you want to learn more about?

**I'd like to learn about . . .**

_____

_____

**I'd like to be involved in . . .**

_____

_____

## IN SUMMARY ▸ Catholics Believe

Faith-filled men and women have made an impact on how the Church responded to the needs of their time.

- The Church grew from a persecuted, illegal religion to the religion of the Roman Empire, and people like Augustine, Benedict, and Pope Gregory the Great helped believers keep their faith despite political and social situations.

- As the Church faced many internal and external challenges to unity and accurate expressions of faith, everyday people tried to maintain their belief, and people like Dominic and Francis tried to help the Church reform.

- The Second Vatican Council encouraged all the members of the Church to give a Catholic response to the challenges and opportunities the modern world presents.

## Our Catholic Life

Over the course of the year, you have learned about many Catholic role models, from the Church's early history to the present day. Think about how your view of your faith has changed since you began the year, and consider how these **role models** have influenced what you now know and believe about being Catholic. Recall some stories you know of people like Pope Saint John Paul II, Blessed Mother Teresa, or another modern Catholic witness. Think of the gifts they shared that helped them be a force for change, and consider how you can use your own gifts and talents to make a change in the world. See what more you can achieve, with God's help and the help of your Church.

> Who is your most consistent Catholic role model, from Church history or today?

## People of Faith

### Saint Marianne Cope, 1838–1918

Maria Anna Barbara Cope came to the United States from Germany with her family when she was a baby. She joined the Sisters of the Third Order of St. Francis in Syracuse, New York in 1862 and became the supervisor of St. Joseph's Hospital. She made it hospital policy to care for the sick, regardless of race or religion. She was called to new work in 1883, joining a Belgian priest, Saint Damien de Veuster, in ministering to the lepers on the island of Molokai, Hawaii. After Father Damien's death, Marianne took charge of the colony. The Church celebrates her feast day on **January 23**.

For more, go to **aliveinchrist.osv.com**

## IDENTIFY AND DESCRIBE

Many things are necessary in order for change to occur. Recall a change in the Church that you learned about in this chapter. Describe what the Church had to do in order to make that change happen. Then describe one change you see happening in the Church now.

_____

_____

_____

_____

_____

_____

_____

_____

_____

_____

## ♥ A Mission Prayer

**Leader:** Since Jesus called the Apostles, there have been faith-filled teachers, Saints, and missionaries for every generation. Today, these brave and prayerful followers inspire us to share the Good News and our Catholic faith.

**Reader 1:** Some of us will become missionaries, people who carry the Gospel message to those who've never heard it.

**Reader 2:** Some may become teachers who help many people to learn about the history of the Catholic Church.

**Reader 3:** Many of us will one day become parents. We will share our faith and values with our children.

**Leader:** All of us can remember and honor the brave witness of Saint Teresia Benedicta. She made many sacrifices and endured rejection, persecution, imprisonment, and execution. Jesus, give us the courage to share your life-giving Gospel wherever our journeys take us.

Let us now read and pray together this Journey Prayer by Saint Teresia Benedicta.

**All:** O my God, fill my soul with holy joy, courage and strength to serve you.

Enkindle your love in me and then walk with me along the next stretch of road before me.

I do not see very far ahead, but when I have arrived where the horizon now closes down, a new prospect will open before me and I shall meet with peace.

Amen.

▶ *Sing or play "Go Make a Difference"*

Go to **aliveinchrist.osv.com** for an interactive review.

**A** **Work with Words** **Circle the letter of the choice that best completes the sentence.**

1. Pope Saint John Paul II lived out the call of the Second Vatican Council to ___ other churches and apply our beliefs to the world's needs.
   a. collaborate with    c. join
   b. ignore    d. defy

2. A ___ is someone who gives up his or her life to witness to Christ.
   a. Saint    c. disciple
   b. martyr    d. monk

3. The sale of ___ was an abuse that centered on the practice relating to avoiding the temporal punishment for sins in Purgatory.
   a. holy water    c. salvation
   b. indulgences    d. Baptisms

4. A(n) ___ is a building where a religious community of men (or sometimes women) who take the vows of poverty, chastity, and obedience join together in spirituality and service.
   a. sainthood    c. monastery
   b. priesthood    d. inquisition

5. The Crusades were military efforts on behalf of the Church to regain the Holy ___.
   a. wealth    c. altars
   b. Land    d. emperor

**B** **Check Understanding** **Indicate whether the following statements are true or false. Then rewrite false statements to make them true.**

6. For over two hundred years, Roman emperors persecuted people who didn't worship their gods, torturing and killing many Christians. **True/False**

   _____

   _____

7. Constantine issued the Edict of Milan in A.D. 313 to free Christians of Roman rule. **True/False**

   _____

   _____

8. Benedict converted the tribes who invaded Europe, and helped make peace in Spain, England, and other lands. **True/False**

   _____

   _____

9. King Henry VIII founded the Anglican Church when the Pope refused to grant him a divorce. **True/False**

   _____

   _____

10. The Council of Trent was part of the Reformation, and worked to make Church teachings clearer and discipline stronger. **True/False**

    _____

    _____

**C** **Make Connections** **On a separate sheet of paper, write a one-paragraph response to the question: What political or theological issues in the Church affect your experience of faith today? Pick one and write about the effect it has on you.**

**A** Work with Words   Match the terms on the left with the correct definitions or descriptions on the right.

____ 1. Communion of Saints

____ 2. sacramentals

____ 3. icons

____ 4. blessings

____ 5. Annunciation

____ 6. Assumption

____ 7. Immaculate Conception

____ 8. devotions

____ 9. martyr

____ 10. Constantine

____ 11. Stations of the Cross

____ 12. iconoclasts

____ 13. monastery

____ 14. Saint

____ 15. Pope Gregory the Great

**a.** the Angel Gabriel's visit to Mary to tell her she would be the Mother of God

**b.** unity of Church members on Earth, in Purgatory, and in Heaven

**c.** the truth that Mary was preserved from Original Sin from the moment of her conception

**d.** when God took Mary—body and soul—into Heaven

**e.** special sacramentals that include praising God for his great works and gifts and praying for others

**f.** sacred blessings, objects, and gestures that help us respond to the grace received in the Seven Sacraments

**g.** Emperor who gave freedom of worship to Christians

**h.** prayers and practices that honor Jesus, Mary, and the Saints

**i.** religious pictures that illustrate Jesus, Mary, and other holy people in a certain style

**j.** someone who gives up his or her life to witness to Christ

**k.** a building where a community of men (or sometimes women) who have taken vows join together in spirituality and service

**l.** fourteen scenes that help us think about Jesus' suffering, Death, and burial

**m.** converted the tribes who invaded Europe and helped make peace in England, Spain, and elsewhere

**n.** a person whom the Pope declares has led a holy life on Earth and is enjoying eternal life with God in Heaven

**o.** were ordered to destroy crucifixes, statues, and paintings

© Our Sunday Visitor

**B** Check Understanding   Indicate whether the following statements are true or false. Then rewrite false statements to make them true.

16. Emperor Constantine ordered that iconoclasts destroy all crucifixes, statues, and paintings.  **True/False**

_____

_____

17. The Mysteries of the Rosary help us focus on events in the lives of Jesus and Mary and apply them to our lives.  **True/False**

_____

18. Visitations are special visions or appearances of Mary, Jesus, or the Saints.  **True/False**

_____

_____

19. A College of Cardinals is a building where a religious community of men (or sometimes women) who have taken vows join together in spirituality and service.  **True/False**

_____

_____

20. The Crusades were military efforts on behalf of the emperor to regain the Holy Land.  **True/False**

_____

_____

21. The Edict of Milan freed Christians from Roman rule.  **True/False**

_____

_____

22. Canonization is the process by which the Pope declares someone a Saint.  **True/False**

_____

_____

**C** Make Connections  **Write a short answer to these questions.**

**23.** Which Saint whom you have learned about has most influenced your
life? How has his or her example affected you?

_____

_____

_____

_____

_____

_____

**24.** Think about the struggles between the Church and government in
the past and today. What is the ideal relationship between Church
and government? Use specific examples from the history of the
Church to support your answer.

_____

_____

_____

_____

_____

_____

**25.** Which sacramentals do you use most in your prayer and worship life?
What connection do they help you keep with God, Jesus, and the
Catholic Church?

_____

_____

_____

_____

_____

_____

**Circle the letter of the response that correctly completes the statement.**

1. By virtue of our ____, we are called to take part in the mission of the Church.

   a. Confirmation

   b. confession

   c. salvation

   d. Baptism

2. The three offices of Christ are Priest, Prophet, and ____.

   a. Savior

   b. Shepherd

   c. King

   d. Pastor

3. Which devotion honors Jesus' Real Presence in the Eucharist?

   a. the Liturgy of the Hours

   b. the Stations of the Cross

   c. Adoration of the Blessed Sacrament

   d. the Litany of the Blessed Virgin Mary

4. Which of the following together are the sources of God's Divine Revelation to us?

   a. Conversion and Confession

   b. Salvation and Grace

   c. Sacred Scripture and Sacred Tradition

   d. Apostles and the Church

5. Saint Paul said that our bodies are temples of ____.

   a. the Church

   b. the Holy Spirit

   c. the Seven Sacraments

   d. sacred meaning

6. This group of people serve(s) through their Baptism and Confirmation in personal life, family life, social life, and parish life.

   a. laity

   b. priests

   c. monks

   d. clergy

7. The Transfiguration is when Jesus ____.

   a. instituted a sacramental remembrance of himself

   b. showed his parents that he would teach others about God

   c. revealed his Divine glory to his disciples on a mountaintop

   d. taught the Beatitudes, which give us a blueprint for living

8. God made a ____, or a sacred promise or agreement, with the Hebrew people, involving mutual commitments.

   a. covenant

   b. vow

   c. conversion

   d. tradition

9. When a Church teaching is ____, it is free from error.

   a. sacramental

   b. traditional

   c. infallible

   d. apostolic

10. Who was the first martyr to be killed for professing belief in Jesus?

   a. Paul

   b. Peter

   c. Stephen

   d. Lazarus

11. The ___ refers to the pilgrim Church on Earth, those being purified in Purgatory, and the blessed already in Heaven.

   a. Holy Communion

   b. Mystical Body of Christ

   c. Communion of Saints

   d. hierarchy

12. The Church is ___, or catholic, because of her mission to share the Gospel with the world.

   a. sacramental

   b. universal

   c. liturgical

   d. righteous

13. Ecumenism is a movement working toward unity and ___ among all Christians.

   a. Church

   b. community

   c. prayer

   d. Sacraments

14. The ___ name some of the minimum requirements given by Church leaders for deepening our relationship with God and the Church.

   a. Ten Commandments

   b. Precepts of the Church

   c. offices of Christ

   d. Theological Virtues

15. When holy water is used in blessings or in a ritual, it is meant to recall ___.

   a. the Eucharist

   b. our Baptism

   c. the Annunciation

   d. the Stations of the Cross

16. What is the name for the practice of making other people or things more important to us than God is?

   a. superstition

   b. blasphemy

   c. idolatry

   d. perjury

17. The ___ is the public prayer that the Church uses to mark each day as holy.

   a. Eucharist

   b. Rosary

   c. Lord's Prayer

   d. Liturgy of the Hours

18. The most important function of a family is to ___.

   a. serve as an economic unit

   b. foster the social life of the parents

   c. cultivate the faith life of its members

   d. stimulate intellectual growth of the children

19. Catholic marriage is a permanent ___ between a baptized man and a baptized woman.

   a. conversion

   b. character

   c. charism

   d. covenant

**20.** Who issued the Edict of Milan in A.D. 313 to give Romans freedom of worship?

    **a.** Saint Benedict

    **b.** Martin Luther

    **c.** the Council of Trent

    **d.** the Emperor Constantine

**21.** This God-given gift allows us to judge whether actions are right or wrong.

    **a.** free will

    **b.** conscience

    **c.** doctrine

    **d.** Tradition

**22.** This Sacrament is founded on the commissioning of the Apostles by Jesus to share in his ministry and work.

    **a.** Baptism

    **b.** Confirmation

    **c.** Holy Orders

    **d.** Matrimony

**23.** Which is a feast honoring Mary that is also a Holy Day of Obligation?

    **a.** feast of the Annunciation

    **b.** feast of the Assumption

    **c.** feast of the Visitation

    **d.** feast of Our Lady of Lourdes

**24.** What do we call showing contempt or lack of reverence for God's name?

    **a.** blasphemy

    **b.** idolatry

    **c.** heresy

    **d.** piety

**25.** Over time, personal sin can become so ingrained into a group of people that it becomes ___.

    **a.** social sin

    **b.** Original Sin

    **c.** mortal sin

    **d.** venial sin

**26.** The Magisterium is the ___ office of the Church.

    **a.** counseling

    **b.** sacramental

    **c.** teaching

    **d.** liturgical

**27.** Pentecost occurred ___ days after Easter.

    **a.** twenty-five

    **b.** forty

    **c.** seven

    **d.** fifty

**28.** A ___ is a formal statement of what is believed about the Holy Trinity and the Church.

    **a.** Gospel

    **b.** creed

    **c.** prayer

    **d.** Sacrament

**29.** These are good spiritual habits that strengthen and enable you to make moral decisions.

    **a.** doctrine

    **b.** virtues

    **c.** Creeds

    **d.** psalms

**Write a short response to the following items.**

Name the Marks of the Church, and describe what each means, in your own words.

30. _____

_____

31. _____

_____

32. _____

_____

33. _____

_____

Explain how the three Divine Persons of the Holy Trinity relate to one another.

34. _____

35. _____

36. _____

37. What is the mission of the Catholic Church?

_____

_____

38. How can the Catholic Church be "one" as Jesus prayed for?

_____

_____

39. What is more important to your faith right now: the fact that the Church is one, or the fact that she is diverse?

_____

_____

40. Describe how the Church is a community to you.

_____

_____

# Live Your Faith

## Catholic Social Teaching

## Life and Dignity of the Human Person

In Scripture, God tells us, "Before I formed you in the womb I knew you" (Jeremiah 1:5). God created each one of us, and every person is unique and valuable to God. He has a special plan for each of our lives. He knows what he made us to be.

Because God made each individual person, we should treat each person with human dignity. We are responsible for taking care of our bodies and minds and using them to do good things. We are called to be kind toward others, and solve problems peacefully instead of fighting. If we see someone being disrespected, we are called to speak up and defend him or her, and get help if necessary. It is our responsibility to protect others because every life is important to God.

Every person is created in the image and likeness of God, and is equally precious in the eyes of God. He wants all of us, not just some of us, to be with him forever. Every person is his child, so we are all sisters and brothers.

In their pastoral letter titled "Brothers and Sisters to Us," the Catholic bishops of the United States reminded us that people of every racial and cultural group are equal in dignity. And as Pope Francis has said, "The Son of God became incarnate in the souls of men to instill the feeling of brotherhood. All are brothers and all children of God." To treat any one person or group as less than fully equal to ourselves is a sin. Racism divides the human family and goes against God's plan to make us all one family.

# Equal Human Dignity

Racism has a terrible history in the world and in our nation. It began with the harmful treatment and displacement of many Native Americans by those who wanted their land. It increased with the slavery of Africans. Over time, other people of color were brought to the United States to do hard labor under brutal conditions.

Racism continues today in unequal treatment and lack of equal opportunity for all. It is our responsibility as Catholics to advocate for change that allows everyone an opportunity to achieve their goals in school and the workplace. Our diversity as humans means that every person brings his or her own God-given gifts to the world, and deserves a chance to share them. Inequalities in schools and workplaces contradict the equal dignity of all God's children and do not contribute to the common good. Therefore, the Catholic Church and her members are called to raise awareness and end these sinful inequalities.

> What has been your own experience with racism?

## Personal Action

Write about a time when you saw someone choose to avoid, exclude, or say or do something mean about someone from another race or culture.

_____

_____

_____

_____

Now write about a time when you or someone you know chose to be with someone from another race or culture or defended that person when others were saying or doing something disrespectful, exclusive, or harmful.

_____

_____

_____

_____

## Group Action

Identify places or situations in which someone or a group of people are treated unfairly or are not included in a community. It could be in your school, on local TV shows, in textbooks, magazine or TV ads, movies, on the covers of greeting cards, featured in kids' toys, or portrayed disrespectfully in cartoons or on sports teams' logos.

Present your research to the entire class. Choose one of these situations and create a plan to address it while maintaining respect for all involved.

# Live Your Faith

## Catholic Social Teaching

## Call to Family, Community, and Participation

From the very beginning, God made people to be in relationship with one another. Scripture tells us, "The Lord God said: It is not good for the man to be alone. I will make a helper suited to him" (Genesis 2:18). God gave us communities of persons so that we could take care of one another.

The family is a special type of community in which we first learn who God is and how to live a Christian life. It is the first place where we learn what it means to live in a community. The family is where we learn how to love others. Family is the first community we are part of. It's the first "school" where we learn virtues and how to care for others. Sometimes the family is even called the "domestic Church," because it's where we first come to know and worship God.

But no family is perfect. All families have to work hard at building a sense of community and rebuilding community when they make mistakes and hurt one another. Learning to apologize, and mean it, when we have hurt others is essential. So is forgiving those who have hurt us. Some families ritualize this by writing down the hurts they've done to others and then burning the papers in a fireplace or burying them. Other families attend the Sacrament of Reconciliation together.

When every member of a family participates in taking responsibility for what needs to be done—chores, prayer, family fun, consoling or encouraging one another, family service, and family decision-making—then that group of people truly becomes a "family."

## Service and Community

Familes are the foundation of every society, and every family has a "mission" to extend its love beyond family members to include others in need around them. This idea of "family service" should be something that all family members participate in, not only in doing what is decided, but also in deciding what to do.

In every community or group you are part of, the Catholic Church says that you are the "subject," not the object. You have the right and the duty to participate both in family discussions and in family service. You can apply these rights and duties at school and in your community as well, and your responsibility extends also to participation in promoting the common good—the good of everyone, with particular concern for people who might be most vulnerable to harm—in every other level of society. We are all part of the human family, a greater community created by God.

> **What do you need to apologize for and make amends for in your family?**

### Personal Action

Think about discussing with the rest of your family different ways of building a greater sense of "family" or "community" in your home. Make a list and decide which ones you all want to do at some time.

_____

_____

_____

_____

_____

_____

_____

Then choose the one you want to start with and make a plan for doing it. Write or draw a picture of what you plan to do and then say a prayer that you will all have the love to follow through.

### Group Action

Discuss with your classmates how you can help younger students at your school:

- feel more a part of the school community
- do better in their schoolwork, in sports, and in art and music
- participate in community service
- participate in prayer and worship

Make a list under each of the categories above. Choose one to start with and create a plan for achieving your goal.

## Rights and Responsibilities of the Human Person

Because God made every person, each of us has rights and responsibilities. Rights are the freedoms or things every person needs and should have. Responsibilities are our duties, or the things we must do.

Jesus gives us these words as part of the Great Commandment: "You shall love your neighbor as yourself" (Mark 12:31). The *Catechism* teaches that when we respect the dignity of another person, we treat them as "another self." We respect the rights that come from their dignity as a human being (see CCC, 1943-44). Everyone has a right to food, shelter, clothing, rest, and the right to medical care. We also have a responsibility to treat others well and work together for the good of everyone.

The dignity of each person is the basis for human equality and basic human rights. These basic human rights start with the right to life and the basic necessities of life—food, shelter, clothing, health care, education, and work—but they go further. Every person has the right to human dignity. This means being respected and appreciated for one's uniqueness. It also means developing mutual relationships with people—learning from them as well as helping them.

Just as you like to be treated as a responsible person and not a completely dependent child, so too the people you visit in the nursing home or the elderly in your parish want you to treat them in the same way.

# A Voice for the Voiceless

Another area of human rights revolves around the right of people to participate in the decisions that affect their lives. Governments especially must respect this fundamental human right and create the conditions for the full political involvement of their people. Everyone has the right to be heard by those in authority, but too often their voices are ignored or silenced. The Church calls us to be the voice of the voiceless.

The Jubliee Campaign was created many years ago to amplify the voices of caring people around the world on behalf of those voiceless men, women, and children falsely imprisoned by their own governments. In the United States, the organization began its work in the early 1990s, and lobbies Congress on behalf of those suffering persecution.

Disciples of Jesus are called to bring the light of the Gospel to bear on these unjust situations. We have a responsibility to speak up for these prisoners of conscience.

> How can you become a "voice" for those who are ignored or for whatever reason are not able to speak for themselves?

## Personal Action

Make a list of the people you, your parish, your school, or your family are serving in some way. Which word would you use to describe each relationship—"mutual" or "one-way helping"?

_____

_____

_____

_____

_____

_____

Choose one of those relationships that is more "one-way helping" and decide one thing you can do to make it a more mutual relationship (for example, asking an elderly person to teach you something). Carry out your decision and tell someone you trust about the experience.

## Group Action

In addition to researching the situation of immigrants in your community, your class might also research some of Jubliee Campaign's and the Catholic Campaign for Human Development's (CCHD) current projects in your area. CCHD is committed to funding projects where the recipients of aid have a direct voice in how the project is organized and carried out.

Share the results of your research and decide whether to create a single class project or divide the class into several projects. Then create a plan for carrying out the project(s).

# Live Your Faith

## Catholic Social Teaching

## Option for the Poor and Vulnerable

In Scripture, Jesus says that whatever we have done for people who are poor or needy, we have also done for him and what we have not done for them, we haven't done for Jesus (see Matthew 25:40). This means we should treat people in need the same way we would treat Jesus himself. We should give special priority to people who are hungry, thirsty, homeless or alone.

Saint Rose of Lima said, "When we serve the poor and the sick, we serve Jesus." Our Church teaches that we should have special love and care for those who are poor and put their needs first. This is called the preferential option for the poor. The *Catechism* also teaches that "God blesses those who come to the aid of the poor" (CCC, 2443).

One contemporary person who can motivate us to "opt for the poor" is Dorothy Day.

Dorothy Day clearly modeled Jesus' special love for the poor. With Peter Maurin, she founded the Catholic Worker movement, and through her Catholic Worker houses of hospitality, she showed us that serving the poor means more than doing things for them or giving things to them. Service means "doing with" more than "doing for." It means getting to know those who are poor and listening to their stories. It means helping people do for themselves, and Dorothy was especially skilled at giving them responsibility, both at the houses of hospitality and on community farms.

## Beyond Comfort Zones

But Dorothy Day went beyond the Works of Mercy and served the poor by challenging the policies and values of our society that allow, or even increase, poverty, including racism. In the Catholic Worker newspaper, she and others pointed out injustices and practices that were hurtful to those in need and urged governments to consider their most vulnerable people when making decisions.

Dorothy opted for the poor each time she demonstrated against military spending and the arms race. As the Catholic Church says, "the harm it inflicts on the poor is more than can be endured" (CCC, 2329).

Dorothy Day challenged all Catholics to go beyond our comfort zones and embrace our calling to bring Christ's sacrificial love to those most in need.

> What is it about the witness of Dorothy Day that inspires you?

> How can you be "the face of Christ" for the poor and vulnerable people in your community?

## Personal Action

Work with your classmates to identify local and regional groups, in addition to the following Catholic groups, that are working to change political or economic policies that are harmful to the poor.

- The USCCB Department of Justice, Peace, and Human Development—for ongoing Catholic justice campaigns
- The Catholic Campaign for Human Development—for many justice projects
- _____
  _____
- _____
  _____
- _____
  _____
- _____
  _____

## Group Action

Work in teams to research the actions that each organization is recommending. Think of ways you could support these organizations on a local, national, or international level.

Choose one organization's recommendation(s) and create a plan for putting it into practice over the next weeks.

## Dignity of Work and the Rights of Workers

All adults have a right and responsibility to work. Work helps people earn money to buy food and other necessities. It also helps to give their lives meaning as they cooperate with God's creation. Everyone should have access to meaningful work, inside or outside the home.

Sacred Scripture and Sacred Tradition teach that workers deserve to be treated with justice by their employers: "You shall not exploit a poor and needy hired servant" (Deuteronomy 24:14). They have a right to a fair wage for their work (see Leviticus 19:13; Deuteronomy 24:15). When there is a conflict between workers and employers, workers have the right to get together and express their opinion. Workers and their employers should treat one another with respect and solve conflicts peacefully.

When students and their parents are starting to think about what high school the students are going to go attend, one of their first concerns often is whether what they learn or take away from that school will help them get into a good college, learn the skills that will help them get a good job, and help them earn a good salary.

Although economic security is an important concern, it's definitely not the bottom line. For Jesus and his Church, the most important thing we do in our lives is participating in God's ongoing work of creation and service to others. Advancing in your education and your career should be about increasing your ability to carry out the reason God created you and the way you respond to his call (your vocation).

# Fairness and Dignity

Work means much more than a job and money. As God's partners in the continuing work of creation, workers have a special dignity that is so much more than the work they do.

But some employers don't treat their workers fairly. The Catholic Church has always supported the rights of workers. Every worker has a right to a fair wage and safe working conditions.

Some Church leaders have said that a fair wage is a "living wage"—what it takes for a family to have the basic necessities of life. Farm workers in the United States are among those who need the support of individual Christians and our Church institutions. But as Catholics, our concern is universal. Workers all over the world, especially children who are forced to work, need our support. Everyone has the right to work in an environment of safety and respect for their human dignity.

> **When you and your family talk about your future, what are you most concerned about?**

## Personal Action

Make a list of jobs that involve serving others and note how they serve. Put a "Y" for "YES" after those professions that appeal to you.

_____

_____

_____

_____

_____

_____

Then make a list of your own talents and interests and match them with your list of professions. Talk your lists over with an adult you respect, and ask for comments. Pray every morning that you will find a way that day to serve someone.

## Group Action

Make a list with your classmates of groups of workers in your community, country, and in other parts of the world who are treated unfairly. Have each classmate research one group and how the class might be able to help them.

# Live Your Faith

## Catholic Social Teaching

## Solidarity of the Human Family

Our world includes people of different nations, races, cultures, beliefs, and economic levels. But God created each one of us. We are one human family. Scripture tells us that the differences that we see between ourselves and others are not important to God (see Romans 2:11). Because God created all people, we have an obligation to treat everyone with love, kindness, and justice. In the Beatitudes, Jesus tells us "Blessed are the peacemakers" (Matthew 5:9). Working for justice between people will help us to live in peace with one another.

We are in solidarity with the human family because we are all brothers and sisters made in God's image. Our solidarity with the whole human family means we must be willing to sacrifice for the common good of everyone. Individuals must be willing to sacrifice some of their time, talents, and possessions for others. Nations must be willing to sacrifice some of their people, wealth, and power for the sake of the well-being of other peoples and nations. Selfishness by individuals and nations is a sin against human solidarity and the Tenth Commandment.

The common good of the human family requires organization of society on the international level. The "right" of one nation to make war against another is limited. War must be a matter of self-defense and a last resort, and actions of warfare must be proportional and mindful of the dignity of life.

## Building Peace

In 2003, Pope Saint John Paul II told a group of international diplomats, "People of the earth and their leaders must sometimes have the courage to say, 'No! . . . No to war!' War is not always inevitable. It is always a defeat for humanity. International law, honest dialogue, solidarity between States, the noble exercise of diplomacy: these are methods worthy of individuals and nation in resolving their differences . . ."

International peacemaking is a an important part of human solidarity, but peacemaking involves many things. It starts with building and rebuilding peaceful relationships with those around you, whether in your school or in your community, even within your own family. It means promoting a caring relationship with creation. And peacemaking also means challenging the violence you see around you, from physical bullying to social media slurs.

> What do you think Pope Saint John Paul II meant when he said war is "always a defeat for humanity"? Do you agree with him? Why or why not?

## Personal Action

Write down one way you have already been a peacemaker:

**At your school**

_____

**At home**

_____

**In your neighborhood**

_____

Choose one situation you are part of, or know about, where you could be a better peacemaker. Write down how you will try to do it and when.

_____

_____

_____

_____

## Group Action

Identify with your classmates different nations or parts of the world where wars are going on and discuss alternative ways for the groups at war to reach their goals without a war or other form of conflict.

# Live Your Faith

## Catholic Social Teaching

## Care for God's Creation

When God created the world—the animals, plants, and all natural things—he looked upon everything that he had made and called it "very good" (Genesis 1:31). God made people the stewards of the "fish of the sea, the birds of the air, and all the living things that crawl on the earth" (Genesis 1:28). That means humans have a special responsibility to care for all of God's creation.

Sacred Tradition teaches us that God created the Earth and all living things for the common good. We are called to take care of the environment and all living things, so they can be enjoyed by everyone today and in future generations. The *Catechism* teaches us that we owe animals kindness, because they give glory to God just by being what they were made to be.

Saint Francis of Assisi learned and lived these principles in an extraordinary way. As a young adult, he rediscovered an appreciation for the beauty of nature God had blessed him with in his youth. His response was to praise God through all the wonders of creation: sun and moon, mountains and rivers, trees and flowers, the wind and rain. And he called them his "brothers" and "sisters." We, too, are called to give God thanks and praise for all these beautiful gifts of creation.

Pope Francis referred back to his namesake Saint Francis of Assisi when he said "Take good care of creation. Saint Francis wanted that. People occasionally forgive, but nature never does. If we don't take care of the environment, there's no way of getting around it."

## Creation and Charity

But Saint Francis also realized that God wants these gifts of creation to be available for everyone. He gave away all his possessions, renounced his inheritance, and began to care for lepers and beg for the poor. Like Francis, each of us is asked by God to be both charitable and just.

God has provided the resources that allow humans to lead comfortable lives. But he wants us to take care of the goods he has given us, to be charitable in sharing those goods with others, and to support efforts that preserve the Earth's resources for all of God's children. Praying for help to Saint Francis, who is the patron Saint of ecology, you can promote recycling at home, at school, and in the community. You can help protect rain forests, rivers, soil, and endangered species, each of which is a revelation of God's wisdom, goodness, and beauty.

> **What most impresses you about the life of Saint Francis?**

> **How could you put this into practice in your own life?**

## Personal Action

Make a list of the things you have (such as clothes, books, electronics, sports equipment, or other items) that you could give to others who don't have as much.

**To whom could you donate these?**

_____

_____

**What could you give up to save money (for example, video games, apps, movies)?**

_____

_____

**With whom could you share these savings?**

_____

_____

**Who else could help you in this effort?**

_____

## Group Action

Identify with your classmates different aspects of creation that are in danger from human activity. Have individuals or teams research those that interest the class most and report their findings. Choose one and create a plan for protecting it.

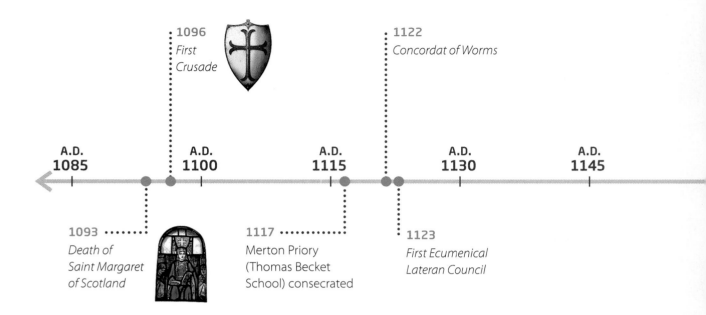

1096
*First
Crusade*

1122
*Concordat of Worms*

A.D. **1085**

A.D. **1100**

A.D. **1115**

A.D. **1130**

A.D. **1145**

1093
*Death of
Saint Margaret
of Scotland*

1117
*Merton Priory
(Thomas Becket
School) consecrated*

1123
*First Ecumenical
Lateran Council*

## ● Death of Saint Margaret of Scotland, A.D. 1093

Saint Margaret was a princess whose family was shipwrecked along the coast of Scotland while escaping from England after the Norman conquest. She married Malcolm, the Scottish king, and became his queen. Margaret used her wealth in service to others, taking care of orphaned children and helping to repair churches that were in desperate need of rebuilding. Margaret encouraged her husband to attend Mass, and she brought the Scottish church's customs and Sacrament practices in line with the Church in Rome.

## ● First Crusade, A.D. 1096

The Crusades were a series of military attempts by Europeans to wrest control of the Holy Land from the Muslims who had controlled it since the seventh century. Pope Urban II called the First Crusade, which lasted until 1099. The knights who answered the call wore a red cross on their chests called *crociati*, and thus became known as crusaders.

## ● Concordat of Worms, A.D. 1122

This agreement between Pope Callistus II and Emperor Henry V gave Popes the power to select bishops and abbots and invest them with their spiritual power, while the Emperor was responsible for their temporal, or worldly, rights and rule.

## ● First Ecumenical Lateran Council, A.D. 1123

While the First Ecumenical Lateran Council may be known for the policy it declared regarding celibacy for priests, it was also concerned with other reforms in the Church. Held in Rome, the Council reestablished freedom from secular domination in the election of bishops and abbots, separated secular and Church affairs, reaffirmed that spiritual authority rests only in the Church, and removed the emperor's claim to a right to interfere in a Pope's election.

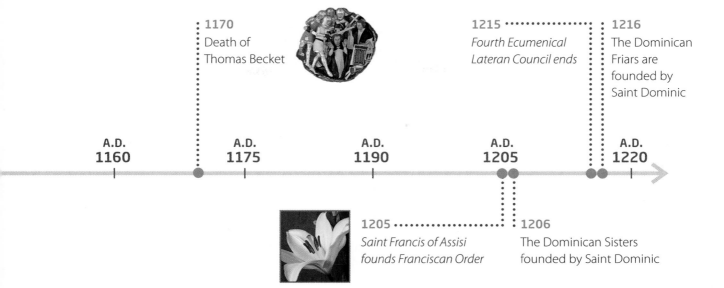

**1170**
Death of Thomas Becket

**1215**
*Fourth Ecumenical Lateran Council ends*

**1216**
The Dominican Friars are founded by Saint Dominic

A.D. **1160**   A.D. **1175**   A.D. **1190**   A.D. **1205**   A.D. **1220**

**1205**
*Saint Francis of Assisi founds Franciscan Order*

**1206**
The Dominican Sisters founded by Saint Dominic

## ● Saint Francis of Assisi founds Franciscan Order, A.D. 1205

A native of Assisi, Saint Francis was the son of a cloth merchant, but renounced his family's fortune and founded what would later become the Franciscan Order. One of the most popular Saints in the world, he is known for his poverty, love of nature, and reforms of the Church. Francis developed rules for those who followed in his ministry, emphasizing poverty, humility, and discipline. He also influenced Saint Clare of Assisi, who founded the Second Order of Saint Francis, also known as the "Poor Clares." He is the patron Saint of animals and the environment, and had the stigmata, the wounds of Christ, on his hands and feet.

## ● The Fourth Ecumenical Lateran Council ends, A.D. 1215

Among other proclamations, this Church council first defined transubstantiation, the teaching that at Mass, the bread and wine truly become the Body and Blood, Soul and Divinity of Christ. The doctrine would later be expanded at the Council of Trent. The Fourth Ecumenical Lateran Council was the most important council of the Middle Ages, and marked a high point in ecclesiastical life and papal power.

**Go to the Document**
Read the *Catechism of the Catholic Church 1376*

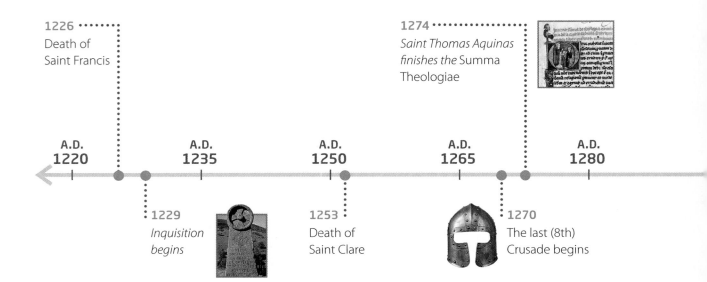

**1226**
Death of
Saint Francis

**1274**
*Saint Thomas Aquinas
finishes the* Summa
Theologiae

| A.D. **1220** | A.D. **1235** | A.D. **1250** | A.D. **1265** | A.D. **1280** |

**1229**
*Inquisition
begins*

**1253**
Death of
Saint Clare

**1270**
The last (8th)
Crusade begins

● **The Inquisition begins,** A.D. 1229

The Cathars taught there were two gods: the "good" god of the New Testament and the "bad" god of the Old Testament who created the natural world. In response to this heresy, the Church began the process of trials for those who persisted in their erroneous beliefs. The trials and subsequent punishments became known as the Inquisition.

**Go to the Document**

Pope Benedict discussed the Cathar heresy and the founding of the mendicant orders on January 13, 2010. His address can be found at www.vatican.va

● **Saint Thomas Aquinas writes the**
  *Summa Theologiae,* A.D. 1265-1274

The *Summa Theologiae* is one of the great classic works of theology and philosophy. In it, Saint Thomas makes arguments for the existence of God as well as outlining and defining the Gifts of the Holy Spirit and other theological doctrines. It is considered Saint Thomas's greatest contribution to the faith and is one of the reasons he is a Doctor of the Church.

**Go to the Document**

Read the *Summa,* which is available as a print book, an ebook and online.

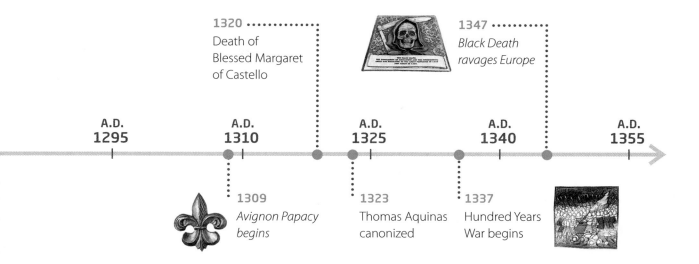

1320 ............
Death of
Blessed Margaret
of Castello

1347 ............
*Black Death
ravages Europe*

A.D.
**1295**

A.D.
**1310**

A.D.
**1325**

A.D.
**1340**

A.D.
**1355**

1309
*Avignon Papacy
begins*

1323
Thomas Aquinas
canonized

1337
Hundred Years
War begins

● **Avignon Papacy,** A.D. 1309-1378

When Bertrand de Got, archbishop of Bordeaux, was elected Pope, he moved the residence of the Pope from Rome to Avignon in France, where it remained for nearly 70 years. Avignon was a more peaceful setting for the center of the Church than the city of Rome, and was closer to Rome than many other centers of Catholicism in Western Europe, but there were many who believed that the Pope should always reside in Rome. Seven Popes lived in Avignon, in a papal palace that still stands near the center of the city. Among those who urged the return of the papacy to Rome was Saint Catherine of Siena, who also encouraged the recognition of Pope Gregory XI's successor, Pope Urban VI.

● **Black Death Ravages Europe,**
   A.D. 1347

The bubonic plague, also known as the Black Death, killed nearly one-third of the population of Europe during the three-year span of its first outbreak. The plague, thought to be carried by rats aboard ships, first appeared in Genoa, Italy, and was carried to humans by fleas on the rats. Church leaders attempted to change sanitation policies to make the European population safer, and many religious communities took care of tending the sick and burying the dead. The Church lost many priests and other religious in the plague as well, and so many of those who were near death were denied the Sacraments in their time of greatest need. Many monasteries also fell into disrepair. During this time of tragedy, Christians turned to the Church for assurance that peace awaited them when their suffering had ended.

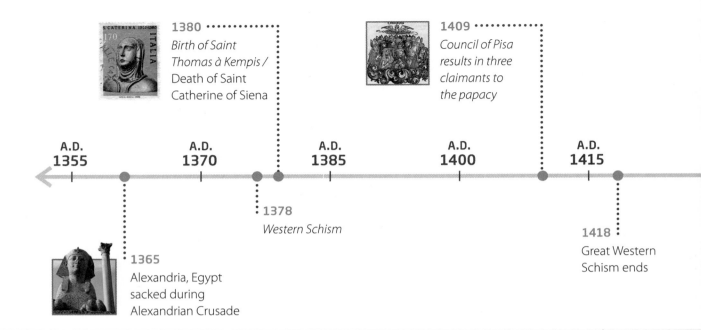

**1380**
*Birth of Saint Thomas à Kempis / Death of Saint Catherine of Siena*

**1409**
*Council of Pisa results in three claimants to the papacy*

A.D. **1355**   A.D. **1370**   A.D. **1385**   A.D. **1400**   A.D. **1415**

**1378**
*Western Schism*

**1365**
Alexandria, Egypt sacked during Alexandrian Crusade

**1418**
Great Western Schism ends

● **Western Schism,** A.D. 1378

Not to be confused with the East/West Schism of 1054, the Western Schism was a division of the Roman Church that lasted until 1418. It began when Antipope Clement VII and Pope Urban VI both claimed rights to the papacy. The Council of Constance ended the split, but at one time three rival factions insisted that their candidate was the true successor of Saint Peter.

● **Birth of Saint Thomas à Kempis,**
   A.D. 1380

Thomas à Kempis was a German scholar who wrote one of the most influential books on Christianity, *The Imitation of Christ*. After leaving school he joined the monastery of Mount St. Agnes and was eventually ordained a priest. Along with writing his own work, Thomas spent time copying Bibles and textbooks, and in devotional practice. There is a shrine dedicated to him at the Assumption of Mary church in Zwolle, The Netherlands.

● **Council of Pisa,** A.D. 1409

The Council of Pisa was not one of the Catholic Church's recognized ecumenical councils, but was significant for its attempt to end the Western Schism. The attempt was unsuccessful, and the cardinals at the council eventually elected a third person as Pope—Alexander V—to try to depose the two men already considered Pope by disagreeing factions of the Schism, Benedict XIII and Gregory XII. Alexander V reigned for less than a full year and was eventually named after the end of the Western Schism by the Catholic Church as an Antipope, or person who stands in opposition to an elected reigning Pope but makes a competing claim to the Papacy that is in some part accepted at its time.

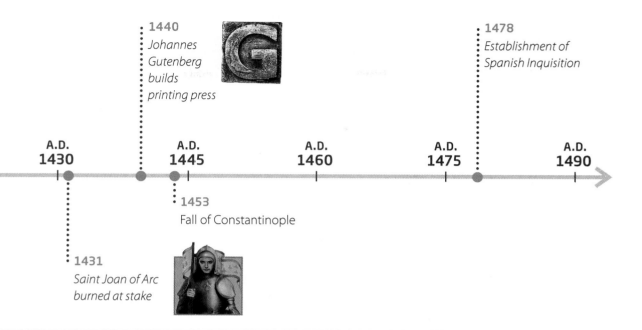

**1440**
*Johannes Gutenberg builds printing press*

**1478**
*Establishment of Spanish Inquisition*

| A.D.<br>**1430** | A.D.<br>**1445** | A.D.<br>**1460** | A.D.<br>**1475** | A.D.<br>**1490** |
|---|---|---|---|---|

**1453**
Fall of Constantinople

**1431**
*Saint Joan of Arc burned at stake*

● **Saint Joan of Arc burned at the stake,** A.D. 1431

A nineteen-year-old French peasant, Joan had visions instructing her to lead her county in battle against the English. She courageously led her troops to numerous victories, but was captured by the English and burned at the stake as a heretic. Twenty-five years later, Pope Callixtus III declared her a martyr. She was canonized in 1920 and is considered one of the patron Saints of France.

● **Johannes Gutenberg builds printing press,** A.D. 1440

The world was revolutionized when Johannes Gutenberg built the first printing press that used moveable type. His invention laid the groundwork for all modern books and printing by making books easier to produce and more affordable. Among the first books to be printed by the new method was the Bible. About 180 copies were made. Forty-eight complete or partial copies of the Gutenberg Bible still exist.

● **Establishment of Spanish Inquisition,** A.D. 1478

In order to rid their land of all non-Christians, especially Jews, Queen Isabella and King Ferdinand of Spain asked the Pope to establish the Spanish Inquisition. Despite Church guidelines, many were tortured and killed for failing to become Christian. In 1483, Tomas de Torquemada became the Grand Inquisitor. It is estimated as many as 2,000 Jews died under his rule. Many thousands more were forced to leave the country.

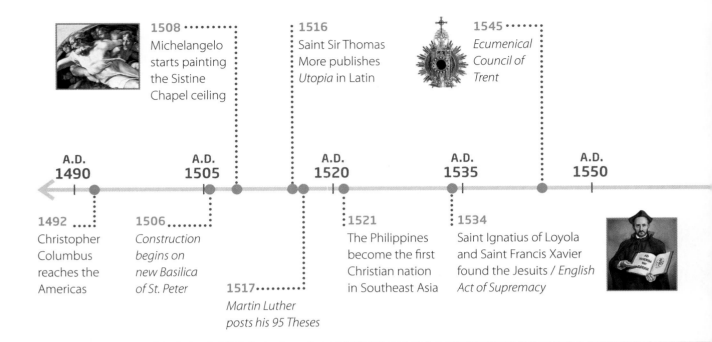

**1508**
Michelangelo
starts painting
the Sistine
Chapel ceiling

**1516**
Saint Sir Thomas
More publishes
*Utopia* in Latin

**1545**
*Ecumenical
Council of
Trent*

A.D.
**1490**

A.D.
**1505**

A.D.
**1520**

A.D.
**1535**

A.D.
**1550**

**1492**
Christopher
Columbus
reaches the
Americas

**1506**
*Construction
begins on
new Basilica
of St. Peter*

**1521**
The Philippines
become the first
Christian nation
in Southeast Asia

**1534**
Saint Ignatius of Loyola
and Saint Francis Xavier
found the Jesuits / *English
Act of Supremacy*

**1517**
*Martin Luther
posts his 95 Theses*

## ● Construction begins on new Basilica of St. Peter, A.D. 1506

Pope Julius II laid the cornerstone of the new Basilica of St. Peter on April 18, 1506. Constantine, the first Christian emperor of Rome, built the first Basilica on Vatican Hill, the site of an ancient Roman cemetery, where Saint Peter is believed to be buried. The old Basilica had fallen into disrepair during the Avignon papacy. The "new" Basilica is the one found in Rome today.

### Explore the Vatican Website

A virtual tour of St. Peter's can be seen at www.vatican.va.

## ● Martin Luther posts his 95 Theses, A.D. 1517

On October 31, 1517, Martin Luther wrote his 95 Theses, outlining his position on a number of theological issues, including his opposition to the sale of indulgences. A devout Augustinian priest at the time, he did not intend for his action to lead to the Protestant Reformation and a division in Christianity that exists to this day. Church officials and Luther spent several years arguing their theological positions. In 1520, Pope Leo X issued a papal bull excommunicating Luther unless he recanted. On December 10, Luther burned the papal letter, and he was officially excommunicated on January 3, 1521.

## ● English Act of Supremacy, A.D. 1534

Because the Pope refused to grant Henry VIII an annulment of his first marriage, the king asked the English Parliament to pass the Act of Supremacy, making him the Supreme Head of the Church of England. This action led to the break between the Anglican and the Roman Church and Henry's subsequent marriage to Anne Boleyn.

## ● Council of Trent, A.D. 1545

The challenge of Protestantism spurred Pope Paul III to call an ecumenical council. Over the 18 years the council was in session, it clarified all the major doctrines of the Church, including clarifying the dogma of transubstantiation, defining the Seven Sacraments and reaffirming priestly celibacy. Its rulings set the tone of the Catholic Church for the next 300 years. *The Catechism of the Council of Trent* served as the official catechism of the Church until the 1992 release of the *Catechism of the Catholic Church.*

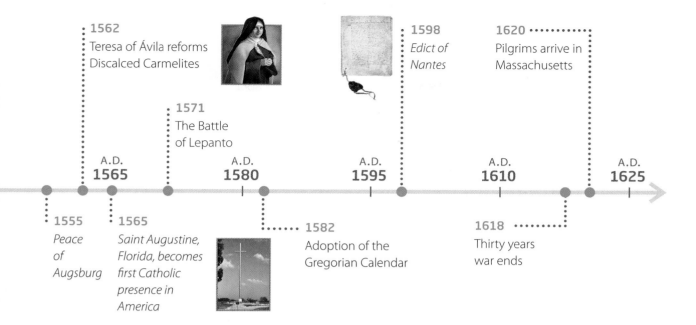

**1562**
Teresa of Ávila reforms
Discalced Carmelites

**1571**
The Battle
of Lepanto

**1598**
*Edict of
Nantes*

**1620**
Pilgrims arrive in
Massachusetts

A.D. **1565**

A.D. **1580**

A.D. **1595**

A.D. **1610**

A.D. **1625**

**1555**
*Peace
of
Augsburg*

**1565**
*Saint Augustine,
Florida, becomes
first Catholic
presence in
America*

**1582**
Adoption of the
Gregorian Calendar

**1618**
Thirty years
war ends

● **Peace of Augsburg,** A.D. 1555

According to this imperial decree, a prince or
king was free to choose either Catholicism or
Lutheranism as the official religion of his territory.
Only Lutheranism was covered by this order; other
Protestant sects were outlawed.

● **Saint Augustine, Florida, becomes
first Catholic presence in America,**
A.D. 1565

Christianity first entered what was to become the
United States by way of Spanish explorers and
missionaries, and later the French. In 1565, Spanish
explorers established a permanent settlement in
a section of northeast coastal Florida they called
St. Augustine. Missionaries built the Nombre de Dios
(Name of God) church on the settlement, and the
building still stands today, claiming to be the oldest
parish in continual use in the United States. In 1598,
a statue of Our Lady of La Leche, depicting Mary
feeding the baby Jesus at her breast, was brought to
the mission, and devotion to Our Lady under this title
still exists at the mission now.

● **Edict of Nantes,** A.D. 1598

Although King Henry IV of France was raised as a
Protestant, he converted to Catholicism, more or less
as a political decision. Thousands of Huguenots had
been killed in Paris in 1572 in what became known
as the St. Bartholomew's Day Massacre. In the Edict
of Nantes, he granted the Protestant Huguenots the
right to build churches and conduct religious services
in selected towns and villages. In 1685 King Louis XIV
revoked the Edict, resulting in the exodus of large
numbers of Huguenots.

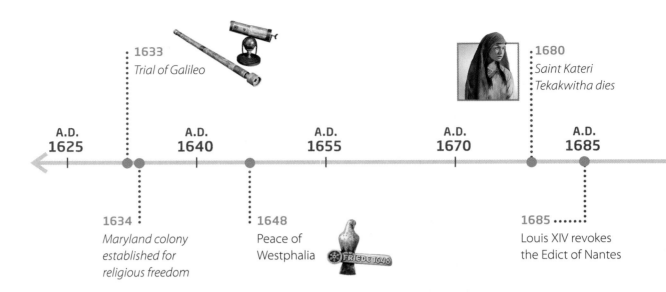

**1633**
*Trial of Galileo*

**1680**
*Saint Kateri Tekakwitha dies*

A.D. **1625**  A.D. **1640**  A.D. **1655**  A.D. **1670**  A.D. **1685**

**1634**
*Maryland colony established for religious freedom*

**1648**
Peace of Westphalia

**1685**
Louis XIV revokes the Edict of Nantes

● **Trial of Galileo,** A.D. 1633

Galileo Galilei was an Italian scientist who supported Nicholas Copernicus' theory that the Earth and other planets revolved around the sun. While Copernicus' theories received support from his local cardinal and he dedicated his work to the reigning Pope of his time, Galileo's research went against commonly held beliefs of his own time, and controversy followed. Many people denounced his views as heresy, because they appeared to contradict certain statements in the Bible. Galileo also offered no firm proof of his findings, and some high-ranking officials of the court of the Inquisition in Rome believed they could present a danger to the faith of the common people if Galileo's work circulated beyond the scientific community. At first, Galileo promised not to write or speak about his views, but he continued to teach them. In 1992, Pope Saint John Paul II acknowledged the errors of the Church during Galileo's tribunal, and in December 2008, Pope Benedict XVI praised Galileo's contributions to astronomy.

● **Maryland colony established for religious freedom,** A.D. 1634

Maryland was one of the original thirteen colonies of the United States. While it began as a safe haven for Catholics, it was not initially founded as a Catholic colony. The first Lord Baltimore, George Calvert, became a Catholic in 1624, and asked permission from King James I to begin a colony in the New World. His son Cecil Calvert received the charter for the new colony, and another son, Leonard, became the first governor of the settlement of Maryland. In 1649, Maryland passed the Act of Toleration granting freedom of religion, including Catholicism in Maryland. At the time it was the only colony to guarantee such freedom. Many prominent Catholics of the colonial era lived or were born in Maryland, including John Carroll, the first Catholic bishop in the United States, and the only one to be elected by members of the clergy rather than be appointed by the Pope.

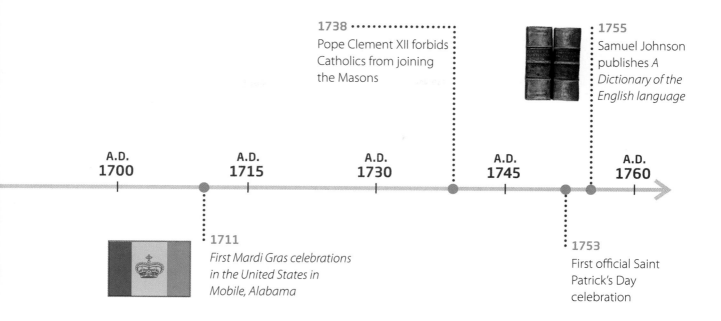

**1738**
Pope Clement XII forbids Catholics from joining the Masons

**1755**
Samuel Johnson publishes *A Dictionary of the English language*

| A.D. 1700 | A.D. 1715 | A.D. 1730 | A.D. 1745 | A.D. 1760 |

**1711**
*First Mardi Gras celebrations in the United States in Mobile, Alabama*

**1753**
First official Saint Patrick's Day celebration

## ● Death of Saint Kateri Tekakwitha, A.D. 1680

Kateri Tekakwitha was the daughter of a Mohawk chief and an Algonquin Christian woman. Kateri's parents died of smallpox, and she became partially blind and had a disfigured face from the effects of the illness as well. When a priest visited her village, Kateri asked to be baptized. Soon afterward, she left her village and traveled to a Christian Native American community near Montreal. She was known for her love and nature and animals, though she covered her face when outdoors to protect her eyes and skin from the sun. When she died, her face was cleared of the blemishes and disfigurement that she had as a child. Kateri was beatified in 1980 by Pope Saint John Paul II, and canonized by Pope Benedict XVI in 2012. She is the first Native American to be canonized.

## ● First Mardi Gras celebrations in the United States in Mobile, A.D. 1703

Mardi Gras is a period of celebration in several countries around the world, beginning on or near the Epiphany (January 6) and ending on the day before Ash Wednesday. This specific day is known as "Mardi Gras", or "Fat Tuesday" in reference to participation in feasts before the season of Lent begins on the following day. In some countries, Mardi Gras is known as Shrove Tuesday. In the United States, many cities that were settled by the French or have historical connections to France celebrate Mardi Gras with parades or carnivals. The most well-known celebrations are in New Orleans, Louisiana, but Mobile, Alabama, which was the first capital of French Louisiana, was the first city to hold an organized celebration of the holiday in the United States. Decorations for the festivities are usually in the traditional colors or purple, green, and gold, which represent justice, faith, and power, respectively. The purple color also represents the Lenten season's liturgical decorations and vestments.

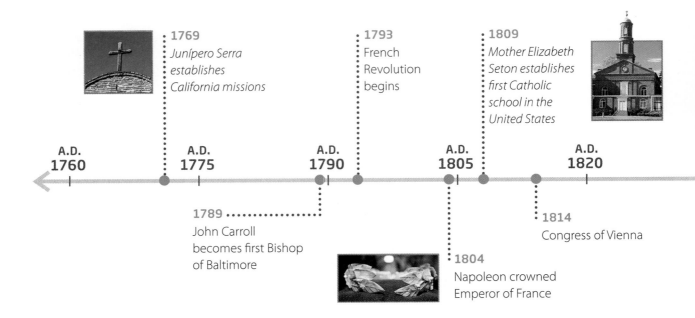

1769
*Junípero Serra establishes California missions*

1793
French Revolution begins

1809
*Mother Elizabeth Seton establishes first Catholic school in the United States*

A.D. **1760**    A.D. **1775**    A.D. **1790**    A.D. **1805**    A.D. **1820**

1789 ················
John Carroll becomes first Bishop of Baltimore

1814
Congress of Vienna

1804
Napoleon crowned Emperor of France

## ● Junípero Serra establishes California missions, A.D. 1769

Franciscan missionary Junípero Serra established the first nine of the 31 California missions, beginning with Mission San Diego de Alcalá. He had been an excellent student, but wanted to go to the missions, and was released from his teaching responsibilities to do so. One of his missions, San Juan Capistrano, built in 1782, is famous for the return of the swallows each year on St. Joseph's Day, March 19. It is believed to be the oldest building in California. By the time of Father Serra's death in 1784, more than 6,700 Baptisms were recorded and more than 4,600 Christian Native Americans were living in the missions.

## ● Mother Elizabeth Seton establishes first Catholic school in U.S., A.D. 1809

Elizabeth Ann Seton was born into an Episcopal family. She lost her husband to illness after his shipping business failed, and soon afterward she began to attend a Catholic Church. She was particularly drawn to the belief in the Real Presence of Christ in the Eucharist, and she became a Catholic in 1805. In 1809, she opened a Catholic school on a property in Emmitsburg, Maryland, that she had received from Bishop John Carroll of Baltimore. Elizabeth, her daughters, and her sisters-in-law began the U.S. foundation of the Sisters of Charity, which endured many years of struggle before the community prospered. In the following decades, inspired by the success of Mother Seton and others, the bishops called for more Catholic schools in their parishes, and for a priest to write a simple catechism that could be used by Catholic schoolchildren. The resulting *Baltimore Catechism* served as the main text of religious education in American Catholic schools until the 1960s.

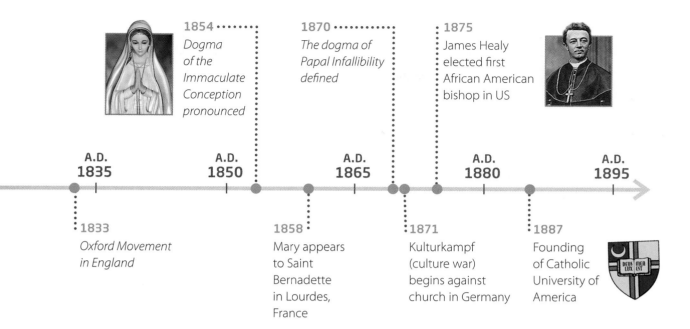

**1854**
*Dogma of the Immaculate Conception pronounced*

**1870**
*The dogma of Papal Infallibility defined*

**1875**
James Healy elected first African American bishop in US

**A.D. 1835**  **A.D. 1850**  **A.D. 1865**  **A.D. 1880**  **A.D. 1895**

**1833**
*Oxford Movement in England*

**1858**
Mary appears to Saint Bernadette in Lourdes, France

**1871**
Kulturkampf (culture war) begins against church in Germany

**1887**
Founding of Catholic University of America

● **Oxford Movement in England,**
A.D. 1833

Blessed John Henry Newman (for whom college campus Newman Centers are named) was one of a number of Anglican priests and bishops who wanted the Church of England to become more Catholic. Because many of these priests and bishops were associated with Oxford University, this attempt was dubbed the "Oxford Movement." Cardinal Newman eventually joined the Catholic Church in 1845.

**Explore the Vatican Website**
Read Pope Benedict's homily for the beatification of Cardinal Newman on September 19, 2010 at www.vatican.va.

● **Dogma of the Immaculate Conception,** A.D. 1854

Pope Pius IX proclaimed the dogma of the Immaculate Conception, stating that God preserved Mary from Original Sin from the moment of her conception and she remained free from personal sin her entire life.

**Go to the Document**
See the *Catechism of the Catholic Church 490-493.*

● **Vatican I defines Papal Infallibility,**
A.D. 1870

Pope Pius IX convened Vatican Council I on June 29, 1868. Among its major accomplishments was the clarification of the doctrine of papal infallibility, which states that the Pope is protected from error, "when, as supreme pastor and teacher of all the faithful—who confirms his brethren in the faith—he proclaims by a definitive act a doctrine pertaining to faith or morals."

**Go to the Document**
Read the *Catechism of the Catholic Church 891.*

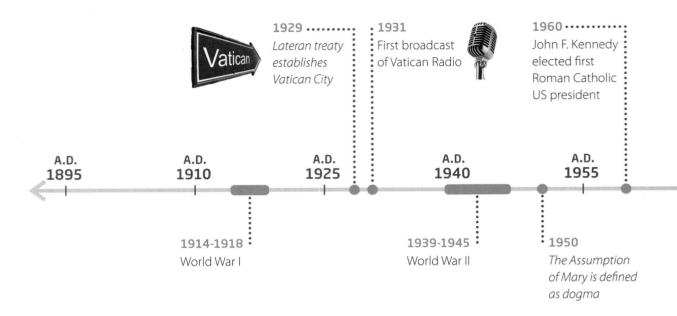

1929
*Lateran treaty establishes Vatican City*

1931
First broadcast of Vatican Radio

1960
John F. Kennedy elected first Roman Catholic US president

A.D. **1895**

A.D. **1910**

A.D. **1925**

A.D. **1940**

A.D. **1955**

1914-1918
World War I

1939-1945
World War II

1950
*The Assumption of Mary is defined as dogma*

● **Lateran treaty establishes Vatican City,** A.D. 1929

On February 11, Benito Mussolini and Cardinal Gasparri signed a treaty creating the independent State of Vatican City. Vatican City is the smallest sovereign state in the world. It consists of about 109 acres, surrounded by ancient walls within the city of Rome. It has a population of about 800; about 450 have Vatican citizenship. According to the Vatican, "Even though Vatican City has no direct access to the sea, by virtue of the Barcelona Declaration of 1921, it is allowed to sail its own vessels flying the papal flag."

● **The Assumption of Mary is defined as dogma,** A.D. 1950

On November 1, Pope Pius XII officially declared that the Virgin Mary was taken body and soul into Heaven. The *Catechism of the Catholic Church* states: "Finally the Immaculate Virgin, preserved free from all stain of original sin, when the course of her earthly life was finished, was taken up body and soul into heavenly glory, and exalted by the Lord as Queen over all things, so that she might be the more fully conformed to her Son, the Lord of lords and conqueror of sin and death."

**Go to the Document**
Read the *Catechism of the Catholic Church 966.*

● **The Second Ecumenical Vatican Council,** A.D. 1962-1965

On October 11, 1962, Pope Saint John XXIII opened Vatican II, the twenty-first ecumenical council of the Catholic Church. The Council enacted many changes, including the use of native languages instead of Latin in the Mass. It also condemned all forms of social and cultural discrimination as incompatible with God's design, saying that each person is created in the image of God and is gifted with dignity equal to all other humans. That equality—guaranteed by the Creator—requires our heartfelt efforts to reduce sinful social and economic inequalities. Pope Saint John XXIII died before the end of the Council, which was closed by Venerable Pope Paul VI on December 8, 1965.

**Go to the Document**

All the documents from Vatican II are available at www.vatican.va.

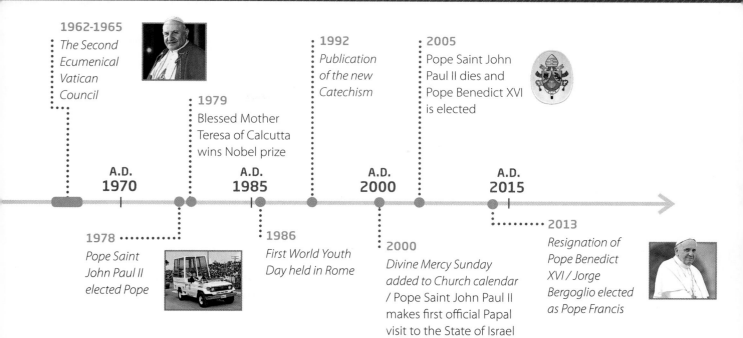

**1962-1965**
*The Second Ecumenical Vatican Council*

**1992**
*Publication of the new Catechism*

**2005**
Pope Saint John Paul II dies and Pope Benedict XVI is elected

**1979**
Blessed Mother Teresa of Calcutta wins Nobel prize

A.D. **1970**

A.D. **1985**

A.D. **2000**

A.D. **2015**

**1978**
*Pope Saint John Paul II elected Pope*

**1986**
*First World Youth Day held in Rome*

**2000**
*Divine Mercy Sunday added to Church calendar / Pope Saint John Paul II makes first official Papal visit to the State of Israel*

**2013**
*Resignation of Pope Benedict XVI / Jorge Bergoglio elected as Pope Francis*

## ● Pope Saint John Paul II elected Pope, A.D. 1978

Karol Józef Wojtyła was the the first non-Italian Pope elected in 450 years and the second longest-serving Pope after Pope Adrian VI. His pontificate was marked with numerous historical events, including the fall of Communism and an assassination attempt. In the 1980s, he showed his support for a workers' movement in his native Poland called "Solidarity." He encouraged workers to rise up for their rights. This led to new freedom in Poland and the end of oppressive governments throughout Eastern Europe, including Russia. He was declared a Saint by Pope Francis on April 27, 2014.

## ● First World Youth Day held in Rome, A.D. 1986

World Youth Day is a gathering of Catholic youth every two to three years in various locations around the world. More than three million pilgrims attended the 2013 World Youth Day, held in Rio de Janeiro, Brazil.

## ● Publication of the new *Catechism of the Catholic Church,* A.D. 1992

The new *Catechism of the Catholic Church* was first published in Latin and French, followed by English and Spanish. A definitive explanation of the teachings of the Catholic Church, it is the preeminent source for understanding the Catholic faith.

## Go to the Document

The *Catechism of the Catholic Church* is available in print and online at www.usccb.org and www.vatican.va.

## ● Divine Mercy Sunday added to Church calendar, A.D. 2000

Pope Saint John Paul II designated the Sunday after Easter as Divine Mercy Sunday in the General Roman Calendar. Divine Mercy is a devotion based on revelations received by Saint Mary Faustina Kowalska emphasizing the merciful love of all.

## ● Resignation of Pope Benedict XVI and Election of Pope Francis, A.D. 2013

On February 28, 2013, Pope Benedict XVI became the first Pope in 598 years to step down from office. Citing declining health due to old age, he took the title of Pope Emeritus and continued to live at the Vatican. Cardinal Jorge Mario Bergoglio, Archbishop of Buenos Aires, Argentina became his successor, taking the name Pope Francis. Pope Francis is the first Pope from the Americas.

# Scripture

## The Catholic Bible

The Catholic Bible has seven Old Testament books or parts of books not included in other Christian Bibles. When these books are included in a Protestant Bible, they are usually found in a section called the Apocrypha or Deutero-canonical Books. The word *apocrypha* comes from a Greek word that means, "hidden things."

The apocryphal books are not found in the present Hebrew Bible but were included in an early Jewish canon that included Greek writings. Protestant Reformers of later centuries did not accept these books. Catholic translations of the Bible include *The New American Bible Revised Edition* and *The New Jerusalem Bible*. Some translations, such as *The New Revised Standard Version*, are accepted by Catholics and Protestants.

## How to Better Understand Scripture

God is the author of Sacred Scripture. But he used human authors and inspired them to write the contents of the Bible, to convey the saving truth he wanted us to know.

Catholics understand the Bible is a religious book and not an eyewitness account of historical events. For this reason, Catholics read Sacred Scripture while taking into account the context in which the human authors were writing. The human authors of the Bible used types of writing and other sources of information that reflected their time. The more we know about how people wrote, thought, and expressed themselves in biblical times, the better we can understand

what they meant. They adapted stories and images from area cultures to make their points about God.

You should always rely on the guidance of the Holy Spirit and the Church to help you understand the Word of God in Sacred Scripture.

# Senses of Scripture

*There are many layers, or senses, of Scripture.*

The **literal** sense of Scripture refers to the actual words that have been recorded.

Understanding the literal sense involves studying the culture in which the words were written—the meaning of those words to the people of that time and place.

The spiritual sense of Scripture has three subcategories:

- The **allegorical** sense of Scripture shows how certain events pointed to Christ, even before his birth. The crossing of the Red Sea, for example, is a sign of Christ's victory over death.

- The **moral** sense of Scripture gives instruction on how to live justly before God.

- The **anagogical** sense of Scripture shows how human events and realities are signs of our heavenly future. The word *anagogical* comes from the Greek word *anagoge*, which means "leading." The Church, for example, is understood as leading to the New Jerusalem of Heaven. You should always rely on the guidance of the Holy Spirit and the Church to help you understand the Word of God in Scripture.

# The Apostles

You can find the names of the Twelve Apostles in Matthew 10:1–4, Mark 3:13–19, and Luke 6:12–16.

**Simon Peter:** The leader of the Apostles, Simon was renamed "Peter" by Jesus. A fisherman from Galilee, he was introduced to Jesus by his brother Andrew. Peter was the first to proclaim Jesus as "the Christ, the Son of the Living God." He is said to have been crucified in Rome under the Emperor Nero. Considered the first Pope, he is believed to buried under St. Peter's Basilica at the Vatican.

**Andrew:** Andrew was originally a follower of John the Baptist. A fisherman like his brother Simon Peter, he is the disciple who brought the young boy with the loaves and fishes to Jesus to feed the crowds. According to tradition, he founded the church in Constantinople, present day Istanbul, Turkey, and was martyred in Southern Greece.

**James:** Considered the first Apostle to be martyred, he was the brother of John. He and his brother were called *Boanerges* or "Sons of Thunder" by Jesus, perhaps because of their tempers.

**John:** John is traditionally known as the author of the Fourth Gospel. Jesus entrusted his mother Mary to John's care during the Crucifixion. He is the only Apostle to live into old age and not be martyred.

**Philip:** Originally from the town of Bethsaida, Philip introduces Nathanael (Bartholomew) to Jesus. At the Feeding of the 5,000, Jesus tested him, asking, "Where can we buy enough food for them to eat?" At the Last Supper, he asks Jesus to show them the Father, prompting Jesus' teaching about the Father and the Son being one. He was martyred in what is now Turkey.

**Bartholomew:** Often identified as Nathanael, he was a friend of Philip. When he learned about Jesus, he had a hard time believing the Messiah could come from Nazareth, saying, "Can anything good come out of Nazareth?" He is said to have traveled to India and was later killed in Armenia.

**Matthew:** Matthew calls himself "the tax collector" and the Gospel according to Mark says his name was "Levi." After Jesus called him, he went to Matthew's house and shared a meal with him. Nothing specific is known about the end of Matthew's life.

**Thomas:** He is sometimes called "Doubting Thomas" because he said he would not believe Jesus had risen unless he could put his fingers in Jesus' wounds. When Jesus appeared and invited him to do so, Thomas proclaimed, "My Lord and my God." He is believed to have been martyred in India.

**James:** Sometimes he is called the "son of Alphaeus" or "James the Lesser" to show he is a different James from John's brother. Tradition says that he was martyred in Egypt where he was preaching the Gospel.

**Simon:** Matthew and Mark call him "the Cananean," and Luke called him a "Zealot," to make sure we know he is not Simon Peter. He is traditionally believed to have traveled and preached with Saint Jude Thaddeus and been martyred with him in the area around present-day Lebanon.

**Thaddeus:** Not to be confused with Judas, Jude Thaddeus is the patron Saint of lost causes. According to legend, he was the son of a cousin of the Virgin Mary.

**Judas Iscariot:** Judas handed Jesus to the authorities to be crucified for 30 coins. He is said to have hanged himself in remorse for his betrayal. Matthias was later chosen to take his place among the Twelve Apostles.

# The Holy Trinity

God is a communion of three Divine Persons: Father, Son, and Holy Spirit. God the Father is the Creator and source of all things. God the Son, Jesus, is the Savior of all people. God the Holy Spirit guides and makes holy all people and the Church.

The Holy Trinity is honored in the Sign of the Cross, in the Doxology, and in the liturgy of the Church. Christians are baptized "In the name of the Father, and of the Son, and of the Holy Spirit." In the blessings, and in the Eucharistic Prayer of the Mass, prayers are directed to God the Father, through the Son, in the Holy Spirit.

## God the Father

The First Divine Person of the Blessed Trinity, God the Father, is Creator of all that is. He is all-powerful and all-knowing. He is the one who journeys with you. He is the faithful and compassionate God who freed his People from slavery. He is as revealed to Moses, "I am who I am." God is gracious and merciful and steadfast in his love.

He is a God whom you can call Father, as Jesus taught in the Lord's Prayer. And, as Jesus also taught, God is love.

## God the Son

Through the power of the Holy Spirit, the Second Divine Person of the Trinity took on human nature and was born of the Virgin Mary. This is known as the Incarnation. Jesus Christ is both true God and true man.

The Paschal Mystery includes Jesus' suffering, Death, Resurrection, and Ascension. By the Paschal Mystery, Jesus completed the work of salvation and won for all people the promise of eternal life. The Paschal Mystery is celebrated in each of the Sacraments, particularly in the Mass, and in Lent, the Triduum, and Easter. Jesus' whole life can be said to be a Sacrament, a sign of God, a sign of God's salvation and love. At the Last Supper, Jesus said, "Whoever has seen me has seen the Father. . . . Believe me that I am in the Father and the Father is in me. . ." (John 14:9, 11).

- In each Sacrament, Jesus is Priest. For example, in the Eucharist, Jesus brings the people's prayers to God and offers himself as a sacrifice.

- Jesus is Prophet because he speaks for God. Jesus announced the Good News of God's mercy and forgiveness. He calls people to love God and one another, to be sorry for their sins, and to live justly.

- Jesus is King, the judge of everything in Heaven and on Earth. His judgments are merciful and just.

## God the Holy Spirit

The third Person of the Trinity, the Holy Spirit, is the guide who helps people to know God as he is revealed in Sacred Scripture and the living Word, Jesus. It is through the power of the Spirit that you come to know the Father and the Son.

The Spirit makes the Paschal Mystery real and present in the Sacraments and the Mass. At Mass it is the Spirit who is called on to transform the bread and wine into the Body and Blood of Christ. Finally, in the Eucharist, the Spirit unites the faithful with one another and with God in Christ. The Holy Spirit brings joy, peace, and reconciliation into the lives of the faithful.

# Creed

A creed is a summary of the Christian faith. The word *creed* means "I believe." There are two main creeds in the Church: The Nicene Creed and the Apostles' Creed

## Nicene Creed

*This creed which is prayed at Mass was written over a thousand years ago by leaders of the Church who met at a city named Nicaea. It is a summary of basic beliefs about God the Father, God the Son, and God the Holy Spirit, the Church, and other teachings.*

I believe in one God,
the Father almighty,
maker of heaven and earth,
of all things visible and invisible.

I believe in one Lord Jesus Christ,
the Only Begotten Son of God,
born of the Father before all ages.
God from God, Light from Light,
true God from true God,
begotten, not made, consubstantial with
the Father;
through him all things were made.
For us men and for our salvation
he came down from heaven,

*At the words that follow up to and including and became man, all bow.*

and by the Holy Spirit was incarnate of the
Virgin Mary,
and became man.

For our sake he was crucified under
Pontius Pilate,
he suffered death and was buried,
and rose again on the third day
in accordance with the Scriptures.
He ascended into heaven
and is seated at the right hand of the Father.
He will come again in glory
to judge the living and the dead
and his kingdom will have no end.

I believe in the Holy Spirit, the Lord,
the giver of life,
who proceeds from the Father and the Son,
who with the Father and the Son is adored
and glorified,
who has spoken through the prophets.

I believe in one, holy, catholic and
apostolic Church.
I confess one Baptism for the forgiveness
of sins
and I look forward to the resurrection
of the dead
and the life of the world to come. Amen.

## Apostles' Creed

*This summary of Christian beliefs has been taught since the time of the Apostles. It is used in the celebration of Baptism and is often used at Mass during the Season of Easter and in Masses with children. This creed is part of the Rosary.*

I believe in God,
the Father almighty,
Creator of heaven and earth,
and in Jesus Christ, his only Son, our Lord,

*At the words that follow, up to and including the Virgin Mary, all bow.*

who was conceived by the Holy Spirit,
born of the Virgin Mary,
suffered under Pontius Pilate,
was crucified, died and was buried;
he descended into hell;
on the third day he rose again from the dead;
he ascended into heaven,
and is seated at the right hand
   of God the Father almighty;
from there he will come to judge
   the living and the dead.
I believe in the Holy Spirit,
the holy catholic Church,
the communion of saints,
the forgiveness of sins,
the resurrection of the body,
and life everlasting. Amen.

# Marks of the Church

The Catholic Church is the Church founded by Christ and his Apostles. There are four marks, or essential characteristics, that distinguish Christ's Church and her mission: one, holy, catholic, and apostolic. These marks are mentioned in the Nicene Creed.

**One** means all the members are united as the Body of Christ, given life by the one Spirit. They acknowledge one Lord, one faith, one Baptism.

**Holy** means the Church is centered in God. It is Christ who, by his sacrifice, makes the Church holy.

**Catholic** means universal. The Church has the fullness of faith and is the means of salvation for all. The Church is for all times and all people.

**Apostolic** means the Church is built on the foundation of the Apostles. It teaches the doctrine of Jesus as it has been handed down through the Apostles and their successors, the Pope and bishops.

© Our Sunday Visitor

# The Church's Mission

The Church's mission is to proclaim and further God's reign in the world. She continues the mission, or work, of Christ through the Holy Spirit, according to God's plan until Jesus comes again in glory. This work is done by all Catholics—clergy, laity, and religious.

Ecumenism is a movement that seeks to bring about the unity of all Christian churches. The word ecumenism comes from a scriptural phrase in Greek that means "the whole household of God."

## The Pope

The Pope's title of "Servant of the Servants of God" began with Pope Gregory the Great. It is stated that "[W]hoever wishes to be first among you will be the slave of all" (Mark 10:44).

The many titles for the Pope include: Bishop of Rome, Vicar of Christ, Supreme Pontiff of the Universal Church, Patriarch of the West, Primate of Italy, Successor of Saint Peter, Prince of the Apostles, Servant of the Servants of God, and Sovereign of Vatican City.

There are several symbols involved in a papacy, including the Pope's ring and his coat of arms. When a Pope is elected, he is given a ring that depicts Saint Peter fishing. This reminds the Pope that he is to be a leader of God's People as Peter was.

The Papal coat of arms changes with each elected Pope, but typically depicts symbols of the papacy including two keys as a representation of the keys to God's Kingdom, an image representing the Holy Trinity, and a motto.

# The Church and Community

Jesus gifted us with the love that the three Persons in the Trinity share with each other. He founded his Church on the Divine love that the Trinity has for humankind. United in the Holy Spirit, the Pilgrim People of the Church lives in the world, as Jesus did, but aspires for a more fulfilling happiness than this world provides. The Church anticipates Jesus' coming again and our eternal reward in Heaven.

Catholics on Earth are united in faith and love with the Saints in Heaven and the souls in Purgatory. We call this the Communion of Saints. Every Sunday at Mass, we pray in the Creed: "I believe in the communion of Saints." After Mass, some Catholics remain and pray the Rosary or before a statue of a Saint. Our grandparent, aunt, or uncle may have a prayer table at home with a picture of a deceased loved one and a candle. Because we on Earth are united with the Saints in Heaven and the souls in Purgatory, we ask all our friends to pray for us—those living on Earth, those being purified in Purgatory, and those rejoicing forever in Heaven.

# The Church as Community

The church is a building in which God's people come together to worship. But the Church is the community of people. It was the plan of God the Father to call together those who believe in Christ. The Church is a gift from God, brought into being by the Holy Spirit to serve the mission of Jesus Christ. The Church, in Christ, can be called a sacrament, a sign of the communion of the Trinity, the union of all people with God, and the unity among people that will reach completion in the fullness of the Kingdom of God.

The Catholic Church is united in her faith, leadership structure, and Seven Sacraments. She is made up of Eastern Rite Catholics (Middle East and Eastern Europe) and Latin Rite Catholics (Rome and Western Europe).

The Catholic Church is governed by the Pope in union with all the bishops. Through the Sacrament of Holy Orders, bishops, priests, and deacons are ordained to serve the Church. Between fifteen and twenty days after the death of a Pope, the cardinals who are under the age of 80 meet in the Sistine Chapel in Rome to vote for a new Pope. Each cardinal writes on a sheet of paper the name of the man (usually one of the cardinals) he wishes to elect. If a candidate does not receive a majority of votes, the papers are burned with straw to produce black smoke. If a new Pope has been chosen, the papers alone are burned, producing white smoke.

The resignation of Pope Benedict XVI in 2013 was the first papal resignation in nearly 600 years. Following his resignation, Benedict XVI's official title became Pope Emeritus (a word that means *retired but retaining a title*). His successor, Cardinal Jorge Maria Bergoglio, took the name Pope Francis. Because he was the Cardinal Archbishop of Buenos Aires, Argentina, Pope Francis became the first Pope from the New World.

Pope Francis is also the first Jesuit to become Pope. The Jesuits belong to the consecrated religious community of the Society of Jesus, founded by Saint Ignatius of Loyola. Religious order priests belong to religious communities and make vows of poverty, chastity, and obedience. They obey a superior and do not own private property.

A diocesan, or secular, priest may own private property. He promises to obey the bishop of his diocese. Celibacy has been required of Latin Rite priests since the thirteenth century; exceptions are made for married men who have been ministers or priests in an ecclesial community and seek ordination after becoming Catholic. Eastern Rite Catholic priests may marry unless they live in countries where celibacy is the rule (such as the United States).

## The Saints

The Saints are holy people, heroes of the Church who loved God very much, did his work on Earth, cooperated with this grace, and are now with him in Heaven. Catholics honor the Saints for their heroic virtue and try to imitate them. They also ask that the Saints join with them in praying to God for special blessings. Saints are remembered in the Eucharistic Prayer and in the Litany of the Saints at Baptisms. Statues and images of the Saints on medals and holy cards are reminders that these "friends of God" can help believers grow in their own friendship with God.

Mary is honored above all other Saints. She is the Mother of God because she is the mother of the Son of God who became a human being. When the Angel Gabriel told Mary that she would be the mother of the Son of God, Mary believed and accepted God's plan. Her "yes" sets the example for all believers. Throughout the liturgical year, the Church celebrates Mary's place in Christian history. Among different cultures and traditions, devotion to Mary takes many forms.

# Life after Death

At the end of the Nicene Creed we profess, "and I look forward to the resurrection of the dead and the life of the world to come." The Church sometimes refers to teaching about this topic as the Last Things.

The Particular Judgment is the judgment made at the moment of a person's death. At this judgment the soul is rewarded with the blessings of Heaven, given a time of purification, or condemned to Hell.

- Heaven is the state of being happy with God forever. The souls of the just experience the full joy of living in God's presence forever.
- The final purification (Purgatory) is a time after death for those who are in God's friendship but need to be purified to be with him in Heaven. It is a state of final cleansing after death and before entering into Heaven.
- Hell is the state of eternal separation from God because of a choice to turn away from him and not seek forgiveness.

The Last Judgment is also called the General Judgment. This refers to God's final triumph over evil that will occur at the end of time when Christ returns and judges all the living and the dead. Then, all will fully see and understand God's plan for creation.

The new Heaven and new Earth is the Kingdom of God (or new Jerusalem) that will come in its fullness at the end of time.

# The Seven Sacraments

## The Sacraments of Initiation

*The Sacraments of Initiation—Baptism, Confirmation, and Eucharist—celebrate membership into the Catholic Church.*

The Sacraments of Initiation—**Baptism**, Confirmation, and Eucharist—celebrate membership into the Catholic Church.

In emergencies and other times of necessity, anyone can baptize another person. The person baptizing must intend to do what the Church does in this Sacrament. He or she needs to pour water over the head of the person being baptized while saying, "I baptize you in the name of the Father, and of the Son, and of the Holy Spirit." *(Rite of Baptism)*

**Confirmation** completes the baptismal grace and strengthens a person to be a witness to the faith through the power of the Spirit.

Catholics in different dioceses in the United States receive the Sacrament of Confirmation at different ages. In the Roman, or Latin, Rite candidates for Confirmation must meet certain criteria. They must believe in the faith of the Church, be in a state of grace, and want to receive the Sacrament. Candidates must be prepared and willing to be a witness to Christ in their daily lives and take an active part in the life of the Church.

**Eucharist** completes the Sacraments of Initiation, nourishing the baptized with Christ's own Body and Blood and uniting the new Christians with God and one another in Jesus.

The Eucharist is known by several different names. These include the Blessed Sacrament, Holy Communion, the Bread of Heaven, Breaking of Bread, the Lord's Supper, Holy Sacrifice, Holy Mass, and the Body of Christ.

## The Sacraments of Healing

*In the Sacraments of Healing—Penance and Reconciliation and Anointing of the Sick— God's forgiveness and healing are given to those suffering physical and spiritual sickness.*

In **Penance and Reconciliation**, through the words of absolution, personal sins are forgiven and relationships with God and the Church are healed.

In the **Anointing of the Sick**, one who is sick or dying is anointed with oil and with the laying on of hands. The person unites his or her suffering with that of Jesus. The Sacrament gives spiritual strength and God's grace. Physical healing also may take place.

## The Sacraments at the Service of Communion

*The Sacraments at the Service of Communion— Holy Orders and Matrimony—celebrate people's commitment to serve God and the community and help build up the People of God.*

In **Holy Orders**, the bishop lays hands on a man and anoints him with Sacred Chrism. The man is empowered to serve the Church as deacon, priest, or bishop.

In **Matrimony**, a baptized man and a baptized woman, through their words of consent, make a covenant with God and one another. Marriage is for the sake of their love and any children God blesses them with.

© Our Sunday Visitor

# Order of Mass

## Introductory Rites

Entrance Chant

Greeting

Rite for the Blessing and Sprinkling of Water

Penitential Act

*Kyrie*

*Gloria*

Collect

## Liturgy of the Word

First Reading

Responsorial Psalm

Second Reading

Gospel Acclamation

Dialogue at the Gospel (*or* Gospel Dialogue)

Gospel Reading

Homily

Profession of Faith (*or* Creed—Nicene Creed or Apostles' Creed)

Prayer of the Faithful

## Liturgy of the Eucharist

Preparation of the Gifts

Invitation to Prayer

Prayer over the Offerings

Eucharistic Prayer

Preface Dialogue

Preface

Preface Acclamation

Consecration

Mystery of Faith

Concluding Doxology

Amen

## Communion Rite

The Lord's Prayer

Sign of Peace

Lamb of God

Invitation to Communion

Communion

Prayer after Communion

## Concluding Rites

Solemn Blessing or Prayer over the People

Final Blessing

Dismissal

# Order of Rite for Reconciliation of Individual Recipients

1. Reception of the Penitent (Welcome)

2. Reading of the Word of God

3. Confession of Sins and Acceptance of Satisfaction (a Penance)

4. Prayer of the Penitent (beginning with the Act of Contrition; see page 387)

5. Absolution, including the words of absolution from the priest:
   God, the Father of Mercies,
   through the death and resurrection of his Son
   has reconciled the world to himself
   and sent the Holy Spirit among us
   for the forgiveness of sins;
   through the ministry of the Church
   may God give you pardon and peace,
   and I absolve you from your sins
   in the name of the Father, and of the Son,
   and of the Holy Spirit.

6. Closing Prayer

## Examination of Conscience

Examining your conscience should be done daily and especially in preparation for the Sacrament of Penance and Reconciliation.

1. Pray to the Holy Spirit to help you examine your conscience.

2. Look at your life in light of the Beatitudes, the Ten Commandments, the Great Commandment, and the Precepts of the Church.

3. Ask yourself:
   Where have I fallen short of what God wants for me?
   Whom have I hurt?
   What have I done that I knew was wrong?
   Have I done penance and tried as hard as I could to make up for past sins?
   Am I working to change my bad habits?
   With what areas am I still having trouble?
   Am I sincerely sorry for all my sins?

4. In addition to confessing your sins, you may wish to talk with the priest about one or more of the above questions.

# The Liturgical Year

The liturgical year celebrates Jesus' life and work for the salvation of the world. During Advent and Christmas, the Church celebrates the Incarnation. The Seasons of Lent, Triduum, and Easter explore the Paschal Mystery. Easter is the high point of the liturgical year because it is the greatest celebration of the Resurrection. The life and ministry of Jesus are the focus of Ordinary Time. Mary and the Saints are also remembered throughout the year in what is known as the sanctoral cycle.

## Holy Days of Obligation

Catholics must attend Mass on Sunday unless a serious reason prevents their doing so. They must also go to Mass on certain holy days. United States Holy Days of Obligation are

- Mary, Mother of God (January 1)
- Ascension (forty days after Easter or the Sunday nearest the end of the forty-day period)
- Assumption (August 15)
- All Saints Day (November 1)
- Immaculate Conception (December 8)
- Christmas (December 25)

## Fasting and Abstinence

To help prepare spiritually for the Eucharist, Catholics fast for one hour before Holy Communion. They take no food or drink except water. (Exceptions are made for those who are sick and for those of advanced age.)

To fast means to eat only one full meal and two smaller meals during the course of a day. All Catholics, from their eighteenth birthday until their fifty-ninth birthday, are required to fast on Ash Wednesday and Good Friday unless a serious reason prevents them from doing so. Another discipline of self-denial is abstinence. Catholics who are fourteen years of age or older are expected to abstain from eating meat on Ash Wednesday, Good Friday, and, in the United States, on all of the Fridays in Lent.

# The Law

Divine law is the eternal law of God. It includes:

**physical law:** the law of gravity is an example of physical law.

**natural moral law:** a moral law is one that humans understand through reasoning (stealing is wrong) and through Divine Revelation (keep holy the Lord's Day).

Natural moral law refers to the precepts about goodness that are written by God in our hearts and accessible through our God-given reason. For example, people everywhere understand that no person may kill another unjustly. Everyone must obey natural moral law because everyone is created by God. God's Commandments are based on natural moral law.

## The Ten Commandments

- ○ I am the Lord your God. You shall not have strange gods before me.
- ○ You shall not take the name of the Lord your God in vain.
- ○ Remember to keep holy the Lord's Day.
- ○ Honor your father and your mother.
- ○ You shall not kill.
- ○ You shall not commit adultery.
- ○ You shall not steal.
- ○ You shall not bear false witness against your neighbor.
- ○ You shall not covet your neighbor's wife.
- ○ You shall not covet your neighbor's goods.

## The Great Commandment

"You shall love the Lord, your God, with all your heart, with all your being, with all your strength, and with all your mind, and your neighbor as yourself." (Luke 10:27)

## The New Commandment

"Love one another. As I have loved you, so you also should love one another." (John 13:34)

## Precepts of the Church

The Precepts of the Church are some of the minimum requirements given by Church leaders for deepening our relationship with God and the Church. They name specific actions that all Catholics are obligated to carry out.

1. Take part in the Mass on Sundays and holy days. Keep these days holy and avoid unnecessary work.

2. Celebrate the Sacrament of Penance and Reconciliation at least once a year if there is serious sin.

3. Receive Holy Communion at least once a year during the Easter Season.

4. Fast and/or abstain on days of penance.

5. Give your time, gifts, and money to support the Church.

## The Beatitudes

Blessed are the poor in spirit,
for theirs is the kingdom of heaven.
Blessed are they who mourn,
for they will be comforted.
Blessed are the meek,
for they will inherit the land.
Blessed are they who hunger and thirst for righteousness,
for they will be satisfied.
Blessed are the merciful,
for they will be shown mercy.
Blessed are the clean of heart,
for they will see God.
Blessed are the peacemakers,
for they will be called children of God.
Blessed are they who are persecuted for the sake of righteousness,
for theirs is the kingdom of heaven.
Matthew 5:1–12

# The Works of Mercy

The Works of Mercy are "charitable actions by which we come to the aid of our neighbor" (CCC, 2447). The Corporal Works show care for the physical needs of people, while the Spiritual Works address the needs of the heart, mind, and soul.

| The Works of Mercy | |
|---|---|
| **Corporal** | **Spiritual** |
| Feed the hungry. | Warn the sinner. |
| Give drink to the thirsty. | Teach the ignorant. |
| Clothe the naked. | Counsel the doubtful. |
| Shelter the homeless. | Comfort the sorrowful. |
| Visit the sick. | Bear wrongs patiently. |
| Visit the imprisoned. | Forgive injuries. |
| Bury the dead. | Pray for the living and the dead. |

## Gifts of the Holy Spirit

The Gifts of the Holy Spirit are seven powerful gifts God gives us to follow the guidance of the Holy Spirit and live the Christian life. We are sealed with these gifts at the Sacrament of Confirmation, and they strengthen the gifts we receive at Baptism.

The spirit of the Lord shall rest upon him;
a spirit of wisdom and of understanding,
A spirit of counsel and of strength,
A spirit of knowledge and of fear of the Lord. Isaiah 11:2–5

**Wisdom** helps you see yourself as God sees you and act as God wants you to act. Wisdom allows you to live in the image and likeness of God.

**Understanding** allows you to get to know God, yourself, and others better. With understanding comes help to make good choices and forgive more freely.

**Right judgment (Counsel)** helps you give good advice to others and hear the Holy Spirit, who speaks to you through the good advice and good example of others.

**Courage (Fortitude)** helps you stand up for what is right even when doing so is difficult, and allows you to overcome your fears, which can lead you to make the wrong choices.

**Knowledge** allows you to be open to God's loving communication and know him in the way that you come to know someone you love and someone who loves you.

**Reverence (Piety)** helps you show faithful love and honor to God, and allows you to recognize the importance of spending time talking and listening to God in prayer.

**Wonder and awe (Fear of the Lord)** allows you to know that God is greater and more wonderful than any created thing, and reminds you to be open to his powerful goodness.

| Fruits of the Holy Spirit | | |
| --- | --- | --- |
| The Fruits of the Spirit are qualities that can be seen is us when we allow the Holy Spirit to work in our hearts. | | |
| Charity | Faithfulness | Gentleness |
| Joy | Modesty | Generosity |
| Peace | Kindness | Self-control |
| Patience | Goodness | Chastity |

# Grace and Sin

**Sanctifying grace** allows you to share in God's own life. It is a permanent gift that builds your friendship with God and assures you of eternal life.

**Actual grace** is a temporary gift that helps you think or act according to God's will for you in a particular situation. Actual grace helps you understand what is right and strengthens you to turn away from sin.

**Sacramental grace** is the gift that comes from the Sacraments. Each Sacrament gives its own particular grace.

## Sin

Sin is a turning away from God and a failure to love. Sin affects both the individual and the community. A person may be sorry for his or her sin, ask forgiveness for it, accept punishment for it, and resolve to do better. In this case, the experience may actually help the person develop as a Christian and avoid sin in the future. However, a person who makes a habit of sin will harm his or her development set a poor example, and

bring sorrow to others. Society suffers when people disobey God's law and the just laws of society. There are many types of sin.

**Original Sin** is the sin that the first humans committed by choosing to disobey God. This sin describes the fallen state that caused the human condition of weakness and tendency toward sin. Baptism restores the relationship of loving grace in which all people were created by God.

**Personal sin** is any thought, word, act, or failure to act that goes against God's law. Sin is a choice, not a mistake.

**Mortal sin** separates you from God. For a sin to be mortal, it must be a serious matter done with full knowledge and complete consent.

**Venial sin** weakens or wounds your relationship with God. Continual venial sin can lead to mortal sin.

**Social sin** results from the effect that personal sin has on a community. People who have been sinned against may sin in return. Violence, injustice, and other wrongs may develop within the community. God created humans in his image and likeness. Because of this, you have dignity and therefore need to respect your dignity and that of others.

Asking forgiveness, accepting punishment, and resolving not to sin again helps a person develop as a Christian. However, one who habitually sins neglects Christian development, sets a poor example, and harms others. When individuals disobey God's law and just civil laws, the entire community suffers.

## Virtue

The Theological Virtues of faith, hope, and charity (love) are gifts from God. These virtues help you live in a loving relationship with God.

The Cardinal Virtues are the principal moral virtues that help you lead a moral life. They help us to live as children of God. We strengthen these virtues through God's grace and our own efforts.

**Prudence** is careful judgment. This virtue helps you be practical and make the right decisions on what is morally good, with the help of the Holy Spirit and an informed conscience.

**Fortitude** is courage, especially in the face of evil and temptation. Fortitude gives you strength to get through difficulties and helps you not give up when you have chosen to do good.

**Justice** is giving to God and to each person what is due to them. Justice helps you build up the community by respecting rights and promoting the common good (see page 377).

**Temperance** means keeping a balance in life. It allows us to use moderation, be disciplined, and have self-control.

# Human Dignity

Human dignity is the worth each person has because he or she is made in the image of God. We are all equal in dignity, each and every one of us worthy of respect and love. Because our common human dignity, people have basic human rights, such as food, clothing, and shelter. No government or social group should fail to recognize those rights.

God's image is his likeness that is present in you because you are his creation. You are called to respect the dignity of all people because everyone is made in God's image.

- Freedom means you are able to choose and act with few limitations. We are given freedom by God that we may choose to good things.
- Free will is the gift from God that allows humans to make their own choices. Because you are free to choose between right and wrong, you are responsible for your choices and actions.
- Conscience is a gift from God that helps us judge whether actions are right or wrong. It is important for us to know God's laws so our conscience can help us make good decisions. Conscience helps you choose what is right. It involves free will and reason working together. You must form your conscience properly. If not formed properly, your conscience can lead you to choose what is wrong.

Forming your conscience is a lifelong process. It involves practicing virtues and avoiding sin and people or situations that may lead you to sin. You can turn to good people for advice, to Church teachings for guidance, and to God for help in educating your conscience.

## Respecting Life

As Catholics, we recognize ourselves as human persons related to one another. From the moment of conception until natural death, we are sacred because God created each of us in his image and likeness. We deepen our relationship with Christ when we love each other as Christ loved us, and when we respect human life through all stages. For more on the Catholic Social Teaching on the Life and Dignity of the Human Person, see pages 334–335.

## Justice and Peace

Justice is a Cardinal Virtue. It is the habit and practice of giving God what is due him, and giving each person what he or she is due because that person is a child of God. Social justice urges individuals to seek the common good of the whole group rather than just his or her individual good.

Peace is a state of calm and harmony when things are in their proper order and people settle problems with kindness and justice. In the Catholic tradition, peace is not just the absence of conflict. It is the result of right relationships with God and others.

## Common Good

The common good refers to the good of everyone, with particular concern for those who might be most vulnerable to harm. It means people are allowed to become who God wants them to become. The common good includes peace, development of groups of people, and respect for every person. These conditions vary from society to society, which is why the Church evaluates each country's system on the basis of whether or not it provides the conditions for human fulfillment.

## Themes of Catholic Social Teaching

The Catholic bishops of the United States have outlined seven themes of Catholic Social Teaching, which call Catholics to address and understand the responsibilities humans have to each other and to creation. For more on these topics see the Live Your Faith section of your book.

**Life and Dignity of the Human Person** All people are created in the image of God and are equal in human dignity. We are called to respect and protect the dignity of all.

**Call to Family, Community, and Participation** As part of our own families and as part of the greater human family, we form one Body of Christ. We are called to promote a sense of community in every level of society.

**Rights and Responsibilities of the Human Person** We are called to respect and recognize the basic human rights of everyone, and work to promote human rights and the common good.

**Option for the Poor and Vulnerable** Catholics are called to use their time, talents, and resources in the service of the poor and vulnerable. We are called to recognize Jesus in the poor and to show them the same respect and love.

**Dignity of Work and the Rights of Workers** Work is one way through which people express themselves and fulfill their human potential using their gifts and talents.

**Solidarity of the Human Family** We are called to recognize the rights and needs of people all over the world, and to stand with them as brothers and sisters. Catholics are meant to respond to those needs personally and sacrificially.

**Care for God's Creation** Our first response to the beauty and goodness of God's creation is to savor and enjoy it. Our second response is to discover God's presence in creation. But our most important response is to care for God's creation and share it with others.

# Vocations

God calls all of us to share in the life and mission of Jesus. A vocation is the purpose for which God made us, and a particular way to answer his call to service. The word vocation comes the Latin word *vocare*, which means "to call." Our vocation helps us see how everything fits together in our lives. It shows us how God created us to love, serve, and work with each other. Our vocation comes from the grace we receive in the Sacrament of Baptism. Every one of us must answer our call from God to work with him as he builds his Kingdom on Earth.

There are three ways you can serve God through your vocation: as a layperson, or member of the laity, as a member of a religious community, or as a member of the ordained ministry.

## The Laity

The laity is all of the baptized people in the Church who share in God's mission but are not priests or consecrated sisters and brothers. Members of the laity can be single people or married couples. They can perform various roles in the Church, such as lector, altar servers, and musicians at Mass, and also serve their parish by acting as good Catholic role models in their daily lives.

## Members of Religious Communities

There are many kinds of communities of religious sisters and brothers. The members of these communities teach, care for the sick, work as missionaries, or do other good works as part of their call from God. Consecrated religious brothers and sisters dedicate their lives to serving God by following the charism, or special grace, of their community and its founder.

## Ordained Ministry

Some men are called to ordained ministry through the Sacrament of Holy Orders. This Sacrament gives a sacred power, through the laying on of hands by a bishop, for serving the faithful by teaching, leading people in worship, and pastoral care. Bishops, priests, and deacons share in this Sacrament. A bishop serves the Church as the pastor and teacher of his diocese. They work with other bishops and the Pope for the good of the whole Catholic Church. Priests assist the bishop within a diocese and celebrate the Sacraments with their parish community. Deacons are ministers who serve by helping in liturgical roles and doing works of charity.

You may not know yet about the vocation to which God is calling you. As you get older, you can continue to think about the gifts God has given you, and through them, you will better understand his plan and purpose for you.

## Charisms

Charisms are special gifts or graces of the Holy Spirit which benefit the Church and help us lead a Christian life. These gifts build up the community and also help us share Christ's message with others, and serve the common good. Members of religious communities follow the specific charisms given to that community and its founder. For example, some communities are devoted to prayer, because their founders built the foundation of the community's spirituality on the power of this special communication with God. Saint Benedict followed a motto of *prayer and work*, and the Benedictans continue to model their ministry on those things. Other communities may be devoted to service, health care, or missions.

## Vows

Members of religious communities profess, or promise aloud, to live three vows, or sacred promises made to or before God, that are found in the Gospel: poverty, chastity, and obedience. These vows are also evangelical counsels that lead to the perfection of the Christian, and therefore apply to all of us.

- **Poverty:** living a simple life and sharing material possessions in community. This helps one free one's self from undue attachment to material things and to rely on God to care for their needs while they provide for others.

- **Chastity:** exercising discipline over sexuality and maintaining the right balance of body and spirit in human sexuality. This shows that for the consecrated religious, their love for God is the most important thing in their lives.

- **Obedience:** following and obeying God's will, expressed through the guidance of the community's leaders, the charism of the community, and the person's conscience. Consecrated religious find peace in discerning and following God's will for them.

We are called to live out these counsels, but men and women religious do so in a radical way.

## Discipleship

The word disciple means "student." If you are a disciple of Jesus Christ, it means you believe in him and follow his teachings. Part of discipleship is studying those teachings and applying them to your life.

From the very beginning of the Church, disciples were sent out to share and teach God's Word and his laws. Discipleship has always involved bringing people to Christ, and bringing all Christians to the Catholic Church. It means deepening your relationship with Christ to understand and live by his teachings, and to be an example of his love to the world. Catholics do not just practice discipleship alone. It is most effective when lived out as part of community of disciples: the entire Catholic Church.

Being a disciple sometimes means being very different from people around you. It means standing up for what you believe and following the Ten Commandments and other teachings from the Bible. The members of your parish support you as you live out God's plan for your life, and share his goodness and truth with others.

Discipleship is part of the Church's mission to continue the work of Jesus Christ, teaching others about God and bringing the Good News of God's Kingdom to the whole world. We have the right and the responsibility to be disciples, and to make sure God's saving message is known and accepted by all.

# Forms of Prayer

Prayer is talking and listening to God. In prayer, we raise our hearts and minds to God. One of the first prayers we learn in the Church is the Lord's Prayer, which Jesus taught his followers. Jesus prayed when he needed help, when he wanted to help others, and when he wanted to praise God his Father. Prayer should be an important part of your life as well. You can pray a prayer you have heard before, or create one yourself. You can pray out loud or in silence. Your prayers will always be heard by God.

On the next pages, you will find several common prayers of the Catholic Church. You will have heard many of them at Mass, and they fit under the categories of these five principal forms of prayer:

## Blessing and Adoration

In this prayer form, we show that we understand God is the Creator of all things, and that we need him. We give him respect and honor his greatness. We bless God, who blesses us. We also bless others who are made in God's image. A blessing is a response to God's gifts. Adoration means giving respect to God by honoring his greatness. Some prayers of adoration you might be familiar with include the Gloria and the Act of Faith.

## Praise

In this prayer form, we give God honor and thanks because he is God. We give him glory not for what he does, but simply because he is. When we praise God in prayer, we give him glory as his children. Praise holds together all of our prayers, and prayer forms, and raises them toward God, who is the source and goal of all prayer. You may be familiar with prayers of praise that include readings from the Psalms.

## Intercession

Intercession, or intercessory prayer, is a form of prayer that involves praying to God on behalf of someone else. We can pray for people who are close to us; for people around the world who suffer from hunger, poverty, disease, war, or other problems; and for those who have died and are not yet with God in Heaven. We use intercessory prayer on behalf of others as Jesus intercedes for us with his Father. Because praying for others is a Work for Mercy, intercessory prayer is vital to the Church and our relationship with God. One important prayer of intercession is the Hail Mary.

## Petition

In this prayer form, we ask God for what we need. We turn to God and ask for his help, and recognize that we need him. In prayers of petition, we might pray for God's mercy, forgiveness, and guidance when we are sad, sick, troubled, confused, or in a state of sin. We also ask God to help others. Possibly the most familiar prayer of petition is the Lord's Prayer, also known as the Our Father.

## Thanksgiving

When we pray a prayer of Thanksgiving, we give thanks to God for all he has given us. We express our gratitude to him for the good things in our lives. When we experience a special reason for happiness, such as good grades or someone feeling better after an illness, or even just for a good day, we can thank God for it in prayer. You may be most familiar with this form of prayer when saying a grace before meals.

## Elements of The Lord's Prayer

The Lord's Prayer is made up of the following parts: praise, hope (a yearning for the Kingdom of God), petition (asking for our needs to be met, and for forgiveness of sins), and a desire for goodness (freedom from testing or evil). There are actually seven petitions in this prayer.

The first three petitions are more theological. They draw us toward the Father's glory, are for God's sake (thy name, thy Kingdom, thy will), and are already answered in Jesus' sacrifice. The last four ask God for improvement in our human situation. With them we put our weaknesses and our poverty of spirit in his hands. We gain strength and richness of spirit in his grace (give us, forgive us, lead us not, deliver us).

## Schools of Prayer

There are several "schools" of prayer and Christian spirituality. They are all part of the Church's living Tradition of prayer, and although they are very different, they all come from the Holy Spirit. The Holy Spirit teaches us through family prayer at home.

**Spiritual direction:** Learning alone from a guide

**Prayer groups:** Learning to pray with others; Church ministers lead and teach liturgical prayer

**Catechesis:** Learning about prayer through classes and ministry involvement; consecrated religious teach contemplative (wordless) prayer

# Basic Prayers

*These are essential prayers that every Catholic should know. Latin is the official, universal language of the Church. As members of the Catholic Church, we usually pray in the language that we speak, but we sometimes pray in Latin, the common language of the Church.*

## Sign of the Cross

In the name of the Father
and of the Son
and of the Holy Spirit. Amen.

## Signum Crucis

In nómine Patris,
et Fílii,
et Spíritus Sancti.
Amen.

## The Lord's Prayer

Our Father, who art in heaven,
hallowed be thy name;
thy kingdom come,
thy will be done
on earth as it is in heaven.
Give us this day our daily bread,
and forgive us our trespasses,
as we forgive those who trespass
 against us;
and lead us not into temptation,
but deliver us from evil.
Amen.

## Pater Noster

Pater noster qui es in cælis:
santificétur Nomen Tuum;
advéniat Regnum Tuum;
fiat volúntas Tua,
sicut in cælo, et in terra.
Panem nostrum
cotidiánum da nobis hódie;
et dimítte nobis débita nostra,
sicut et nos
dimíttus debitóribus nostris;
et ne nos indúcas in tentatiónem;
sed líbera nos a Malo.

## Glory Be

Glory be to the Father
and to the Son
and to the Holy Spirit,
as it was in the beginning
is now, and ever shall be
world without end. Amen.

## Gloria Patri

Gloria Patri
et Filio
et Spíritui Sancto.
Sicut erat in princípio,
et nunc et semper
et in sæ´cula sæ´culorem. Amen.

## The Hail Mary

Hail, Mary, full of grace,
the Lord is with thee.
Blessed art thou among women
and blessed is the fruit of thy womb, Jesus.
Holy Mary, Mother of God,
pray for us sinners,
now and at the hour of our death.
Amen.

## Prayer to the Holy Spirit

Come, Holy Spirit, fill the hearts of
    your faithful.
And kindle in them the fire of your love.
Send forth your Spirit and they shall
    be created.
And you will renew the face of the earth.
Let us pray.
Lord, by the light of the Holy Spirit you
    have taught the hearts of your faithful.
    In the same Spirit help us to relish
    what is right and always rejoice in
    your consolation.
We ask this through Christ our Lord. Amen.

## Ave, Maria

Ave María, grátia plena,
Dóminus tecum.
Benedícta tu in muliéribus,
et benedíctus fructus ventris tui, Iesus
Sancta María, Mater Dei,
ora pro nobis peccatóribus,
nunc et in hora mortis nostræ.
Amen.

## *Memorare*

Remember, most loving Virgin Mary,
never was it heard that anyone who turned
    to you for help was left unaided.
Inspired by this confidence, though
    burdened by my sins, I run to your
    protection for you are my mother.
Mother of the Word of God, do not despise
    my words of pleading but be merciful
    and hear my prayer. Amen.

## Hail, Holy Queen

Hail, holy Queen, Mother of mercy,
hail, our life, our sweetness, and our hope.
To you we cry, the children of Eve;
to you we send up our sighs,
mourning and weeping in this land of exile.
Turn, then, most gracious advocate,
your eyes of mercy toward us;
lead us home at last
and show us the blessed fruit of your womb,
Jesus:
O clement, O loving, O sweet Virgin Mary.
Salve, Regina

# Prayers from the Sacraments

## Holy, Holy, Holy Lord

Holy, Holy, Holy Lord God of hosts.
Heaven and earth are full of your glory.
Hosanna in the highest.
Blessed is he who comes in the name of
   the Lord.
Hosanna in the highest.

## Sanctus, Sanctus, Sanctus

Sanctus, Sanctus, Sanctus
Dominus Deus Sabaoth.
Pleni sunt coeli et terra gloria tua.
Hosanna in excelsis.
Benedictus qui venit in nomine Domini.
Hosanna in excelsis

## Lamb of God

Lamb of God, you take away the
   sins of the world,
     have mercy on us.
Lamb of God, you take away the
   sins of the world,
     have mercy on us.
Lamb of God, you take away the
   sins of the world,
     grant us peace.

## Agnus Dei

Agnus Dei, qui tollis peccata mundi:
miserere nobis.
Agnus Dei, qui tollis peccata mundi:
miserere nobis.
Agnus Dei, qui tollis peccata mundi:
dona nobis pacem

## Gloria

Glory to God in the highest,
and on earth peace to people of good will.

We praise you,
we bless you,
we adore you,
we glorify you,
we give you thanks for your great glory,
Lord God, heavenly King,
O God, almighty Father.

Lord Jesus Christ, Only Begotten Son,
Lord God, Lamb of God, Son of the Father,
you take away the sins of the world,
   have mercy on us;
you take away the sins of the world,
   receive our prayer;
you are seated at the right hand of the
Father,
   have mercy on us.

For you alone are the Holy One,
you alone are the Lord,
you alone are the Most High,
Jesus Christ,
with the Holy Spirit,
in the glory of God the Father.
Amen.

## Confiteor

I confess to almighty God
and to you, my brothers and sisters,
that I have greatly sinned,
in my thoughts and in my words,
in what I have done
and in what I have failed to do,
through my fault, through my fault,
through my most grievous fault;
therefore I ask blessed Mary ever-Virgin,
all the Angels and Saints,
and you my brothers and sisters,
to pray for me to the Lord our God.

# Prayers from the Liturgy of the Hours

## The Canticle of Zechariah

*This hymn is sung during the Liturgy of the Hours, Morning Prayer.*

Blessed be the Lord, the God of Israel;
he has come to his people and set them free.

He has raised up for us a mighty savior,
born of the house of his servant David.

Through his holy prophets he promised of old
that he would save us from our enemies,
from the hands of all who hate us.

He promised to show mercy to our fathers
and to remember his holy covenant.

This was the oath he swore to our father
   Abraham:
to set us free from the hands of our enemies,
free to worship him without fear,
holy and righteous in his sight
all the days of our life.

Based on Luke 1:68–75

## The *Magnificat* (Mary's Canticle)

*This hymn is sung during the Liturgy of the Hours, Evening Prayer.*

My soul proclaims the greatness of the Lord,
my spirit rejoices in God my Savior;
for he has looked with favor on his lowly
servant.
From this day all generations will call me
blessed:
the Almighty has done great things for me,
and holy is his Name.
He has mercy on those who fear him
in every generation.
He has shown the strength of his arm,
he has scattered the proud in their conceit.

He has cast down the mighty from their
thrones,
and has lifted up the lowly.
He has filled the hungry with good things,
and the rich he has sent away empty.
He has come to the help of his servant Israel
for he has remembered his promise of mercy,
the promise he made to our fathers,
to Abraham and his children for ever.

Based on Luke 1:46–55

# Personal and Family Prayers

*The Holy Spirit teaches us through family prayer at home. Below are some common prayers Catholics pray at home. The Act of Contrition (see page 386) should be prayed before receiving the Sacrament of Reconciliation.*

## Act of Faith

O God, we firmly believe that you are one God in three divine Persons, Father, Son, and Holy Spirit; we believe that your divine Son became man and died for our sins, and that he will come to judge the living and the dead. We believe these and all the truths that the holy Catholic Church teaches because you have revealed them, and you can neither deceive nor be deceived.

## Act of Hope

O God, relying on your almighty power and your endless mercy and promises, we hope to gain pardon for our sins, the help of your grace, and life everlasting, through the saving actions of Jesus Christ, our Lord and Redeemer.

## Act of Love

O God, we love you above all things, with our whole heart and soul, because you are all-good and worthy of all love. We love our neighbor as ourselves for the love of you. We forgive all who have injured us and ask pardon of all whom we have injured.

## Act of Contrition

My God, I am sorry for my sins with all my heart.
In choosing to do wrong
and failing to do good,
I have sinned against you
whom I should love above all things.
I firmly intend, with your help,
to do penance,
to sin no more,
and to avoid whatever leads me to sin.
Our Savior Jesus Christ
suffered and died for us.
In his name, my God, have mercy.

# Devotional Practices

## Novenas

The Novena was a popular expression of faith for Catholics in previous generations that is still used today. A novena is a recitation of prayers or spiritual devotions with a specific request or intention that are performed nine times in a row. Sometimes that means nine hours in a row, nine weekdays (such as nine Fridays) or nine days of the month (such as First Fridays or First Saturdays). These devotions can include fasting, almsgiving, or receiving Holy Communion as well as prayer.

The name novena comes from the Latin word for nine (novem, meaning "nine each") and is based on the nine days the Apostles and Mary spent in prayer between the Ascension of Jesus Christ in Heaven (forty days after Easter) and Pentecost (the coming of the Holy Spirit). Novenas may be private devotion or public prayer. They often focus on a particular Saint, Mary, image (such as the Sacred Heart of Jesus), or occasion (such as the Annunciation).

© Our Sunday Visitor

## Praying with the Saints

When we pray with the Saints, we ask them to pray to God for us and to pray with us. The Saints are with Christ. They speak for us when we need help.

As the Mother of Jesus, the Son of God, Mary is called the Mother of God, the Queen of all Saints, and the Mother of the Church. There are many prayers and practices of devotion to Mary. One of the most revered is the Rosary. It focuses on the twenty mysteries that describe events in the lives of Jesus and Mary.

## How to Pray the Rosary

1. Pray the Sign of the Cross and say the Apostles' Creed.
2. Pray the Lord's Prayer.
3. Pray three Hail Marys.
4. Pray the Glory Be.
5. Say the first mystery; then pray the Lord's Prayer.
6. Pray ten Hail Marys while meditating on the mystery.
7. Pray the Glory Be.
8. Say the second mystery; then pray the Lord's Prayer.

Repeat 6 and 7 and continue with the third, fourth, and fifth mysteries in the same manner.

9. Pray the Hail, Holy Queen (see page 383).

## The Mysteries of the Rosary

### The Joyful Mysteries
The Annunciation
The Visitation
The Nativity
The Presentation in the Temple
The Finding in the Temple

### The Sorrowful Mysteries
The Agony in the Garden
The Scourging at the Pillar
The Crowning with Thorns
The Carrying of the Cross
The Crucifixion and Death

### The Glorious Mysteries
The Resurrection
The Ascension
The Descent of the Holy Spirit
The Assumption of Mary
The Coronation of Mary in Heaven

### The Luminous Mysteries
The Baptism of Jesus
The Wedding at Cana
The Proclamation of the Kingdom
The Transfiguration
The Institution of the Eucharist

## Stations of the Cross

The devotional practice of the Stations of the Cross began in the early Church. Pilgrims would visit the various sites in Jerusalem that were associated with Christ's suffering and death. The Stations of the Cross focus on fourteen scenes of Christ's Passion.

**First Station:** Jesus is condemned to death on the Cross.  John 3:16
"For God so loved the world that he gave his only Son, so that everyone who believes in him might not perish but might have eternal life."

**Second Station:** Jesus accepts his Cross. Luke 9:23
"Then he said to all, 'If anyone wishes to come after me, he must deny himself and take up his cross daily and follow me.'"

**Third Station:** Jesus falls the first time. Isaiah 53:6
"We had all gone astray like sheep, all following our own way; but the LORD laid upon him the guilt of us all."

**Fourth Station:** Jesus meets his sorrowful mother.  Lamentations 1:12
"Come, all who pass by the way, pay attention and see: Is there any pain like my pain …"

**Fifth Station:** Simon of Cyrene helps Jesus carry his Cross.  Matthew 25:40
"And the king will say to them in reply, 'Amen, I say to you, whatever you did for one of these least brothers of mine, you did for me.'"

**Sixth Station:** Veronica wipes the face of Jesus. John 14:9
"… 'Whoever has seen me has seen the Father'…"

**Seventh Station:** Jesus falls the second time.  Matthew 11:28
"Come to me, all you who labor and are burdened, and I will give you rest."

**Eighth Station:** Jesus meets and speaks to the women of Jerusalem.  Luke 23:28
"Jesus turned to them and said, 'Daughters of Jerusalem, do not weep for me; weep instead for yourselves and for your children …'"

**Ninth Station:** Jesus falls the third time. Luke 14:11
"For everyone who exalts himself will be humbled, but the one who humbles himself will be exalted."

**Tenth Station:** Jesus is stripped of his garments.  Luke 14:33
"In the same way, every one of you who does not renounce all his possessions cannot be my disciple."

**Eleventh Station:** Jesus is nailed to the Cross.  John 6:38
"Because I came down from heaven not to do my own will but the will of the one who sent me."

**Twelfth Station:** Jesus dies on the Cross. Philippians 2:7–8
"… And found human in appearance, he humbled himself, becoming obedient to death, even death on a cross."

**Thirteenth Station:** Jesus is taken down from the Cross.  Luke 24:26
"Was it not necessary that the Messiah should suffer these things and enter into his glory?"

**Fourteenth Station:** Jesus is placed in the tomb. John 12:24
"Amen, amen, I say to you, unless a grain of wheat falls to the ground and dies, it remains just a grain of wheat; but if it dies, it produces much fruit."

## Litany of Saint Joseph

| | |
|---|---|
| Lord, have mercy. | Lord, have mercy. |
| Christ, have mercy. | Christ, have mercy. |
| Lord, have mercy. | Lord, have mercy. |
| Good Saint Joseph, | pray for us. |
| Descendant of the House of David | pray for us. |
| Husband of Mary, | pray for us. |
| Foster father of Jesus, | pray for us. |
| Guardian of Christ, | pray for us. |
| Support of the holy family, | pray for us. |
| Model of workers, | pray for us. |
| Example to parents, | pray for us. |
| Comfort of the dying, | pray for us. |
| Provider of food to the hungry, | pray for us. |
| Companion of the poor, | pray for us. |
| Protector of the church, | pray for us. |

Merciful God,
grant that we may learn from Saint Joseph
to care for the members of our families
and share what we have with the poor.
We ask this through Christ our Lord. Amen.

## *Angelus*

V. The angel spoke God's message to Mary,
R. and she conceived of the Holy Spirit.
Hail, Mary. . . .
V. "I am the lowly servant of the Lord:
R. let it be done to me according to your word."
Hail, Mary. . . .
V. And the Word became flesh,
R. and lived among us.
Hail, Mary. . . .
V. Pray for us, holy Mother of God,
R. that we may become worthy of the promises of Christ.
Let us pray.
Lord,
fill our hearts with your grace:
once, through the message of an angel
you revealed to us the incarnation of your Son;
now, through his suffering and death
lead us to the glory of his Resurrection.
We ask this through Christ our Lord.
R. Amen.

## The Chaplet of Divine Mercy

**1.** Begin with the Sign of the Cross.

**2.** Pray the Our Father.

**3.** Pray the Hail Mary.

**4.** Say the Apostles' Creed

**5.** Then pray, on the large bead before each decade on the rosary:

Eternal Father,
I offer you the Body and Blood,
Soul and Divinity,
of Your Dearly Beloved Son,
Our Lord, Jesus Christ,
in atonement for our sins
and those of the whole world.

**6.** On the small beads of each decade say:

For the sake of his sorrowful Passion,
have mercy on us and on the whole world.

**7.** Then say three times:

Holy God,
Holy Mighty One,
Holy Immortal One,
have mercy on us
and on the whole world.

The Jesus Prayer

Lord Jesus Christ, Son of God, have mercy
on me, a sinner.

**actual grace** the help God gives us in our particular need or to do a particular good act or to avoid evil **(256)**

**angels** spiritual beings that praise God and serve him as messengers to help people understand God's plan or to keep them safe from harm **(79)**

**Apostles** the twelve men Jesus chose to be his closest followers and to share in his work and mission in a special way **(134)**

**Apostles' Creed** one of the Church's oldest creeds. It is a summary of Christian beliefs taught since the time of the Apostles. **(159)**

**apostolic** a Mark of the Church. The Church is apostolic because her teaching authority comes directly from Jesus and his chosen Apostles handed down through the bishops of the Church, who are direct successors of the Apostles. **(159)**

**Apostolic Succession** the term used to describe that the authority to lead and teach the Church can be traced through the centuries from the Apostles to their successors, the Pope and bishops **(175)**

**Ascension** the event of the Risen Christ being taken up to Heaven forty days after his Resurrecion **(138)**

**Assumption** the Church teaching that, at the end of her life, Mary, body and soul, was "taken up" (assumed) into Heaven. The Church celebrates the Feast of the Assumption on August 15. **(307)**

**beatification** the second step in the process of becoming a Saint, in which a venerable person is recognized by the Church as having brought about a miracle through his or her prayers of intercession **(311)**

**blasphemy** the sin of showing contempt or lack of reverence for God and his name **(218)**

**Blessed Sacrament** a name for the Holy Eucharist, especially the Body of Christ reserved in the Tabernacle **(254)**

**canonization** a declaration by the Pope naming a person a Saint. Canonized Saints have special feast days or memorials in the Church's calendar. **(311)**

**catholic** a Mark of the Church. The Church is catholic because her mission is to the whole world. **(188)**

**character** a permanent, sacramental, spiritual seal that strengthens us to do God's work. A seal is given in the Sacraments of Baptism, Confirmation, or Holy Orders. **(120)**

**Church** the community of all baptized people who believe in the Holy Trinity and follow Jesus **(68)**

**clergy** men who are ordained and given sacred authority to serve the Church by teaching, divine worship, and pastoral leadership **(199)**

**common good** the good of everyone; the Christian principle that all people, either in groups or as individuals, have the opportunities to reach their fulfillment more fully and easily **(238)**

**Communion of Saints** the pilgrim Church on Earth, those being purified in Purgatory, and the blessed already in Heaven **(294)**

**consecrated religious life** a state of life lived by religious sisters, brothers, and priests in community and characterized by the vows of poverty, chastity, and obedience **(202)**

**consecration** the part of the Eucharistic Prayer in which the priest prays the words of Jesus over the bread and wine, and these elements become the Body and Blood of Christ **(280)**

**conscience** the God-given ability that helps individuals judge whether actions are right or wrong **(230)**

**conversion** a sincere change of mind, heart, and desire to turn away from sin and evil and turn toward God **(150)**

**councils** gatherings of bishops during which they speak about the faith of the Church, her teachings, and important issues (**68**)

**covenant** a sacred promise or agreement between humans or between God and humans (**56**)

**Creed** a formal statement of what is believed about the Holy Trinity and the Church. The word *creed* comes from the Latin for "I believe." There are two main creeds of the Church: the Nicene Creed and the Apostles' Creed. (**98**)

**Decalogue** another name for the Ten Commandments; from the Greek phrase meaning "ten words" (**59**)

**devotions** popular prayers or practices that honor Jesus, Mary, and the Saints (**308**)

**disciple** one who learns from and follows the example of a teacher. The disciples of Jesus are those who believe in him, follow his teachings, and put them into practice. (**134**)

**domestic Church** a term for the Catholic family, because it is the community of Christians in the home. God made the family to be the first place we learn about loving others and following Christ. (**108**)

**ecumenism** an organized effort to bring Christians together in cooperation as they look forward in hope to the restoration of the unity of the Christian Church (**162**)

*ekklesia* the original term for church in Scripture, meaning "convocation" or "those called together" (**108**)

**eternal life** life forever with God for all who die in his friendship (**148**)

**evangelical counsels** poverty, chastity, and obedience. Those in consecrated religious life take public vows to live these counsels. (**202**)

**Evangelists** the four inspired human authors of the Gospels: Matthew, Mark, Luke, and John (**187**)

**faith** the Theological Virtue that makes it possible for us to believe in God and all that he has revealed. Faith leads us to obey God. It is both a gift from God and a free, human choice. (**68**)

**Feast of the Holy Family** the day celebrating the special family relationship among Mary, Joseph, and Jesus (**226**)

**fidelity** faithful presence; it is the most important rule of loving and lasting relationships (**266**)

**filial respect** the response children are called to have toward their parents, which includes obedience, respect, gratitude, and assistance (**226**)

**free will** the God-given freedom and ability to make choices. God created us with free will so we can have the freedom to choose good. (**54**)

**Fruits of the Holy Spirit** the qualities that can be seen in us when we allow the Holy Spirit to work in our hearts (**120**)

**Gifts of the Holy Spirit** seven powerful gifts God gives us to follow the guidance of the Holy Spirit and live the Christian life. We are sealed with the Gifts of the Holy Spirit at Confirmation. (**120**)

**grace** God's free, loving gift of his own life and help to do what he calls us to do. It is participation in the life of the Holy Trinity. (**98**)

**Great Commandment** the twofold command to love God above all and your neighbor as yourself. It sums up all of God's laws. (**215**)

**holiness** a state of becoming more God-like, living in his presence and with his love (**79**)

**holy** a mark of the Church. The Church is holy because she is set apart for God and his purposes and God is holy. Christ gave himself up to make the Church holy and gave the Church the gift of the Holy Spirit to give her life. (**80**)

**Holy Days of Obligation** all Sundays, as well as designated holy days that Catholics are required to participate in the Mass (**282**)

**Holy Orders** the Sacrament at the Service of Communion in which a baptized man is ordained to teach the faithful, lead divine worship, and govern the Church; ordained ministers serve as bishops, priests, and deacons (**269**)

**Holy Trinity** the mystery of one God in three Divine Persons: Father, Son, and Holy Spirit (**98**)

**icons** religious pictures that illustrate Jesus, Mary, and other holy people; icons are traditional among many Eastern Christians (**298**)

**idolatry** the sin of putting other people or things in God's place, or before God, in our lives (**216**)

**Immaculate Conception** the truth that Mary was preserved free from Original Sin from the first moment of her conception. The Church celebrates the Feast of the Immaculate Conception on December 8. (**308**)

**infallible** the quality of being free from error. A teaching is Infallible when the Pope, as head of the Magisterium, speaks officially on a matter of faith or morals that is to be believed by everyone in the Church. (**176**)

**informed conscience** a conscience that is educated and developed through constant use and examination and learning about the teachings of the Church (**230**)

**in persona Christi** term referring to the mission and ability of priests and bishops, granted through Holy Orders, to act in the person of Christ (**269**)

**justification** the forgiveness of sins and the return to the goodness for which humans were first created (**148**)

**laity** all baptized members of the Church who share in Jesus' mission and witness to him and his message but are not priests or consecrated sisters or brothers; sometimes called lay people (**199**)

**liturgical year** the feasts and seasons of the Church calendar that celebrate the Paschal Mystery (**279**)

**liturgy** the official public worship of the Church. It includes the Seven Sacraments and forms of daily prayer. (**254**)

**Liturgy of the Hours** the Church's public prayer offered at set times during the day and night to mark each day as holy (**282**)

**Magisterium** the teaching office of the Church, which is all the bishops in union with the Pope. The Magisterium has the teaching authority to interpret the Word of God found in Sacred Scripture and Sacred Tradition. (**176**)

**Marks of the Church** the essential characteristics that distinguish Christ's Church and her mission: one, holy, catholic, and apostolic (**80**)

**martyr** a holy person who gives up his or her life to witness to the truth of Christ and the faith. The word *martyr* means "witness" (**319**)

**Matrimony** the Sacrament at the Service of Communion in which a baptized man and a baptized woman make a permanent covenant of love with each other and with God (**266**)

**missionaries** people who answer a call from God to devote a period of their lives to bringing Christ's message to people in other places (**190**)

**missionary mandate** the responsibility given by Jesus to the Church to bring his saving message to everyone (**187**)

**monastery** a building where a community of religious men (or sometimes women) join together in spirituality and service (**319**)

**Mystical Body of Christ** a name for the Church, whose baptized members are all united to Christ and one another through the Holy Spirit, forming one holy people with Christ as her head (**122**)

**New Commandment** Jesus' command for his disciples to love one another as he has loved us (**241**)

**Nicene Creed** a summary of foundational truths about the Holy Trinity, the Church, and eternal life. We usually say the Nicene Creed during Mass. (**176**)

**offices of Christ** the three roles of Jesus (Priest, Prophet, and King) that describe his mission and work among God's People; all those baptized share in these three roles (**110**)

**one** a Mark of the Church. The Church is one because the power of the Holy Spirit unites all the members through one faith and one Baptism. (**159**)

**P – R**

**Paschal Candle** a large, white candle that is lit from the Easter fire, and is used during the Easter season and at Baptisms and funerals as a symbol of the Resurrection (**296**)

**Pentecost** the feast that celebrates the coming of the Holy Spirit upon the Apostles and first disciples fifty days after Easter (**96**)

**perjury** making a promise under oath which the maker does not intend to keep (**218**)

**personal sin** a deliberate thought, word, deed, or omission that violates the law of God (**242**)

**Pope** the successor of Peter, the bishop of Rome, and the head of the entire Catholic Church (**175**)

**Precepts of the Church** some of the minimum requirements given by Church leaders for deepening our relationship with God and the Church (**256**)

**righteous** to act in accordance with God's will, being in his friendship, free from guilt or sin (**148**)

**sacramentals** sacred blessings, objects, and actions that remind us of God, are made sacred through the prayers of the Church, and that help us respond to the grace received in the Sacraments (**296**)

**Sacred Tradition** is God's Word to the Church, safeguarded by the Apostles and their successors, the bishops, and handed down verbally—in her Creeds, Sacraments, and other teachings—to future generations (**67**)

**Saints** those whom the Church declares led holy lives and are enjoying eternal life with God in Heaven (**282**)

**salvation** the loving action of God's forgiveness of sins and the restoration of friendship with the Father brought by Jesus Christ (**108**)

**sanctifying grace** God's Divine life within us that makes us his friends and adopted children (**256**)

**Seven Sacraments** effective signs of God's grace, instituted by Christ and given to his Church. In the celebration of each Sacrament, there are visible signs and Divine actions that give grace and allow us to share in God's work. (**254**)

**social sin** a term that refers to the sinful social structures that result from personal sin and that lead to social conditions that do not reflect or promote the New Commandment (**242**)

**solidarity** a Christian principle that motivates believers to share their spiritual gifts as well as their material ones (**241**)

**soul** the spiritual principle of a human person that is individual, created by God, and will exist forever (**54**)

**Stations of the Cross** images of fourteen scenes that help us think and pray about Jesus' suffering, Death, and burial (**296**)

**Tabernacle** the special place in the church where the Blessed Sacrament is reserved after Mass for those who are ill or for Eucharistic Adoration (**254**)

**Temple of the Holy Spirit** the way Saint Paul describes how the Holy Spirit resides within the body (**118**)

**Ten Commandments** the ten fundamental moral laws given by God to Moses, and recorded in the Old Testament, to help his People live by the covenant (**59**)

**Theological Virtues** gifts from God that help us believe in him, trust in his plan for us, and love him as he loves us; they are faith, hope, and charity (**71**)

**Transfiguration** the revelation of Jesus' Divine glory to the Apostles Peter, James, and John (**94**)

**virtue** a good spiritual habit that strengthens and enables you to do what is right and good. They develop over time with our practice and openness to God's grace. (**71**)

**vows** solemn promises that are made to or before God (**266**)

**Boldfaced numbers refer to pages on which terms are defined.**

**Endnotes**

1. P. Hansen, Vita mirabilis (Louvain, 1668)
2. LG 59; cf. Pius XII, *Munificentissimus Deus* (1950): DS 3903; cf. Rev 19:16.